FUNNY BUSINESS

FUNNY BUSINESS

David Housham &
John Frank-Keyes

BⓉXTREE

Produced in association with Tiger Television

Acknowledgments

The authors and publishers wish to thank Sarah Williams, producer of the Funny Business series, for all her advice and help.

Thanks are also due to the following companies for providing pictures for this book:Retna Pictures Ltd., The Hulton Picture Library, The Kobal Collection, and Syndication International.

First published in the UK 1992 by
Boxtree Limited
Broadwall House
21 Broadwall
London SE1 9PL

13579108642

Text © copyright Tiger Television Ltd 1992

Cover design: Triffic Films

Designed and typeset by Blackjacks, London

Printed and bound in Great Britain by
Redwood Press Ltd., Melksham, Wiltshire

ISBN 1 85283 792 6

Foreword

When we first came up with the idea for a television documentary series about comedy we were greeted with a certain amount of cynicism from friends and colleagues in the business: "You can't analyse comedy," they said. "To explain humour is to destroy it," and in many respects they were right. However, if they'd only let us finish (which they didn't) we would have gone on to say that we were certainly not going to attempt an analysis of humour, but simply look at some of the traditions and techniques that funny people have employed over the years in order to make us laugh. In other words, the how, rather than the why of comedy, the nuts and bolts rather than the grand purpose.

Similarly with this book, intended, as I'm sure you are aware, to be a companion to, rather than a transcript of, the television series, there will be no pontificating on the function of the comic in society, no theorising on the impact of humour on perception, and no Freud will be mentioned. Neither Clement nor Emma. This book is quite simply a collection of brief accounts of the lives and work of some of the best comics this century. Indeed it is simply a perfect companion, a priceless and timeless work for you to hug to your bosom and cherish always. The limitations of time and space have meant that omissions are inevitable, and if we have not included your own particular favourite comic, then obviously the whole book is completely worthless, and we apologise for bringing it to your attention.

If you are still trying to decide whether to buy this book, I am delighted to recommend it to you. If you are reading this after making a purchase, I am sure you will share annoyance that this foreword has served no useful commercial purpose whatsoever.

Rowan Atkinson.

Abbott and Costello

"Bud Abbott was a genius. Lou Costello was one of the greatest comics in movies; his 'scare' take was the best I've ever seen. Together Bud and Lou were sublimely funny" – Mel Brooks.

Bud Abbott (the straight man) and Lou Costello (the little fat one) are the archetypal 'low comedy' double act that critics like to look down on.

They've always lacked the artistic and intellectual approval bestowed on the likes of Laurel and Hardy and the Marx Brothers, but they were brilliant exponents of rapid-fire 'cross-talk' or 'patter' comedy

Catchphrases

Costello (loud and afraid):
"Heeey Aaaaaa-bott!"

Costello (infantile, for pathos):
"I'm a b-a-a-a-d boy!"

Along with W.C. Fields, their film work is the best record of the kind of skilled but unsubtle, populist comedy that flourished amid the bump n'grind of America's sleazy, stripteasey burlesque theatres of the 1930s and 1940s.

Their Work

It's a comedy biz maxim that in a double act the clown is only as funny as his straight man makes him. Like a war-time spiv, Abbott was dapper, tough and smart – the hectoring father to Costello's innocent, childish clown. Abbott's timing and delivery were superbly judged; Costello had the vital natural quality of looking funny, with a big expressive face that could register endless variations of fear, incomprehension and foolishness.

During World War II Abbott and Costello were America's most popular comics and their hallmark

routines, based on street corner scams, dice games and easy money, reflected both the leisure pursuits of burlesque audiences and also the escapist mood of the times.

The 'Lemon Table' routine is a version of the sleight-of-hand Find The Lady fairground swindle still relieving suckers of their cash to this day. Abbott and Costello's cross-talk routines were rococo structures of linguistic misunderstanding (eg. the baseball team with players named 'Who' and 'What' and 'I Don't Know'), irresistibly inviting audiences to laugh at the fathead who doesn't cotton on.

Their Life

William Abbott (born 1895) and Louis Francis Cristillo (born 1906) were showbiz backstagers (respectively a box office manager and silent movies stuntman) before becoming performers who met up on the vaudeville and burlesque theatre circuits in the 1930s.

The more family-oriented entertainment of vaudeville was suffocated by the rising success of talking pictures, but burlesque's heavy-breathing appeal survived, as did its theatres' function as a craft school for young comedians. Abbott and Costello honed their patter act and kept it clean, which eased their progression to radio shows in the late 1930s.

As burgeoning radio stars, they were signed up by Hollywood's unfashionable B-movie factory, Universal Studios, and in 1941 they began churning out cheap, armed forces comedies which stunned the film industry by their immediate and enormous popularity.

Abbott (1895-1974), Costello (1906-1959)

Abbott and Costello's on-screen characters were the inverse of their true selves. Abbott may have shouted and slapped the contrite Costello about for big laughs in public, but in real life he was a mild-mannered epileptic. Off-stage Costello flaunted a Napoleonic ego. At the height of their fame, Costello demanded that their hitherto equal pay packets should be adjusted to 60:40 in his favour, and Abbott meekly complied. Their most famous, typically petty, feud occurred in 1945 when the Abbotts hired a maid who had just been fired by the Costellos. Contractual obligations clamped them together, but for a while Costello not only demanded, with Chaplinesque delusions, that his film roles should have more pathos, but also that he should not have to share scenes with Abbott – with unhilarious consequences on screen.

In truth, they could never afford to split up. Both men were generous spendthrifts with expensive homes and entourages, and both were hopeless gamblers. In addition to making four films a year, they were constantly recording radio shows and doing live work just to keep pace with their debts.

Even when they were scarcely on speaking terms, Abbott and Costello passed the time on film sets playing fiercely competitive, high stakes poker games. Led on by Costello, they trampled all over their directors, rarely did more than one take of a scene and showed little interest in learning or developing new material. Costello usually insisted that the classic burlesque routines they knew by heart should be shoehorned into their films, regardless of the setting or plot.

The duo's declining box office appeal was revived in the late 1940s when Universal stuck them in a new series of films that were cheap because they used the same 'stars' (ie. Frankenstein's monster, the Wolf Man and the Invisible Man) and sets from the studio's more consistently profitable line of horror movies.

The same old burlesque routines got a final and popular airing in Abbott and Costello's TV shows in the 1950s – the cash from which was immediately subsumed by the enormous tax bills neither of them had paid. Their slide into relative poverty was proceed by even tackier films like *Abbott And Costello Go To Mars* (though bizarrely it's Venus in the film) and Universal dropped them in 1955.

The final split came in 1957. Costello found himself back in burlesque, fronting 'Minsky's Follies' in Las Vegas. Two years later at 53 his heart, weakened by earlier illnesses, gave out. Abbott lived on for another 15 years of intermittent TV work and harassment by tax collectors. He was latterly reduced to adding his own voice to a Hanna-Barbera Abbot And Costello cartoon series, before poor health overcame him in 1974.

Key Films

Buck Privates (Universal 1941);
In The Navy (Universal 1941) – includes the 'Lemon Table' routine;
Hold That Ghost (Universal 1941);
The Naughty Nineties (Universal 1945) – notably only for its inclusion of the famous 'Who's On First' routine;
Abbott And Costello Meet Frankenstein (Universal-International 1948).

Performance Extract

From the 'Who's On First' routine:

Abbott: Who is on first.
Costello: Well, what are you asking me for?
Abbott: I'm not asking you. I'm telling you – Who is on first.
Costello: I'm asking you – who's on first?
Abbott: That's the man's name!
Costello: That's whose name?
Abbott: Yes.
Costello: Well, go ahead and tell me.
Abbott: Who.
Costello: The guy on first.
Abbott: Who.
Costello: The first baseman!
Abbott: Who is on first.
Costello: Have you got a first baseman on first?
Abbott: Certainly.
Costello: Then who's playing first?
Abbott: Absolutely!

Dave Allen

"In case you wonder what I do, I tend to stroll around and chat. I'd be grateful if you'd refrain from doing the same." – Dave Allen (addressing a theatre audience).

Dave Allen was one of British television's best and certainly most controversial stand-up comedians in the 1970s, and the only one whose trademark was to deliver his material sitting down. His current TV appearances, though less frequent, still pack a potential for public outrage.

Perched on his stool, at the height of his popularity the Irish-born Allen used his intelligence and charm to make his dark comic obsessions – especially religious hypocrisy – uniquely accessible to a mainstream audience.

His Work

Allen, at heart a satirist and story-teller rather than a conventional comedian, developed a style of delivery through his TV career that increasingly led him away from gag/set-up/gag to less structured comic meditations. The objects of his scorn are often provocatively but seldom cruelly chosen: "I hate any sort of gags where you are putting people down. It's much better to laugh at yourself," he said.

A Director General of the BBC in the 1970s, Sir Charles Curran, was moved personally to defend Allen against one of the many gusts of criticism howling over the Irish sea from Catholic priests upset by the decidedly 'fallen' comedian's love of anti-Pope jokes.

Allen defended himself: "I do not ridicule religion. I ridicule some concepts of what men believe religion is. I firmly believe that if anybody wants to do anything in their life, they have the right to do it."

The enormous energy under the surface of his highly crafted monologues was only hinted at by his constant recourse to his two essential props – a tumbler of (apparently) whisky and chain-smoked cigarettes. These may have calmed him; but in sips and drags they undoubtedly provided him with wonderfully timed comic pauses.

His Life

David Tynan O'Mahoney was born in Templegate near Dublin on 6th July 1936 into a family with great journalistic and literary traditions.

His aunt was the poet Kathleen Tynan, a friend of W.B. Yeats.

Catchphrase

"Good night, good luck and may your God go with you."

(1936-)

His grandmother edited the Dublin newspaper, the *Freeman's Journal*, and his father was managing director of the *Irish Times*.

Allen was educated, unhappily, at a Catholic school where he looks back on his experience with the nuns: "it was like the Gestapo in drag". He sought a career in journalism, joining the *Irish Independent* at 16, before moving as a junior reporter to the *Drogheda Argus*.

At 20 he came to Britain to take Fleet Street by storm, but ended up as a Butlins holiday camp 'redcoat' in Skegness, before moving on as a comic to the bottom, literally, of the club circuit: his first professional job was with one of England's last touring nude shows.

With the advice and help of the singer, Sophie Tucker, in 1963 Allen was booked into a nightclub tour of Australia, where, as has happened to many British entertainers, he stayed and quickly became a huge TV star.

Tonight With Dave Allen, his live chat show, earned record-breaking ratings and had a reputation for the unexpected. This was notoriously sealed when Allen, engrossed in an interview with Peter Cook and Dudley Moore, allegedly told a producer who was winding him into a commercial break to "go away and masturbate" instead.

Despite such tendencies to frank-speaking, on returning, aged 30, to club work in Britain, Allen was soon offered the job of resident comic on the TV series of the squeaky clean, pullover-clad Irish crooner, Val Doonican.

After a couple of successful series, his star ascended through compering *Sunday Night At the London Palladium* to his first solo show in 1968, for ATV, *Tonight With Dave Allen*.

He hit his stride in 1971 with a move to the BBC and the first of many acclaimed series of *Dave Allen At Large*, produced and directed by Peter Whitmore (whose later work included BBC TV's *Yes Minister*). Allen's status as a comedy star also helped him revive his earlier journalistic ambitions in a number of documentaries, shot in Britain and America, in which he typically went in search of the kinds of oddballs and eccentrics who drift unnoticed into the backwaters of modern society. He also flirted with theatre, and toured in Britain and Australia, though a first and last attempt at a Broadway show in 1981, *An Evening With Dave Allen*, was not greatly appealing to American audiences.

In 1990 he was given a show on BBC1, comprising only his monologues and recorded in a theatre rather than a TV studio. This attempt at a less restrictive

Key TV

Sunday Night At the London Palladium (Compere; ITV, 1967); Tonight With Dave Allen (ITV, 1968); Dave Allen At Large (BBC2, 1970s).

atmosphere paid off spectacularly with a relatively innocuous 'bad language' incident which nonetheless rattled the watchdogs' cages and even caused questions to be asked in the House Of Commons.

Twenty five years after British TV's first four-letter furore, thanks to Kenneth Tynan, Allen proved its durable potency for hitting the headlines in a routine about workers' enslavement to time – "we clock on and clock off, and take prearranged lunch-hours and holiday breaks and when we retire what do they give us? A fucking watch!"

Where once upon a time the BBC's Director General had defended him, the BBC now meekly apologised, leaving a bemused and amused Allen to explain: "I mean, bloomin' watch wouldn't have worked; bloody watch would only have been half as funny..."

Dave Allen has recently made a new series for Carlton Television.

Performance Extract

'They say to me if I'm not good in life then I'll go to Hell; then I think I've met a lot of what I would call good people, and they are goody-goodies, creepy goodies, 'God I love you' and thinking 'me' all the time. That means Heaven is going to be full of that lot. Can you imagine being stuck with that lot for eternity? I mean hell is going to be full of the most interesting people, so I'll be happy to go to Hell. But then I suppose that God would know that Hell would be Heaven to me, so he'll send me to Heaven, and that's going to be boring!"

Woody Allen

"When you do comedy, you're not sitting at the grown-ups' table, you're sitting at the children's table" – Woody Allen in a 1978 *Newsweek* interview.

Woody Allen is the supreme contemporary example of that age-old archetype – the clown who wants to play *Hamlet*.

It is, curiously, the case that comedians with the greatest ability to make people laugh often value that talent the least, and long for the 'respect' bestowed on 'serious' artists. Allen has struggled in recent years to create films (*Interiors, September, Another Woman*) with the intellectual depth and resonance of the Russian theatre and Scandinavian cinema he fervently admires, so his critics (like Allen himself) have tended to under-rate his achievements as a comedy actor.

His Work

A TV writer turned stand-up comedian turned film writer/actor/director, Allen's brand of humour has proved genuinely inimitable: so distinctive, personal and innovative that few have tried to emulate or imitate it.

Allen took the inflections, the smart, self-deprecatory sparkle of American-Jewish humour and injected it with an eclectic mixture of slapstick, often surreal comedy, knockabout sexuality and a satirical view of urban (New York) pseudo-intellectualism.

Allen is arguably best-loved for his one-liners, but his films have frequently featured some of the most striking visual comedy since the hey-days of Keaton, Lloyd and

Chaplin. For instance, stealing giant-sized vegetables in the sci-fi spoof *Sleeper*, being pursued by a zepplin-sized breast in *Everything You Wanted To Know About Sex But Were Afraid To Ask*, or the shoot-out amid giant carnival floats in *Broadway Danny Rose*.

Most Quoted One Liners

"My one regret in life is that I'm not somebody else."

"It's not that I'm afraid to die – I just don't want to be around when it happens."

"Don't knock masturbation – it's sex with someone I love."

His Life

Woody Allen was born Allan Stewart Konigsberg on December 1st 1935 in the unglamorous Bronx suburb of New York. He grew up in Brooklyn and decided at 17 that Woody Allen was a hip name to append to the jokes he was selling precociously to PR flacks and newspaper gossip columns.

The young Allen loved jazz, sports, magic and comedy but was unable to cope with the academic demands of college – a failing for which, like most self-made people, he has since conspicuously over-compensated.

However, the teenage Allen's ability to knock out 50 jokes a day gave him an early taste of showbiz success that soon led to his arrival as a wunderkind scriptwriter on

(1935-)

big '50s American TV comedy shows like *The Colgate Variety Hour* and specials starring the celebrated Sid Caesar.

Typically, the simple populism of TV comedy soon palled in Allen's eyes and he turned his back on the lucrative world of TV to become a nightclub comedian, partly with the encouragement of newly acquired managers, Jack Rollins and Charles H Joffe – still his business partners to this day.

By 1964 Allen's fame as trendy, cerebral stand-up comic was such that a major Hollywood producer, Charles Feldman, commissioned his first film script. The resulting energetic, but uneven, Peter Sellers and Peter O'Toole farce, *What's New Pussycat?*, was nonetheless an international box office hit in 1965. Allen's additional well received, if minor, comic acting performance in *Pussycat* confirmed his position as a hot young comedy star. The ensuing flood of offers led to him writing absurd comic prose in *The New Yorker* magazine, and two hit plays on Broadway, *Don't Drink The Water* and *Play It Again Sam*.

Allen's attempts at building his film career proved more tricky. Having persuaded a studio to let him direct his first film, he ended up with a chaotic mountain of rushes which only the film editor, Ralph Rosenblum (who continued to work with Allen on his next five films, teaching him filmmaking along the way), was able to turn into 1969's *Take The Money And Run*.

Allen astutely capitalised on its success to carve out the model deal as writer, actor and director by which he has worked ever since: by taking ungreedy fees and making (by Hollywood standards) modestly budgeted films, he has retained, uniquely among his peers, absolute creative control over his work.

He is famous for his isolation and rigid working methods: only using leading actresses who are or have been his lovers – Mia Farrow, Louise Lasser, Diane Keaton; never letting his actors see the script other than their own lines and never letting them know a film's ending; latterly working only in New York; re-writing and re-shooting often well into the editing stage; retaining a core team of technicians from film to film; and being subdued on the set.

The turning point in his career was his 1977 Academy Award-winner, *Annie Hall*. It was his first film not parodying a genre, and his first homage to New York life. It was also his first film to show that after eight years of brilliantly inventive cinematic joke-making inspired by the films of his comedy hero, Bob Hope, he had

Key Films

Bananas (1971);
Play It Again Sam (1972);
Sleeper (1974);
Love And Death (1975);
Annie Hall (1977);
Manhattan (1979);
Broadway Danny Rose (1984);
The Purple Rose Of Cairo (1984)
{Allen's favourite};
Hannah And Her Sisters (1986);
Radio Days (1987);
Crimes And Misdemeanours
(1989).

started to master the formal, narrative skills of film-making.

No doubt Allen will continue to turn out films of varying styles and success for as long as the American film industry accords him his unrivalled 'untouchable' status, letting him wander wherever his whimsies and obsessions take him.

There have latterly been signs that Allen is uneasy about the relatively small financial reward of his creative autonomy. In 1990 he took a lead acting role with Bette Midler in a Walt Disney comedy, *Scenes From A Mall*, and the following year took a well-paid assignment directing (very funny) TV commercials for an Italian supermarket chain.

Performance Extract ➔

From a *New Yorker* piece, 'A Little Louder Please':

On not being able to appreciate mime: "I tried raging impotently again, but mime is a quiet neighbourhood, and several minutes later two red-necked spokesmen for the Nineteenth Precinct dropped by to inform me that raging impotently could mean a 500 dollar fine, six months' imprisonment, or both. I thanked them and made a beeline for the sheets, where my struggle to sleep off my monstrous imperfection resulted in eight hours of nocturnal anxiety I wouldn't wish on Macbeth."

American Film Comedy

The 1930s

When silent movies became the 'talkies', they were well named. Talk is exactly what the actors in early comedies did – at a breath-taking rate of knots.

Crackling cross-fire patter was common among the top vaudeville comedians, and found in fast-moving Broadway plays of the 1920s. One such play, by Ben Hecht and Charles MacArthur, *The Front Page* was turned into the first classic screen 'talkie' in 1931. Produced by Howard Hughes, it starred Adolphe Menjou and Pat O'Brien in a breathlessly paced portrayal of sensationalist yellow journalism in Chicago.

Rapid-fire dialogue, crisp witticisms and mismatched romance were the hallmarks of America's greatest film comedy genre, the 'screwball comedy', which was to flourish through the 1930s and early 1940s in the hands of brilliant writers and directors like Howard Hawks, Garson Kanin, George Cukor, Frank Capra and Preston Sturges.

Capra's Oscar-winning 1934 movie, *It Happened One Night*

provided a basic blueprint for screwballs to come, as Clark Gable and Claudette Colbert overcame their initial resistance to each other to fall in love.

Nineteen-thirty-four also saw the start of William Powell and Myrna Loy's popular *Thin Man* series of comedy mysteries. Howard Hawks and stars, Cary Grant and Katherine Hepburn, skillfully turned up the 'screwy' factor in 1938 with *Bringing Up Baby*.

The 1940s

The 1930s' advances in film-making were crystallised in three fabulous years at the start of the 1940s. In 1940 Cary Grant gave three outstanding comedy acting performances: opposite Irene Dunne in Garson Kanin's bigamy farce, *My Favourite Wife*; opposite Katherine Hepburn in George Cukor's *The Philadelphia Story*; and in Howard Hawks' breakneck re-make of *The Front Page*, *His Girl Friday* with Rosalind Russell.

In 1941 Preston Sturges wrote and directed two of his best films,

The Lady Eve, starring Henry Fonda and Barbara Stanwyck, and the Hollywood satire, *Sullivan's Travels*, with Joel McCrae and Veronica Lake.

McCrae turned up again in another Sturges masterpiece, *Palm Beach Story* in 1942, the year in which Hawks directed Cooper and Stanwyck in *Ball Of Fire*; and in which Lubitsch made *To Be Or Not To Be* – its urbane attack on Nazism misunderstood at the time. The experiences of war-time, the decline of theatrical comedy and the continuing rise of radio seemed to mark a sea-change in film comedy styles and audiences' tastes during the mid-1940s.

The pace and sophistication of screwball comedies gradually gave way to the broader, Forces-style comedy of Abbott and Costello's films; and Bob Hope and Bing Crosby's series of *Road To...* movies, kicking off in Singapore in 1940.

The 1950s

As comedy thrived on the rapidly pervasive small screens of television, and Hollywood started to lose its studio production-lines and grappled with new epic, colour and wide-screen formats, so movie comedy faltered.

Jerry Lewis and Bob Hope were the kings of big screen comedy, and the audience for smarter comedy had, in the main, only the work of Billy Wilder as a comedy director to be grateful for. In 1957 he directed Marilyn Monroe in *The Seven Year Itch*, and show-

Marilyn Monroe and Jack Lemon from the 1959 hit, Some Like It Hot.

cased her natural comedy talent in 1959's *Some Like It Hot*, with Jack Lemmon and Tony Curtis.

The 1960s

The Wilder-Lemmon link-up worked again for two more Oscar-reaping classics: *The Apartment*, with Shirley MacClaine and Fred McMurray; and *The Fortune Cookie* with Walter Matthau.

Peter Sellers gave two tremendous performances under the directorial guide of the Anglophile American, Stanley Kubrick – first, in 1962 in *Lolita* and then, in 1963 in *Doctor Strangelove*.

The big trend in the 1960s, however, was a return to slapstick on a spectacular scale: eg, Stanley Kramer's 1963, *It's A Mad Mad Mad Mad World*; in 1965 there was Blake Edwards' *The Great Race* and its airborne equivalent, *Those Magnificent Men In Their Flying Machines*.

In 1963-4 Edwards shot two funny French police farces, *The Pink Panther* and *A Shot In The Dark*, with Peter Sellers as Inspector Clouseau, the character to which he (unusually) returned in the 1970s for further, even more popular sequels.

In 1967 former young sophomore satirist turned director, Mike Nichols, drew the first great comedy performance out of Dustin Hoffman in *The Graduate*.

The 1970s

The 1970s witnessed a revival in literate film comedy: in 1970 Robert Altman directed Donald Sutherland and Eliott Gould in *M*A*S*H*, whose black comedy was matched by Mike Nichols' version of Joseph Heller's anti-war novel, *Catch 22*.

In 1972, Peter Bogdanovich lovingly directed a slick blend of slapstick and screwball comedy, with Barbara Streisand and Ryan O'Neal falling crazily in love in *What's Up Doc?*

While the decade really belonged to Woody Allen and Mel Brooks, it didn't do too badly by Neil Simon, whose screenplays were done justice to by Arthur Hiller (*The Plaza Suite* in 1971) and Herbert Ross (*The Sunshine Boys*, 1975; *The Goodbye Girl*, 1977; and *California Suite*, 1978).

The 1980s

Movie comedy mushroomed like never before in the 1980s. The decade began on a feminist note with Jane Fonda, Dolly Parton and Lily Tomlin's office comedy smash *9 to 5*, while Goldie Hawn established herself as Hollywood's top female comedy star with *Private Benjamin*.

Nineteen-eighty also saw the first major hit by the writer/director/producer team of brothers David and Jerry Zucker and Jim Abrahams, *Airplane*, from which they spun off a series of popular and influential movies, heavily reliant on parody and silly, bawdy visual comedy: *Airplane II* (1982) *Top Secret* (1984); *Naked Gun* (1988) and *Naked Gun 2 1/2* (1991).

Dustin Hoffman scored his biggest comedy hit in drag in Sidney Pollack's 1982 soap opera satire, *Tootsie*.

The major trend in the 1980s was the emergence of former TV sitcom actors as successful film comedy directors. Bob Reiner, son of Carl and ex-*All In The Family* hit a hot streak with *This Is Spinal Tap* (1984), *The Sure Thing* (1985), *Stand By Me* (1986), *The Princess Bride* (1987) and *When Harry Met Sally*.

Ron Howard, ex-*Happy Days*, helmed *Splash* (1984), *Cocoon* (1985), *Gung Ho!* (1986) and *Parenthood* (1989); Danny DeVito, ex-*Taxi*, directed the delightfully dark *Throw Momma From The Train* (1987) and *War Of The Roses* (1989); while Penny Marshall, ex-*Laverne And Shirley*, made a spectacular debut with *Big* in 1988.

The 1990s

So far, television has continued to have a strong influence over American film comedy. The 1991 success of Barry Sonnenfeld's updating of *The Addams Family*, portended a rush of 1960s TV show re-makes.

Saturday Night Live's spin-off, *Wayne's World*, directed by Penelope Spheeris and starring Mike Myers and Dana Carvey, was the major hit of 1992 and evinced a new style of dumb/ironic MTV sensibility in comedy, also found in actors, Keanu Reeves and Alex Winter's *Bill And Ted's Excellent Adventure* (1989) and its 1991 sequel, *Bill And Ted's Bogus Journey*.

However, producer John Hughes and director Christopher Columbus were responsible for the biggest comedy phenomenon for many years, *Home Alone* (1990), whose star, Macauly Caulkin, was just ten-years-old.

➤ American Radio Comedy ←

Unlike in Britain, where the BBC's licence fee has helped fund a vigorous and productive radio comedy department for the past 35 years, American radio comedy almost entirely expired with the rise of television in the 1950s.

The most popular American radio show of the 1930s and 1940s crossed over into television, an especially inevitable process since the TV networks were set up by the same corporations, NBC, CBS and ABC, that had owned and run the radio networks.

Radio comedy really began to make its mark in America after the Wall Street Crash and the onset of the Depression years into the 1930s, when it was the cheapest and most widely available form of entertainment.

With the unusual exception of *Amos 'n' Andy*, the popular early radio shows were built round performers from the vaudeville stage. Eddie Cantor (born Edward Israel Iskowitz in 1892 in New York) worked in vaudeville as a blackface singer, and wowed Broadway as a singer/comedian before becoming, by 1931, a radio superstar with weekly audiences of 60 million.

Cantor suffered teething problems with the medium. He had to be given a portable microphone since at first listeners could only hear part of his act clearly – his tough apprenticeship in front of missile-throwing vaudeville crowds had left Cantor with a ducking and bobbing style of delivery that he couldn't change.

It was through their guest appearances on Cantor's Sunday night NBC shows, that future radio stars, George Burns and

George Burns and Gracie Allen recording one of their shows in 1936.

Gracie Allen, got their break in the medium. The latter were not the only successful husband and wife act on radio.

The vaudevillian pairing, Jim Jordan and Marian Driscoll, were first hired as radio singers in 1926, before getting their own comedy show in 1931, *The Smackouts*, followed by their most famous domestic sitcom, launched in 1935, *Fibber McGee and Molly*.

Another hugely popular domestic comedy series was *The Goldbergs*, which was written by and starred, Gertrude Berg. She was the first person to immortalise the Jewish mother as a mass medium comedy character. Between 1929 and 1949 Berg personally wrote the scripts for 4,500 shows, all of which were written in longhand

One of American radio's best and most popular performers was Fred Allen, who was also one of the radio business's most laconic critics. American radio shows, like the early TV shows, were editorially subject to the whims of the companies that sponsored them, funded their production and provided revenue to the networks.

In one show Allen made a passing joke about Scottish meanness and several hundred angry Scotsmen in Pittsburgh wrote to the sponsor announcing they would boycott its product. which was a laxative. Allen later commented "The prospect that (the protesters) will go through life constipated so frightened (the sponsor) that they made me apologise."

From his first venture into radio in 1932 until his switch to

TV in 1950, Allen's career was based on his own considerable talents as a mordant comedy writer and caustic commentator on contemporary events.

His radio shows underwent exotic name changes as sponsors came and went – eg *The Linit Bath Club Review*, *Best Foods Salad Bowl Show* and *Ipana And Sal Hepatica Hour Of Smiles* – but the format remained fairly constant. There were Allen's monologues, singers and celebrity guests and, most notably, *Allen's Alley* – a collection of characters which Allen would interview each week in the guise of an opinion pollster.

Among the most celebrated characters was the loud Southerner, Senator Claghorn, played by Kenny Delmar. Allen wrote Claghorn as an oafish blusterer, yet the Senator was loved in the South. In Washington the Senate received bags of mail addressed to him, while Warner Brothers' cartoonists characterised him as the cocky Rooster, Foghorn Leghorn.

The notion of Allen's Alley was similar to the whole format of the show of Allen's on-air rival, Jack Benny. These two comics' famous feud was begun by Allen in 1938 when he challenged Benny not to carry out a promise to play Schubert's *The Bee* on his show. The insult-swapping escalated to national headlines status, and, to the delight of their audiences, was sustained by both for many years.

The most successful female comedy star in the hey-day of American radio was the vaudevillian, Fanny Brice, who entertained listeners with her squeaky-voiced portrayal of a bratty child, dubbed Baby Snooks, and initially conceived as a private party trick.

Brice (whose life was enacted by Barbara Streisand's Oscar-winning 1968 movie, *Funny Girl*) was born Fannie Borach in New York in 1891. She became famous as the vivacious singer/comedienne in Florenz Ziegfeld's Broadway *Follies* revues between 1910-1923.

In the *Baby Snook* shows Brice got sterling support from Hanley Stafford as her long-suffering Daddy, but for all the ten-year success of the show it never demanded more than a fraction of the amazing talent that Brice had displayed on stage in the 1920s.

The most extraordinary radio success was undoubtedly that of the ventriloquist Edgar Bergen and his dummy, Charlie McCarthy. The oddity of ventriloquism on radio never seemed to register with Bergen, who always performed with the dummy at the microphone and didn't attempt to hide his own short-comings in the voice-throwing business.

Nonetheless, McCarthy was a decidedly unsentimental, prickly character and indulged in lively repartee with the show's regular guests – W.C. Fields in particular. The often vituperative tone of the show was reflected in another of its highly successful spinoffs, *The Bickersons* in which Don Ameche and Frances Langford played a supremely bad-tempered married couple.

Through the 1940s radio audiences were also regularly treated to shows featuring their favourite film comedy stars – Bob Hope and Bing Crosby, The Marx Brothers, Abbott and Costello, Martin and Lewis. Some could still be heard on radio through the '50s, but by the 1960s television had effectively killed off US radio comedy.

Since then, comedy shows have occasionally cropped up on commercial radio when a sponsor can be found, such as the comedy magazine, *National Lampoon's* 1970s radio shows that were the forerunners to TV's *Saturday Night Live*.

In the mid-1970s, however, a small radio station, Minnesota Public Radio, gave birth to what became in the 1980s a national and international success – the comic stories of Garrison Keillor, set in the fictional mid-West small town, Lake Wobegon.

Keillor was born in Minneapolis in 1942. As a youngster he was a keen fan of radio and the humour of *The New Yorker* magazine. After university, in 1968 he began presenting a drive-time classical music show for Minneapolis Public Radio.

Writing an article about Nashville's grand Ole Opry for *The New Yorker* in 1974 gave Keillor the inspiration for the Lake Wobegone monologues, modelled after the rustic radio shows he had listened to as a boy.

From its debut in 1974, Keillor's show, *A Prairie Home Companion* reached ever-larger audiences, until 1980 it achieved, through satellite link-up to all American Public Radio stations, a coast-to-coast audience of two million, the second biggest in public radio.

The first compilation of the stories was published in 1985, being a best-seller in America and Britain, and subsequently followed by several equally successful sequels. Keillor is now as established an American humorist as his childhood idols like James Thurber and S.J. Perelman.

American Sitcom

The 1950s

The earliest sitcoms in the pioneer era of American television were simply transferred, lock, stock and laughter, from radio. Radio hits like *The Goldbergs*, *Amos 'n'Andy*, *The George Burns And Gracie Allen Show* made some concessions to their new visual forms, but didn't divert too far from their original blueprints.

Lucille Ball's *I Love Lucy*, launched in 1951, didn't so much discover new territory in domestic comedy; rather, it demonstrated how effective a showcase for a dominant comic talent the sitcom format could be. Similarly, Jackie Gleason's blue-collar, *The Honeymooners*, actually existed for much of its life only as a segment within Gleason's own CBS variety show. Phil Silvers' innovative and influential army sitcom, has only latterly been known as *Bilko*: two months after its inception as *You'll Never Get Rich*, its title was changed to *The Phil Silvers Show*.

The three 1950s sitcoms that arguably most decisively set the pattern for the nuclear family-based domestic sitcoms of the next 30 years were *The Adventures Of Ozzie And Harriet*, *Father Knows Best* and *Leave It To Beaver*.

The former, moving from radio to TV in 1952, was a barely re-fracted small screen version of the actual family happenings of band-leader, Nelson (though on TV he had no clearly defined employment), his wife and their two sons, David and Eric.

Father Knows Best (broadcast between 1954-63), starred Robert Young as a typical mid-western insurance salesman, with a typical loving wife (Jane Wyatt) and three typical teenage kids whose typical adolescent problems were always somehow resolvable within the span of the show's half-hour.

Leave It To Beaver was the first family sitcom to focus on children as its prime source of comedy. Theodore 'Beaver' Cleaver, played by Jerry Matthews, was just seven when the series began in 1957, and his elder brother, Wally (Tony Dow), 12: the sons of all-American accountant, Ward Cleaver (Hugh Beaumont) and his nice-as-the-apple-pie-she-baked-herself wife June (Barbara Billingsley). The boys were created by writers Bob Mosher and Joe Connelly as an antidote to the too-perfect kids in all the other 1950s sitcoms.

The 1960s

The first two new hits of the 1960s were still treading the family way, though their polarised settings – the town and the country – marked a trend that was to develop through the decade.

The Beverley Hillbillies pose with their faithfull hound-dog, Duke.

Carl Reiner's *The Dick Van Dyke Show* revolved around Rob Petrie's hip, urban job as a TV writer and his successful, liberal, modern marriage to Laura (Mary Tyler Moore).

CBS's other hugely popular sitcom, launched in 1960, was most definitely set in the country. In *The Andy Griffith Show*, Andy Taylor played Griffith, a widower sheriff in a small southern town, and Ronny (later film director Ron) Howard played his chipmunky preteen son.

In the mid-'60s sitcoms moved away from ordinary domestic sitcoms to a host of surreal and silly shows with a broader and more slapsticky sense of humour: – the magical *Bewitched*, *I Dream Of Jeannie*; the monstrous *The Addams Family* and *The Munsters*; the spy-spoof *Get Smart*, the talking horse, *Mr Ed*, and so on.

Of the country comedies, the most successful was *The Beverly Hillbillies*, launched in 1962, about a Tennessee backwoods family that strike oil and move to California; while *Green Acres* concerned a frustrated city lawyer (Eddie Albert) who moves his wife (Eva Gabor) and family to a ramshackle farm he has bought sight unseen.

The 1970s

This was the decade when as never before American sitcoms both soared to sublime new heights and sank to ridiculous depths.

In 1972 former Sid Caesar writer, Larry Gelbart, and producers Gene Reynolds and Burt Metcalfe, brought *M*A*S*H* to CBS. Set in an army field hospital during the Korean War, it was undoubtedly the high standard of writing and ensemble performing, centred round Alan Alda as the witty, subversive, skirt-chasing surgeon, 'Hawkeye' Pierce, that kept the show fizzing into the 1980s.

*M*A*S*H*'s 11-year, 251 episode run was only beaten in the 1970s by the 12-year, 325-episode *All In The Family*. This show was adapted from the BBC/Johnny Speight's controversial 1960s sitcom, *Til Death Us Do Part*. Carrol O'Connor played the multi-prejudiced reactionary, Archie Bunker; Jean Spapleton his devoted, dim-witted wife, Edith; Sally Struthers, their politically aware daughter; and Rob (son of Carl) Reiner her raving, right-on boyfriend.

The show broke previous sitcom taboos about mentioning death, homosexuality, the menopause, etc. Another Brit-com, *Steptoe and Son* was turned into the black hit, *Sanford And Son*.

Mary Tyler Moore was sitcom's first single career girl in *The Mary Tyler Moore Show* (1970-1977), from which stars and shows such as *Lou Grant* (Ed Asner), *Rhoda* (Valerie Harper) and *Phyllis* (Cloris Leachman) spun off, seeing her being the co-founder of an eponymous production empire, MTM, in the process.

Tyler Moore's show was also the first to make the most of an ensemble cast of contrasting but complementary characters, a feature of two other top 1970s shows (and many since). *Barney Miller* (1975-1982), starring Hal Linden, gave viewers a dryly funny view of everyday life in a run-down New York police-squad room. *Taxi* (1978-1983), produced by MTM and starring Judd Hirsch and Danny DeVito, was set in a cab company, with brilliantly written and performed comedy from characters such as the East European Latka, played with genius by the late Andy Kaufman.

The 1980s

Two *Taxi* writers, brothers Glen and Les Charles, with director James Burrows, left the show to make, from 1980, the most consistently fine sitcom of the 1980s, *Cheers*, which is still running.

Cheers, set in a comfy Boston bar, refined the ensemble comedy of the great 1970s shows and gave it the extra boost of classic sex comedy, firstly between ex-baseball player and reformed alcoholic bar owner Sam Malone (Ted Danson) and beautiful, pseudo-intellectual snob waitress Diane Chambers (Shelley Long); and then, on Long's departure, between Malone and sexy, neurotic businesswoman, Rebecca Howe (Kirstie Alley).

Susan Harris, the creator and writer behind the 1970s sitcoms, SOAP (black comedy soap-spoof) and *Benson* (black butler spin-off), hit pay dirt in 1985 with *The Golden Girls*, an intelligent comedy upturning conventional prejudices about the elderly, starring Bea Arthur, Betty White, Rue McLanhan and Estelle Getty.

Meanwhile the family sitcom staged a comeback: Bill Cosby presented the new face of middle class black America in *The Cosby Show*, while Michael J Fox launched his career as a teen movie idol in *Family Ties*.

Roseanne Arnold

"I think Roseanne's comedy comes from the background she had growing up Jewish in Salt Lake City in a community of Mormons – that would tend to make one an outsider. All the knocks and hardships that she's overcome have made her a very keen observer of people, things and places. She has something to say about everything and it's almost always funny" – John Goodman.

American television has had its blue-collar sitcoms before: *The Honeymooners*, *All In The Family*. It has had comedy shows built around female stars: *I Love Lucy*, *The Mary Tyler Moore Show*.

But the success of Roseanne has been unlike any other TV phenomenon. Not only does the show defy TV's standard sanitised portrayals of ordinary family life, it's completely dominated by the powerful, unalloyed personality of Roseanne Arnold, a stand-up comedian rather than an actress.

Her Work

In the past 15 years America's comedy club circuit has provided TV and movies with a string of male stars – Robin Williams, Billy Crystal, Jay Leno, Richard Lewis, Jerry Seinfeld.

Of all the many female comics who have become established in that time, only Roseanne has broken through from the clubs and cable TV specials to a mass prime-time audience. It's hardly a theory, but interesting to consider that while most women stand-up comedians in the 1980s did routines about the troubles and strife of single life, Roseanne

chose to present herself as the 'housewife from Hell', ripping into domestic drudgery.

That attitude and other ingredients of Roseanne's stand-up act – that people can be fat and not be losers; that a healthy dose of cynicism doesn't cure life's ills but at least it makes them bearable – provided the blueprint for her sitcom and gave it a wide appeal.

Her Life

Roseanne Barr was born on November 3rd 1952 in Salt Lake City, home of the strict Mormon religion. She had two sisters and a brother and describes her upbringing as Jewish on weekends and Mormon on weekdays.

Finding herself married with three children in her 20s and need-

ing money, she worked as a cocktail waitress and learned to handle difficult customers by being funny: "it was because of those men that I knew I had a place in comedy."

She began to perform in local coffee shops, and, deciding that she needed to do something different, Roseanne with her sister worked out the character of the 'housewife from Hell' and quickly realised its potential.

She travelled to Los Angeles to audition for Mitzi Shore, owner of the legendary Comedy Store, which had provided a launch-pad for Robin Williams and Richard Pryor. Shore soon promoted Roseanne to the club's main stage and told her "You are going to be the one who breaks down the doors of comedy for women".'

An appearance in a TV showcase for women comics, organised

(1952-)

by Shore, on the cable channel HBO led to Roseanne being asked to appear in a network TV special celebrating *The Tonight Show*. Again, such was her impact that after just two years Roseanne had outgrown the clubs circuit where other comics have had to work for up to ten years before getting a break. "I was able to go directly to a concert tour. I never really had to work clubs and be ground down – they would have killed me, I would never have made it," she says.

Marcey Carsey and Tom Werner, the TV producers behind Bill Cosby's hugely popular 1980s sitcom, *The Cosby Show*, developed an initial idea for a female blue-collar sitcom with writer Matt Williams. They wanted Roseanne to be one of three main leads, but after talking with her, decided to base the show around her alone, as a housewife and mother of three kids.

Launched on the ABC network in the autumn of 1988, *Roseanne*, unlike most new sitcoms, rapidly attracted a big audience, and eventually overtook *The Cosby Show* and *Cheers* to become America's Number One show. Although it's recently been overtaken by a new blue-collar sitcom, *Home Improvement*, *Roseanne* can still attract over 30 million viewers a week.

A vital ingredient in the show's success is the remarkable, often unashamedly sexy, rapport that Roseanne has with her on-screen husband, Dan, played by John Goodman. A fine actor, Goodman has found himself propelled by Roseanne's popularity from supporting roles in films like *Raising Arizona* and *Sea Of Love* to becoming an out-size, genuine Hollywood star, though his starring-role films like *King Ralph* and *The Babe* have yet to match his talents.

An equally vital counter balance to the over-whelming natural charisma of Roseanne is the superb actress, Laurie Metcalfe, who plays her unlucky-in-love sister, Jackie, and Sara Gilbert, Lecy Goranson and Michael Fishman who play Roseanne's (for the most part) mercifully un-cute children.

In recent years Roseanne has been attracting more attention for what she's been doing behind the scenes rather than on the screen.

Firstly, there were arguments about how the show should develop which ended up with Matt Williams, the original writer and executive producer of the show, plus director, Ellen Falcon leaving the team.

Roseanne subsequently explained that she had felt the show was losing touch with its earthy realism. Now she is certainly able to wield huge influence over new executive producer Jay Daniel and his team of writers, as each week

Key TV

Roseanne
(ABC network, 1988-present).

As a stand-up comedian: Rodney Dangerfield - It's Not Easy Being Me (HBO special, 1986); The Tonight Show – 24th Anniversary Special (NBC network, 1986); The Roseanne Barr Show (HBO special, 1987).

they struggle to turn round new scripts in three days; she has final veto over what is in or out.

One character that has come in, a schmucko neighbour, is played by Tom Arnold, a former stand-up comedian and Roseanne's second husband and also co-executive producer of the show with her. Such is Roseanne's clout and the value of her show to ABC that in 1992 she was even able to persuade the network to give Arnold a series of his own as well.

In addition to her controversial home-and-work relationship with Arnold, and the proprietorial his-and-hers tattoos they both share, Roseanne has also attracted major headlines attention with fashionable confessions of having been abused by her parents as a child. None of which has seemed to damage her or the show's appeal.

Performance Extracts

Typical Roseanne material:

I hate the word housewife; I don't like the word home-maker either. I want to be called – domestic goddess.

My husband complained to me, he said "I can't even remember when we last had sex", and I said, "Well I can and that's why we ain't doin' it."

You may marry the man of your dreams, ladies, but 14 years later you're married to a couch that burps.

Rowan Atkinson

"Rowan completely focuses the audience on his lips, face or body. His talent is mysterious, baffling, magical and inimitable as he conjures things out of nowhere" – Stephen Fry

Rowan Atkinson is one of Britain's most outstanding modern comedy talents. Though a highly skilled comic actor, Atkinson is best known for reviving visual comedy and slapstick for 1990s TV audiences with his Mr Bean character.

He has the natural gift of highly pliable facial features (newspapers perennially dub him 'the rubber-faced clown'). His rich repertoire of silly movements betray his great admiration for Buster Keaton, John Cleese and the French visual comedian, Jacques Tati.

Lip and limb-twitching aside, Atkinson has also shown in four series of his hugely popular historical sitcom, *Blackadder*, that he possesses the equally impressive comic ability of playing a two-faced, bad-tempered, amoral character which audiences nevertheless take to their hearts. In British television only the late Leonard Rossiter has made such a relentlessly unpleasant character (Rigsby in *Rising Damp*) so popular.

His Work

Atkinson, a neurotic perfectionist, spends a great deal of time working on Mr Bean ideas with his writers, and is loathe to spread the material over more than one or two half-hour Mr Bean specials a year.

He says: "Mr Bean is an anarchic, childish and asexual character. Buster Keaton and Jacques Tati's characters were the same. He is a child not only in the sense of his innocence but also in his viciousness and vindictiveness when things do not go his own way.

"Comedians in the silent films were schooled in vaudeville where their movements had to be large to get the audience's attention. An awful lot of what Mr Bean does is quite small and discreet – which you can do on TV and in films now, with more close-ups and definition."

His Life

Rowan Atkinson was born in 1955 into a family with no show-biz aspirations, though his father's father had owned a chain of cinemas in the 1930s. Rowan ran the film society at school and there first came across Jacques Tati's films.

Apparently an unremarkable, slightly nerdy teenager, Atkinson studied Electrical and Electronic Engineering at Newcastle University, and then went to Oxford University to do his research for an MSc in Engineering Science.

At Oxford, a latent desire to perform emerged and he joined the Oxford Revue, taking part in its show at the 1977 Edinburgh Fringe Festival and stealing the best notices.

The following year he staged a critically acclaimed one-man show in a small London theatre and was snapped up to form a team with Mel Smith, Griff Rhys Jones, Pamela Stephenson and Chris Langham in a new BBC sketch show, *Not The Nine O'Clock News*. Produced by John Lloyd and Sean Hardie, the show was a new experiment in satirical television, a co-venture between the BBC's comedy and current affairs departments.

The show was a huge hit, and in its wake Atkinson put together a new one-man theatre show with his collaborators since Oxford, writer Richard Curtis and music composer Howard Goodall, which ran for a sell-out season in the West End and which he then toured round Australia, New Zealand and the Far East.

The first series of *Blackadder*, written by Curtis and produced by Lloyd, had Atkinson playing a weevilish young nobleman at the time of the Crusades. It had a big budget and big ideas that were disappointing in their execution.

But Lloyd managed to persuade to BBC to back a second, far more financially constrained, series, set in the Elizabethan era. Surrounded by a strong supporting cast, including Stephen Fry, Tim McInnerny and Miranda Richardson, and with Ben Elton teaming

up as co-writer with Curtis, both Atkinson and the series took off in a fast-moving whirl of witty and bawdy comedy.

The next two series, set in the Regency period with Hugh Laurie as the Crown Prince George, and then during the First World War in *Blackadder Goes Forth*, confirmed Atkinson's position as a great comic actor who can, unusually, combine broad popular appeal and subtlety and thoughtfulness in his comedy.

In this period, though, Atkinson had less success pursuing a theatrical career. He starred in a critically panned production of an American farce, *The Nerd*, and later suffered the traumatic experience of having his first one-man show on Broadway savaged by the critics and shut down after 14 performances. He made a happier return to the West End in 1989 in *The Sneeze*, acting in a collection of one-act plays by Chekhov, translated by Michael Frayn.

Despite the public pressure for more *Blackadders*, Atkinson turned his attention to Mr Bean, the first pilot for which (made at Thames Television) was transmitted on New Years Day 1990, and since when half a dozen more shows have been made. Thames Television was the company that had earned many millions of pounds through its worldwide

distribution of *The Benny Hill Show*, and the company clearly saw Atkinson's visual comedy export potential.

Atkinson has his own television production company, Tiger Television – producer of the documentary series, *Funny Business*, to which this book is a companion.

Professionally, his sights are now set on establishing a following for Mr Bean in America, where a special short-film was shown in cinemas across the States last year; but it remains to be seen whether Mr Bean will strike such a resoundingly popular – and silent – chord there as he has done in Britain.

Key TV/Films

TV: Not The Nine O'Clock News; The Black Adder; Blackadder II; Blackadder The Third; Blackadder Goes Forth; Mr Bean.

Films: The Tall Guy (1990); The Witches (1990) and the 1989 BBC/HBO co-production, The Appointments Of Denis Jennings which won an Oscar for Best Short Film.

Performance Extract

From a *Not The Nine O'Clock News* sketch:

DOCTOR, IN A NHS HOSPITAL, TO A ROOM FULL OF SICK PEOPLE: "Right, you all know the procedure... we are in the unusual position of having a hospital bed to spare... award goes to the most deserving case... who's going to start the bidding?... measles anyone?... do I hear measles?... thank you, sir... pneumonia... double pneumonia... malaria... I

have a telephone offer of rabies... deep depression to the man on the window ledge... going to the man on the window ledge... going... going... going... gone... I'll have to start the bidding again..."

Dan Aykroyd

"Frankly, I wish I had the money and not the fame. I don't believe in low profile, I believe in no profile." – Dan Aykroyd.

America's *Rolling Stone* magazine once declared that comedy was the "rock n'roll of the '80s".

No-one contributed more than Aykroyd and his partner John Belushi to the notion that comedy stars could give performances full of the kind of druggy, volatile aggression and self-regarding sexuality more usually associated with 1970s rock stars – especially in their most famous creation, Jake and Elwood, the Blues Brothers.

His Work

Aykroyd cites as his comedy influences Peter Sellers, Jackie Gleason, Jerry Lewis and The Three Stooges, and elements of all those exuberant styles could be seen in his performances as an original cast member of the ground-breaking TV show, *Saturday Night Live*.

He was hailed for his wildly exaggerated impersonations of Presidents Nixon and Carter and crazy characters like Beldar of the conically disfigured family of aliens – the Coneheads, and numerous crooks and implausible fast-buck salesmen.

As a performer, writer and recently director in films, Aykroyd's comedy acting talent has actually been most successfully employed under the guidance of strong comedy directors: John Landis in *The Blues Brothers*, *Trading Places* and *Spies Like Us*; fellow-Canadian Ivan Reitman in *Ghostbusters* and its sequel.

Unlike fellow SNL alumnus, Chevy Chase, Aykroyd is not really cut out for the conventional male leads in Hollywood's romantic comedies, but his Oscar-nominated supporting performance in *Driving Miss Daisy* underlined the depth of his acting abilities.

His Life

Daniel Edward Aykroyd was born in Ottawa, Ontario on July 1st 1952. He had a strict Catholic upbringing in Quebec but was expelled from the St Pius X Preparatory Seminary for "minor acts of delinquency."

He dropped out of university, but through working in commercials and comedy shows on cable TV, was able to co-write and co-star in a children's TV series, *Coming Up Rosie*, for the Canadian Broadcasting Corporation.

In 1972 he joined the Toronto off-shoot of Chicago's legendary improvisational comedy group, Second City. Two years later, he moved to Chicago to join the main group. His impersonation of Richard Nixon as a used car salesman was a local hit and helped him get recruited in 1975 to the cast for the debut season of *Saturday Night Live* by its producer, Lorne Michaels.

(1952-)

Aykroyd immediately fell into a close relationship with Belushi both in and outside *Saturday Night Live*, even sharing for a time the New York apartment of the latter and his wife, Judy Jacklin.

As their reputations soared, so did their apparent desire to elevate recreational drug habits to Olympic levels; their upward trajectory seemed unstoppable. They introduced the Blues Brothers to SNL's audience in 1977, and within a year, backed by a band of authentic blues giants, they were playing stadium gigs and releasing an album, *Briefcase Full Of Blues*, which sold two million copies.

Their involvement in 1979 in Steven Spielberg's colossal flop of a comedy movie about America's hysterical response to Pearl Harbour, *1941*, was a minor hiccup. They quit SNL and made *The Blues Brothers* film with John Landis, an enduring and highly profitable comedy classic with young audiences.

The inevitable toll of their private indulgences on their professional judgement began to emerge with the next film they made together in 1981, *Neighbours*, a sloppy suburban farce.

When Belushi died in infamously sad and squalid circumstances in 1982, of all the 'rock n' roll' comedians who had tagged along for the seemingly endless party, Aykroyd was naturally the most deeply affected.

Aykroyd's first solo film appearance came in 1983 with the disappointing college-professor-becomes-a-mobster comedy, *Doctor Detroit*. But then came the box office bonanzas: 1983's *Trading Places*, with Aykroyd a worthy foil to Eddie Murphy at his best; and, in 1984, the wonderfully off-beat paranormal comedy *Ghostbusters* (the highest earning comedy ever until *Home Alone*), which Aykroyd wrote with co-star Harold Ramis (and which he had initially conceived as a vehicle for himself and Belushi).

Apart from its 1989 sequel, Aykroyd has found it hard to pin down the right parts in the right films since *Ghostbusters*. Mostly he's been the best thing in otherwise disappointing movies, like *The Great Outdoors* or 1988's *My Stepmother Is An Alien*. Arguably the best was 1987's *Dragnet*, the Tom Mankiewicz-directed spoof of the 1950s TV cop series, in

which Aykroyd sends up in splendidly dead-pan style the show's original granite-featured hero, Jack Webb.

The most unlikely facet of Aykroyd's character, in fact, is his life-long fascination with the police – the career he says he would have chosen if he hadn't become a comedy actor. He's devoted to motorcycles and collects police badges, and was once part-owner with a number of police officers of a bar in Toronto (he later owned a private bar in Chicago with Belushi). He's married to the actress Donna Dixon, and they have one child.

> # Key TV/Films
>
> **TV:** Saturday Night Live.
>
> **Films:** The Blues Brothers (1980);
> Trading Places (1983);
> Ghostbusters (1984);
> Dragnet (1987);
> Ghostbusters II (1989);
> Driving Miss Daisy (1989).

Performance Extract

From a *Saturday Night Live* sketch:

AYKROYD IS FRED GARVIN, A GROSSLY UNSEXY MIDDLE-AGED MAN IN A BROWN PLAID JACKET WHO HAS ENTERED A CONFUSED YOUNG FEMALE BANK EXECUTIVE'S HOTEL ROOM AT NIGHT, ANNOUNCING HIMSELF AS A BUSINESS PERK PROVIDED BY GREAT LAKES FEED & GRAIN.

Woman: I don't think you understand – I'm not that kind of girl.

Fred: Let me reassure you ma'am. I can assure you professional hygiene, discretion and animal gratification.

Woman: I've never had to pay for that in my life.

Fred: Well don't worry about it, Great Lakes Feed & Grain is picking up the tab. You've got me for the whole night.

Woman: (NOT EXCITED BY THE THOUGHT) Hey...

Fred: Hay is for horses, young lady, no ifs and ands and buts about it. You're spending the night with (TURNING SMUGLY TO CAMERA LIKE A COP SERIES HERO) Fred Garvin – Male Prostitute! (SHOWING HER A CHIT) I have a work order here which specifies that I am to roger you roundly until 6.15 tomorrow morning.

Lucille Ball

"Lucy is the female Charlie Chaplin... there's nobody else who can do what she does with her face, with her walk, with her action... in a Lucy show, everything starts with Lucy" – Desi Arnaz.

Lucille Ball is the red-headed Godmother of TV comedy whose clever clowning in her and husband Desi Arnaz's sitcom, *I Love Lucy*, has never been surpassed, as continued re-runs of the 1950s series still testify today.

Her Work

The panoply of Ball's clowning skills are well demonstrated in some of the best loved Lucy shows. For instance, 1952's 'Lucy Does A TV Commercial', in which rehearsing a pitch for a television commercial for a vitamin syrup (which, she doesn't know, chiefly comprises alcohol) Ball gets progressively smashed: an object lesson in the art of playing stage-drunk.

In 1955's 'Harpo Marx' show, Lucy, trying to impress a friend that movie stars are always dropping by her home, has disguised herself as Harpo Marx. Then the real Harpo unexpectedly turns up and Lucy does a memorable version of a classic mime routine, pretending to be a mirror-image of the Marx brother.

Ball's story in movies was the time-honoured tale of the beautiful chorus girl who steps into the limelight; except she caught producers' attention through her vanity-free willingness to make herself look silly.

I Love Lucy's domestic 'situation' – neighbours and house-

wives, Lucy and Ethel (Vivian Vance), are constantly embroiled in schemes that exasperate their respective husbands, Ricky (Arnaz) and Fred Mertz (William Frawley) – was no more exceptional than that of other sitcoms of the period and the hundreds of family-and-friends-based television comedy series that have trailed in its wake.

What the show had was a tremendous comic energy, inventiveness and relentlessly good writing (courtesy of writers like Bob Carroll Jnr, Madelyn Pugh, Jess Oppenheimer, Bob Weiskopf and Bobby Schiller) plus the benefit of great comic acting from Vance and Frawley and (after 1955) the general glamour of its Hollywood setting and numerous guest stars.

Her Life

Lucy Desiree Ball was born on August 6th 1911. At the age of 15 Lucy enrolled in a New York drama school (where Bette Davis was the star pupil), but left after six weeks when her teacher told the 'gawky girl' she was wasting her money. She tried to make an impact on Broadway as a

chorus girl, but had more success as a model.

At 17 she was stricken with a crippling illness, a form of arthritis, from which she took a couple of years to recover. But bouncing back into New York City she secured a high profile modelling job as the Chesterfield Cigarette Girl, and then in 1933 Busby Berkeley brought her to

Catchphrase

"Waaaaah!"
(approximately the noise made by Ball, regularly bursting into tears in *I Love Lucy*)

Hollywood as one of the glamorous 'Goldwyn Girls', firstly to appear in the Eddie Cantor musical, *Roman Scandals*, and then ten more in the following year.

In 1934, anxious to become a star, she left Goldwyn, taking a big salary drop, to become a B-picture bit player with Columbia. Quickly moving on to RKO's charm school she began to be noticed for her tireless zeal for learning and her demands to be given better parts, which, gradually, she got – the star's best-friend kind of roles – until cracking the big time in RKO's back-stage comedy hit, *Stage Door*, in 1937.

Her comic talents were more fully exploited by radio, and in the late '30s she worked successfully as the featured comedienne in top radio shows hosted by Phil Baker and Jack Haley.

By 1940 Ball was known as the 'Queen of RKO's B pictures', and on one of them, *Too Many Girls*, she met Cuban band leader, Desi Arnaz, who later, after a cautious on-off-on courtship (he was a notorious womaniser), became her first husband and crucial business partner.

Praise from the critics for her first serious acting role as a crippled night club singer in RKO's *The Big Street* (1942), led to a contract with MGM. However, her first vehicle, a musical with Red Skelton, *Dubarry Was A Lady*, was not the incandescent launch-pad she had hoped. Though she did receive an education at MGM in slapstick and prop comedy from Buster Keaton, also under contract to the studio at the time, who had spotted her potential.

Again it was radio to the rescue. In the late '50s she starred in a radio sitcom, *My Favourite Husband*. When CBS wanted to adapt it for TV, Lucy suggested that Arnaz should play her husband but, strangely, the network said the public wouldn't accept that she could be married to a Cuban band leader.

To prove them wrong, the couple formed their own company, Desilu Productions, toured a comedy act version of the idea based on their own married life, financed their own pilot of the show and finally convinced CBS to buy the show, after Lucy and Desi had agreed that they should not be playing themselves but a more mundanely married couple.

I Love Lucy was not just a hit with audiences, it changed the nature of the TV business. Lucy and Desi refused to do the show live in New York (as was the norm). Instead they recorded it, multi-camera, on film, and having done a deal with CBS whereby they retained ownership of the shows, were able to earn a

fortune through Desilu Productions by selling them over and over again in syndication.

For a while Desilu Productions was a major force in Hollywood, producing many other television comedy series and specials and even feature films. Lucy and Desi divorced in 1960 (she remarried, to stand-up comic, Gary Morton, in 1961), and she bought Arnaz out of their company for two and a half million dollars, remaining closely involved herself in the running of the company.

Key TV/Films

TV: I Love Lucy (CBS, 1951-57); The Lucy Show (CBS, 1962-68); Here's Lucy (CBS, 1968-73).

Films: Stage Door (1937); Room Service (with the Marx Brothers, 1938); A Girl, A Guy, and A Gob (screwball comedy directed by Harold Lloyd, 1941); The Big Street (1942); Dubarry Was A Lady (1943); Her Husband's Affairs (1947); Fancy Pants (with Bob Hope, (1950); Mame (1974).

Performance Extract

From *I Love Lucy*:

Ricky: These have been the best 15 years of my life...(LUCY IS UPSET)... what's the matter?
Lucy: We've only been married 13 years.

Ricky: Oh, well... I mean, it seems like 15 years.
Lucy: What?
Ricky: No, uh... what I mean is that it doesn't... uh... seem possible... that all the fun could have been crammed into

only 13 years.
Lucy: Well, you certainly wormed out of that one. Waaaaah!

Ronnie Barker

Catchphrase

"And it's goodnight from me...",
"and it's goodnight from him"
(Barker and Corbett's
familiar sign-off at the end
of *The Two Ronnies*)

"Thank you for your inquiry, but I am retiring from public and professional life so I am unable to undertake any more commitments. To those people with whom I have worked, I would like to express my gratitude and good wishes. So it's a big thank you from me and it's goodbye from him. Goodbye" – message on Ronnie Barker's answering machine after his abrupt withdrawal from showbiz in 1988.

Ronnie Barker is one of British television's greatest post-war comic actors, equally admired for his starring performances in BBC sitcoms like *Porridge*, *Going Straight* and *Open All Hours*, and achievements as a sketch performer and writer in *The Two Ronnies* with Ronnie Corbett.

When Barker first appeared on television in the mid-1960s he had a solid background in repertory theatre behind him, but once famous, with one or two exceptions, he chose to concentrate his talent on television work, rather than pursuing a parallel career as a character actor in the West End.

A master of accents and possessing a superbly assured sense of how and when to deliver a punch-line, Barker once confessed: "I'm not one of those people who can reel off funny story after funny story. I must have a script and a character."

His Work

Barker's first notable comedy work was as a mid-run addition to the cast of BBC Radio's hugely successful sailoring sitcom, *The Navy Lark*, which greatly benefited from his ability to reproduce voices across the range of regional accents and the class spectrum.

At the same period in the mid-1960s he came to the public's attention as one of the regular team of comedy performers which David Frost employed in his satirical comedy shows for the BBC and latterly ITV. Barker worked with up-and-coming talents like John Cleese, Tim Brooke-Taylor and Ronnie Corbett.

In his greatest role, the habitual crook, Norman Stanley Fletcher ('Fletch'), banged up in Slade Prison in *Porridge* (written by Dick Clement and Ian LaFrenais), Barker pulled off the considerable dramatic feat of making what could have been a seedy or pathetic character into a hugely likable tower of wit and University-Of-Life-style wisdom.

His Life

Ronnie Barker was born in Bedford on September 25th 1929, the son of an oil company clerk. After school he worked in a bank and trained as an architect in Oxford, while at 17, making his first steps into amateur dramatics.

His talent turned a hobby into a profession, beginning with stints in repertory theatre in Aylesbury, Manchester and Oxford. As Ronald Barker he gave his first

(1929-)

West End performance in a production of *Mourning Becomes Electra* at the Arts Theatre, and was subsequently in five plays at the Royal Court Theatre.

When Barker was first offered work in radio he changed his name to Ronnie, thinking it sounded friendlier and was more suited to the comedy shows he was doing.

His radio success led to the offer in 1966 to become one of the comedy team on *The Frost Report*, David Frost's first major British show following *That Was The Week That Was.*

It was on *The Frost Report* that Barker struck up his off-screen friendship and on-screen rapport with Ronnie Corbett. They were the two grammar school 'oiks' amid the crowd of thrusting young Oxbridge comics and the visual disparity between the large, rotund Barker and the diminutive, hamster-faced Corbett made them a naturally funny and obvious double-act.

In 1970 the BBC launched Barker and Corbett in *The Two Ronnies* which established itself through the 1970s as TV's classiest variety show. The shows had a precise structure: sketches and music interspersed with their solo

spots – Corbett's artfully rambling jokes and Barker's mock-public information lectures spun from puns, double-entendres and spoonerisms; plus the weekly serial, usually spoofs of cinema genres. It was only after several years that Barker modestly revealed to the production team and Corbett that sketches apparently contributed to the show by writers, Gerald Wiley, Jonathan Cobbold and Jack Goetz, had actually been written by him.

Porridge came along for Barker in 1974 from writers Clement and LaFrenais who had previously penned the outstanding 1960s sitcom, *The Likely Lads*, and its even better 1973 sequel, *Whatever Happened To The Likely Lads?*

The follow-up show, 1978's *Going Straight* in which Fletch was stranded in the outside world, was by comparison a disappointing venture. However, in the same year he kicked off another sitcom which was to draw even higher ratings, playing the stuttering, tight-fisted north country shopkeeper, Arkwright, in Roy Clarke's *Open All Hours*. Like Porridge, this was produced by Sydney Lotterby, and once again Barker had excellent comic support, particularly from David Jason as his assistant, Granville.

Clarke, Lotterby and Barker later combined on another altogether weaker sitcom about a Welsh photographer, *The Magnificent Evans*. But when a doctor informed Barker in 1988 that he was seriously endangering his health through over-work, he immediately decided to retire at a point that could be described as the peak of his career.

Barker marked his retirement by opening an Oxfordshire antiques shop with his wife, Joy – free to indulge such passions as his enthusiasm for collecting saucy Victorian postcards, two books of which – *Gentlemen's Relish* and *Sugar And Spice* – he has published with some success.

Performance Extract ➤

From The Two Ronnies:

AN ELDERLY GENERAL AND ANCIENT ADMIRAL ARE SITTING IN A HOTEL LOUNGE. A PRETTY WAITRESS SERVES THEM TEA...

Ronnie Barker: ...Fond of women are you?
Ronnie Corbett: I used to be..

Barker: Gone off 'em, have you?
Corbett: Not at all. Just as keen as ever...
Barker: ...How long is it?
Corbett: What?
Barker: How long is it – since you had, since you made, since you were, er... since you did, er... the... er, made love to a woman, I mean?

Corbett: ... When did you last make love?
Barker: If you must know, it was around 1945.
Corbett: 1945? Ha, well that's a damn long time ago!
Barker: Not really (LOOKS AT WATCH). It's only 22.30 now.

John Belushi

Rolling Stone magazine: "The '60s and the Woodstock legacy applied a subcultural legitimacy to the consumption of drugs for both mind expansion and mind impairment. John, and, in fact, all of us from *Saturday Night Live*, were participants in that new social phalanx. It was the touch of the hippie, the beatnik, the hipster that helped us to impart a weird, novel approach to our work."

Belushi was a performer of huge physical strength and stamina, but he didn't have the grace normally associated with great clowns and slapstick technicians. He didn't have the quick-fire verbal dexterity of a stand-up comedian.

What he did possess was a comedic equivalent to that element in the screen performances of actors like Marlon Brando (a Belushi hero), Paul Newman and Robert DeNiro that might be called 'attitude'.

His Life

John Belushi was born on January 25th 1949 in Chicago, the son of an Albanian father who had moved to America at 16 in 1934 and built a small restaurant business. He had a brother, Jim (now a moderately successful comedy movie actor), and sister, Marian.

He went to high school in Illinois, but was more interested in drama, playing in rock bands and sport (he was football captain) than classes.

He didn't get good enough grades to win a chosen football scholarship at Illinois Wesleyan, and ended up at the University of Wisconsin instead where there was no football team but a good

"He was 50% clown, 50% rock star and 50% actor" – Bernie Brillstein, John Belushi's manager.

John Belushi could have been the unrivalled towering presence in post-war American comedy. Instead, following his death from a drugs overdose in 1982, his name has become synonymous with the gruesome flipside of contemporary fame and the opportunities for unfettered excess it can offer.

Belushi filled *Saturday Night Live*, the influential American TV comedy show in whose success he was a pivotal player, with a kind of brooding, aggressive physical comedy that had never been seen before. Either as a berserk Samurai warrior or frenetically jiving Blues Brother or as a super-slob in the hit film, *National Lampoon's Animal House*, Belushi's comic performances were so imbued with commitment and intensity as to be unnerving.

His Work

After Belushi's death in 1982, his best friend, SNL partner and Blues Brother, Dan Aykroyd, said in drama department. He told his girlfriend (later his wife), Judy Jacklin, that he was going to be an actor and that she might have to support him.

In 1970 he began performing sketches in a Chicago coffee house he had opened with friends and this led to an audition with the city's renowned improvisational comedy troupe, Second City (a training ground and springboard for other future stars like Bill Murray and Gilda Radner).

In 1972 Tony Hendra, the editor of the hip, counter-culture humour magazine, *National Lampoon*, was putting together an off-Broadway stage show aimed at capturing live the exuberant outrageousness it displayed in print.

Hendra recruited Belushi to the cast of the show, *National Lampoon's Lemmings*, which also included Chevy Chase. The show opened in 1973 and was a long-running hit; it was Belushi's introduction to trendy acclaim and the casual intake of cocaine that was rife across the whole of the entertainment industry.

Belushi also wrote and performed on a syndicated *National Lampoon* radio show, which he ended up directing. One new comedian he tried to recruit to the radio show was a member of Second City's Canadian off-shoot,

Dan Aykroyd. Aykroyd had too many commitments to be able to move, but in 1974 Belushi brought Gilda Radner and Harold Ramis into a new Lampoon stage show.

In 1975 Lorne Michaels was preparing to launch a hip new television comedy and music show for the NBC network with a group of young performers and writers, to be centred on Chevy Chase. Michaels hired Aykroyd, Radner, Garrett Morris, Jane Curtin and Laraine Newman, and – at Aykroyd and Chase's prompting – Belushi.

Saturday Night Live took off on October 11th 1975 and took the youth of America by storm. Although Belushi earned the inside reputation as the show's most explosive performer, it was Chase who initially got all the publicity and left for Hollywood in 1976.

However, it was Belushi, now confirmed as SNL's major star, who in 1978 appeared in the first film to spectacularly hit home with the new comedy audience that SNL had identified. *National Lampoon's Animal House*, directed by John Landis, was a low-budget high-earning smash ("a panty raid on respectability... low humour of a high order", raved *Newsweek*) and the critics saluted Belushi as a new comic powerhouse.

Key TV/Films

TV: Saturday Night Live.

Films: National Lampoon's Animal House (1978); Goin' South (1978); The Blues Brothers (1980).

Straight after *Animal House* Belushi also filmed an excellent cameo role in Jack Nicholson's laconic Western, *Goin' South*, then an unexpectedly downbeat part in director Joan Tewkesbury's feminine revenge drama, *Old Boyfriends*, and, with Aykroyd, a leading role in Steven Spielberg's exorbitant WWII comedy turkey, *1941*.

Belushi and Aykroyd enjoyed greater personal success with their SNL spin-off characters, the Blues Brothers, who spawned a number one album and another high-earning (though critically panned) Landis movie, *The Blues Brothers*, in 1980.

After their first post-SNL movie together, *Neighbours (1981)*, flopped, Belushi had a respectable starring role in Michael Apted's 1981 romantic comedy, *Continental Divide*. He was found dead from a cocaine-and-heroin overdose in a hotel off Sunset Boulevard on March 5th 1982.

Performance Extract ➤

From a *Saturday Night Live* sketch:

CHEVY CHASE SIGNING OFF FROM HIS 'WEEKEND UPDATE' SEGMENT IN THE SHOW.

Chase: Last week we made the comment that March comes in

like a lion and goes out like a lamb. Now to reply is our chief meteorologist, John Belushi.

Belushi: Do you know that March behaves differently in other countries? In Norway, for example, March comes in like a polar bear and goes out like a

walrus. Or take the case of Honduras, where March comes in like a lamb and goes out like a salt-marsh harvest mouse. Let us compare this to the Maldive Islands where March comes in like a wildebeest and goes out like an ant.

Jack Benny

"He is secure on stage. He never sweats. The tempo is easy. If he tells a pointless joke and fails to get a response, he'll stop and do the look and the hand gesture. And if he holds it long enough, he'll get the laugh. He's such an institution, they'll laugh because they're afraid there really is a point." – George Burns on Benny.

Jack Benny was among the handful of comedians who dominated American radio, films and TV between the 1930s and 1960s, and he was the comedian most admired by his peers.

Benny developed a unique comic style which had little to do with the traditional, pushy, punchline-crazy vaudeville comedians who strove to shove jokes down the throats of their boisterous audiences like trainers force-feeding fish to seals.

He used the more intimate nature of radio to coax the audience into his world, trading on his own supposed meanness and vanity, and unselfishly surrounding himself with outspoken supporting players who turned the swapping of insults with Benny into a great spectator sport. He understood that by making his mock displays of pride look foolish, his audiences would love him all the more.

His Work

One of the most important lessons that a stand-up comedian can learn is not to be afraid of silence: you don't have to gabble on and on at an audience. You can stop, pause, intimidate or entice an audience into laughing; you can use a pause to make the audience do the work. Unlike many comics he was endlessly respectful of his writers, including Hal Goldman, Sam Perrin, George Baizer and Al Gordon, and the degree to which he depended on their talents.

The format developed in the 1930s for his radio show – presenting a 'back-stage' view of events supposedly happening in the run-up to its broadcast – was innovative and influenced many subsequent radio and TV shows in America and Britain.

His Life

Jack Benny was born Benjamin Kubelsky on February 14th 1894 in Waukegan, Illinois, to Lithuanian immigrant parents who ran a saloon.

He took violin lessons as a child and became proficient enough on leaving school at 16 to get work playing in vaudeville theatre bands. For a while he performed in vaudeville in a musical duo, but after a bizarre in-land spell with the US Navy in 1917-18, he developed a solo act, mixing dry monologues with his violin playing, and in the 1920s as 'The Aristocrat Of Humour' he became a sizable success, graduating to Broadway shows and Hollywood musicals.

NBC gave him his first radio series in 1932, and within a couple

(1894-1975)

of years it had taken residency at the top of the popularity polls. Each week, listeners heard Benny trying to control his 'stock company' of regular sidekicks: his (real-life since 1926) long-suffering wife, Mary Livingstone; boozy, skirt-chasing band leader, Phil Harris; jovial announcer, Don Wilson; and, later, his irreverent valet, Rochester (played by Eddie Anderson), and the annoying, gauche young singer, Dennis Day. Another important addition was Benny's violin teacher, Professor LeBlanc, played by Mel Blanc (the voice behind immortal Warner Brothers cartoon characters like Bugs Bunny, Sylvester and Tweety Pie).

One of the main highlights of American radio comedy in the 1940s was the long-running 'feud' which Benny invented with the acerbic comedian, Fred Allen, whose show *Allen's Alley*, had a similar format to Benny's. They hurled insults at one another from their respective shows ("Benny couldn't ad-lib a belch after a Hungarian dinner") and occasionally guested on each other's shows.

Despite his huge popularity on radio, Benny never quite clicked on a massive scale with cinema audiences. He made films regularly between 1934-45, all kinds of

comedies from Western spoof, *Buck Benny Rides Again* (1940), to classic farce, *Charley's Aunt* (1941), but, as Benny himself remarked, it seemed that Hollywood's writers never quite understood how his idiosyncratic humour worked.

However, Benny did give a stunning starring performance in *To Be Or Not To Be*, director Ernst Lubitsch's brilliant 1942 black comedy about a Polish theatre troupe accidentally embroiled in espionage and trying to outwit their country's Nazi occupiers. The film's darkly urbane humour was not much appreciated by wartime audiences but Benny and co-star Carole Lombard's work, as married, bitchy Shakespearian bill-toppers, has since been highly lauded by critics.

Moving to television in the 1950s, Benny began with occasional, then biweekly shows until he and his writing team had developed a show that they felt was strong enough to run on a weekly basis. The show became less complex than it had been on radio, though still boldly (for TV) set 'behind-the-scenes'.

After 1965, Benny reduced his workload to a couple of specials a year; *Jack Benny's Second Farewell* was the final one, broadcast on January 24th 1974, and the following year he died at the age of 80.

Key Radio/TV/Films

Radio: The Jack Benny Program (NBC, 1932-55. Sponsors included Canada Dry, Chevrolet, Jell-O, Grape Nuts Flakes and Lucky Strike).

TV: The Jack Benny Program

Films: Artists and Models (1937); Charley's Aunt (1941); To Be Or Not To Be (1942); George Washington Slept Here (1942); The Meanest Man In The World (1943); The Horn Blows At Midnight (1945); It's In The Bag (1945).

Off-stage Benny was known to his friends as a warm and big-hearted man; as a comedian who made his career on a comic reputation for stinginess, it's perhaps unsurprising that he was at pains to be a big tipper, always ensured that his employees were among the highest paid in the business, and raised many millions for charity. One thing he truly was serious about was his violin playing – he owned a Stradivarius and liked to practise for a few hours each day.

Performance Extract

From a sketch from his TV show:

BENNY IS ORGANISING A CHARITY SHOW AND WANTS GREGORY PECK TO APPEAR IN IT – THOUGH NATURALLY HE DOESN'T WANT TO PAY HIM AND IS PREPARED FOR SOME TOUGH BARGAINING, THE KIND HE

ENJOYS. BENNY VISITS PECK AT HOME AND NERVOUSLY SPENDS A LONG TIME HEDGING ROUND THE QUESTION OF PAYMENT, THEN HE BLURTS OUT:

Benny: Now – look, Greg – what fee would you ask for appearing

at this function?
Peck (AMIABLY): Jack – I'll do it for nothing.
Benny (SO WOUND UP TO HAGGLE HE CAN'T STOP HIMSELF): We weren't thinking of going that high.

Milton Berle

working class families; televisions having previously been more of a smart, luxury purchase for the well-to-do.

Milton Berle was a brash vaudevillian comedian who loved dressing up in all kinds of costumes and zany, glitzy outfits, hurling custard pies around and relentlessly rattling off corny one-liners. It was also said that he wasn't too fussy about where his jokes originated, and that his fellow comics had dubbed him 'the Thief of Badgags'.

His Work

The author, David Nathan, in his 1971 book, *The Laughtermakers*, recorded an explanation from veteran British comic, Bob Monkhouse, on how Berle gave him a lesson in comedy theory in the 1960s.

Prior to a New York concert, Berle asked Monkhouse to give him two words plus any joke of Berle's that Monkhouse could recall. The words were "last Thursday" and the joke "This suit is made from virgin wool – it comes from the sheep that runs the fastest." Berle promised Monkhouse he could switch the punchline to "It came from a sheep last Thursday" and still get the laugh. Monkhouse said: "(Berle) cracked a series of one-

liners, progressively shorter, one after the other, doing about ten, until the audience was laughing in pulse, until he got them into an absolutely neurotic state with laughter. Then he said "How about this suit? That's virgin wool. Came from a sheep last Thursday!" and they roared. He was completely the master, he had them hypnotised.

His Life

Mendel Berlinger was born on July 12th 1908 in New York, the youngest of four boys. His mother was the archetypal Jewish 'stage mother', desperate for her youngest to become a star.

At the age of five he won a talent contest imitating Charlie Chaplin. By the time he was ten he was appearing in silent movies with Mary Pickford at the Biograph studios, and from the age of 11 he began touring (as 'The Wayward Youth') New York's vaudeville circuits. Rapidly successful as a singer, dancer and clown he moved up the vaudeville bills into musical comedies, Broadway's biggest theatres and spectacular shows like *The Ziegfeld Follies*. Constantly seeking to expand his range of skills, he also began turn his hand to mimicry, magic and straight acting.

En route to Broadway stardom, Berle worked for a while as master of ceremonies at the Loew's State Theatre, where he is said to have honed his brash comic style, his ability to swat hecklers down mercilessly and his tendency to 'edit' other comedians' material into his own brand of patter. One particularly shrill laugh that could

"**H**is programs are said to have so powerful a hold on the TV public that shopkeepers who would ordinarily be open for business between eight and nine on Tuesday evenings now close down their stores for lack of customers" – the extent of Milton Berle's TV success in the late 1940s, as quoted by *The New Yorker*.

Milton Berle was the first comedy star of American television. His variety shows were garish confections of slapstick and schmaltz, and if television made 'Uncle Miltie' a star, he more than returned the favour.

It was said that his show, *Texaco Star Theatre*, was not only the most popular one in the country on its launch in 1948, but did more than any other show to boost sales of TV sets to ordinary always be heard in the audience wherever Berle played was that of his mother, who never missed one of her son's performances.

The popular Broadway singer and clown didn't really have much impact on Hollywood until the late 1930s and such B-picture formula entertainment as *New Faces* of 1937 and *Radio City Revels* (1938), and then in the 1940s he didn't progress much beyond supporting roles in nondescript 20th Century Fox comedies and whodunits.

It was frustrating at the time, but it was just as well for Berle in the light of his forthcoming television career. This was, naturally, because, when the networks ventured seriously into television after the Second World War, it was initially seen as a novelty and no threat to the big business of movies and radio shows.

A performer like Berle, experienced, funny, well known but not a major star, was a perfect prospect for the early days of television. The wary sponsors would not have to pay him a movie star salary, and unlike movie stars he wouldn't turn his nose up at the new medium.

In 1948 when NBC gave him what was initially called *The Texaco Star Theatre Vaudeville Show*. Berle made sure the show lived up to its title and stuffed it with every bit of slapstick and 'two-act' (ie, two-hander) sketch business he had learned in vaude-

ville. One of the show's writers, Goodman Ace, said that Berle told him to make the jokes 'lappy' – in other words, to avoid subtlety and let the jokes fall right into the audience's lap.

Berle insisted on supervising everything in the shows from costumes to choreography, and claimed to have been the first person to install monitors for the studio audiences to see what was going on better, and to use cameras on cranes.

Berle's reign as the king of TV comedy was spectacular but brief. NBC cancelled his show after it began haemorrhaging viewers to Phil Silvers' army sitcom, *You'll Never Get Rich* (aka *Bilko*), launched by CBS in 1955.

Berle, to his great distress, subsequently fell victim to a 30-year exclusivity contract he had signed with NBC in 1951. The network kept paying him $100,000 a year, but wouldn't take up his ideas for new TV shows, or release him to work for shows on other networks until he later renegotiated a drop in his 'salary'.

Apart from deputising for Ed Sullivan and appearing in a legal drama series, *Defenders*, Berle actually did little TV work, but maintained a heavy schedule of nightclub and theatre appearances. When vaudevillian and silent movie comedy enjoyed a trendy revival in the 1960s he starred, along with Sid Caesar, Buddy Hackett, Ethel Merman, Phil

Silvers, Jimmy Durante and others, in director Stanley Kramer's attempt at slapstick on an epic Cinerama scale, *It's A Mad, Mad, Mad, Mad World*. With its mayhem-filled chase after a secret stash of ill-gotten cash, the destruction-crazy film was like a *Blues Brothers* of its time.

Berle has never lost his appetite for stand-up comedy, and as recently as 1991 was cracking jokes at the prestigious Montreal *Just For Laughs* Comedy Festival. He plans to donate to the Library of Congress his files containing over five million jokes, cross-indexed by subject and by the comics who first told each gag and where.

Performance Extract

A typical Berle one-liner:

"Of course on TV today they are much more daring. I saw a show the other night about a surgeon who became intimate with his patient. But he was a tree surgeon."

→ Sandra Bernhard ←

"In dredging up her own adolescent dreaminess and scrutinising it with such an intense mixture of rapture and scorn, Sandra Bernhard proves both satirist and shaman, exposing the narcissism of rock culture... it is a brilliant, risky performance that brings comedy and music together in an altogether new way" – *New York Times* review of her stage show, *Giving Til It Hurts*.

Bernhard in some ways represents a meeting of comedy and performance art – her (public) life her great comic creation: as a performer, a singer, fashion model, journalist and writer, talk show guest, film actress, she swims easily through all the media's streams. She courts publicity, needing the media's many outlets for her provocative, camp outrageousness, yet whenever the media seems to think it has her trapped and tamed, she slips from its grasp, mocking its presumption and foolishness.

She is just about the only major comedy performer ever to trade on sexual ambiguity (Monty Python's the late Graham Chapman was comedy's only openly gay star prior to her, though he didn't make an issue of his homosexuality in his work). This reached its apogee in 1990 when she teased television talk show host, David Letterman, and subsequent gossip hacks that she might be the lover of pop superstar Madonna.

Her Work

We live in a media age and an age when the media is dominated by the sound, images and cultural values of pop music more than anything else.

So it makes sense that Bernhard should have chosen pop music as the increasingly central component of her stage shows. She has sent up pop singers as diverse as Diana Ross, Nina Simone and Liza Minelli, and interspersed her songs with caustic reminiscences of her childhood, weird fantasies about Steve Hicks, Patti Smith and Barbara Streisand, and any number of bitchy asides about celebrities in the news. She also takes pop's MTV-approved titillation to its discomforting extreme – for instance, singing Prince's *Little Red Corvette* in nothing but a star-spangled G-string.

She says: "My whole career is about creating false mythology because I think it's a fantastic way of manipulating the media". Bernhard's comedy attacks racial and gender stereotyping, white America's appropriation of black culture and all kinds of complacency, including any self-satisfaction she perceives in herself or her audience.

Her Life

Bernhard was born in 1955 in Flint, Michigan, the youngest of four children. Her father was a proctologist, her mother an artist. During her childhood the family moved to Scottsdale, Arizona, where, she says, she was completely misunderstood. Michigan had "black music and things with life and soul and emotion", but in Scottsdale "it was very uptight, a white, white atmosphere... the kids just didn't know how to take me."

After graduating from high school, she lived on a kibbutz in Israel, before returning to America in 1974, winding up in Los Angeles as a Beverly Hills manicurist. She took acting classes and began developing some routines in Los Angeles' comedy clubs, her ambition at the time was "to become famous so that I can have a nervous breakdown." She decided to devote herself full-time to comedy in 1978.

(1955-)

Bernhard got a considerable break in 1982 when acclaimed director Martin Scorcese cast her in a major role in his film *The King Of Comedy*, in which Robert DeNiro plays a man obsessed with the notion that he can become a top TV comedian overnight. Bernhard was a revelation as the fanatical groupie of a talk show host (played by Jerry Lewis) that she and DeNiro decide to kidnap.

She reaped a ton of favourable reviews, but Hollywood's homogeneity has meant a dearth of similar stand-out roles since then, beyond her playing a kinky nurse in Nic Roeg's film of a Dennis Potter script, *Track 29*; an unexpected appearance in 1985's *Sesame Street Presents Follow That Bird*; and then, more appropriately, a leading role as a camp villainess in the otherwise badly flawed Bruce Willis comedy flop, *Hudson Hawk*.

It was in 1988 that Bernhard began to make her mark as a comedy performer, putting together *Without You I'm Nothing* with long-time writer/ director collaborator John Bosk-ovich, which ran off-Broadway for six months and then became a best-selling comedy record.

She also published a well received collection of autobiographical prose pieces, *Confessions Of A Pretty Lady*; its apercus as incisive as: "There was a time when you spent the night with someone, and the next day they would send you a dozen long-stem roses with a sexy little note. Now people send a bunch of balloons with cute cards saying such things as 'Being with you last night was like having my own circus'."

Bernhard has been a regular guest/performer on the cultish NBC talk show, *Late Night With Letterman*, and it was with David Letterman in 1990 that she and Madonna flirted suggestively. The world's media immediately trumpeted that the two women enjoyed an intimate relationship, engulfing Bernhard in the biggest publicity blitz of her career.

Bernhard later featured in Madonna's controversial documentary film, *Truth Or Dare*; but however much she might have revelled in the story's shockwaves at first, she has since become highly impatient with the lingering and restrictive label of being 'Madonna's girlfriend' first and foremost in the public's eyes. The singer is now a taboo topic with her.

In 1990 she and Boskovich adapted and broadened out the one-woman nightclub show setting off *Without You I'm Nothing* for an eponymous feature film, of which one reviewer wrote: "...there's a dark genius here... that realizes how much commercial time has speeded up in America, which makes every cultural impulse instantly convertible to kitsch."

In 1991 she launched her new cabaret show, *Giving Til It Hurts*,

Key Shows/Films

Stage Shows: Without You I'm Nothing (1988); Giving Til It Hurts (1991).

Films: The King Of Comedy (1983); Track 29 (1988); Without You I'm Nothing (1990); Hudson Hawk (1991).

to yet more high praise from American critics, and in 1992 from British critics when she brought it over for her West End debut in London. The show retains its predecessor's mix of monologues and big campy production numbers, the music provided by her backing band, *The Strap-Ons*.

Since the Madonna episode Bernhard seems to have become more assured of her physical looks (she's increasingly seen modelling at international fashion shows), and less coy about her sexuality; though she continues to confound expectations – posing recently, for instance, naked under a covering of gold paint in Playboy magazine.

Performance Extract

From *Confessions Of A Pretty Lady*:

I took a couple of acting classes my first year in LA. We would meet on hot nights in a room with no air-conditioning. A bunch of waiters with hangovers and girls who sold make-up at Bullock's would lie on the floor doing relaxation exercises and deep breathing and letting go; that was always my favourite part.

British Film Comedy

The 1930s

British music hall had supplied Hollywood's silent cinema with great clowns such as Chaplin and Laurel, but the British stage stars of the 1930s struggled to make much impact on screen.

This was not for a lack of opportunity since by law Britain's booming circuit of 5,000 cinemas had to show (and thereby finance) a quota of homemade films alongside the American product.

Thus, between 20 to 30 comedy films were produced each year, but in pure comedic terms only the films of Will Hay stand up to scrutiny now. Musical comedy films were among the most successful of the era, and made the reputations of cheeky Northerners, Gracie Fields and George Formby, while Jack Hulbert and his wife Cicely Courtenidge had the stylish corner of the market sewn up.

Fields was an established, successful stage singer by the time she found the role which would make her an icon, an irrepressible Lancastrian millgirl, in *Sing As You Go* in 1934. The following year the irrepressible Lancastrian Formby scored his first big celluloid hit in *No Limit*, directed by Field's husband, Monty Banks. Formby's gawky brand of nudge-nudge innuendo and ukulele-strumming proved surprisingly popular with overseas audiences; his spouse, Beryl, was famous for the ferocity with which she managed his career, even forbidding George to kiss the leading ladies in his films.

Through the 1930s comedy film fans could see low budget, low aspiration films starring the cream of music hall and radio talent – Max Miller, Will Fyffe, Tommy Trinder, The Crazy Gang, Arthur Askey, Tommy Handley, Sandy Powell, Arthur (Old Mother Riley) Lucan, Sydney Howard and Frank Randle – but sadly nothing to match their reputations as live performers.

The 1940s

During World War II the comedy stars of the 1930s donned their uniforms for patriotic propaganda purposes, and though such films undoubtedly cheered wartime audiences they were thin stuff – Hay's *The Ghost Of St Michaels* (1941) and Askey's remake of the 1931 hit *The Ghost Train* (1941) being exceptions.

After the war, the focus switched from vehicles for music hall and radio stars to the output of one of Britain's small film studios. 1947 saw the release of *Hue And Cry*, 1948 *Whisky Galore* and 1949 *Passport To Pimlico* and *Kind Hearts And Coronets* – brilliant, imaginative, distinctive films from Ealing Studios. Ealing had been the home of outstanding wartime documentary-making, but in the late 1940s the studio championed intelligent, urbane comedy directors like Robert Hamer and Alexander Mackendrick and in particular the superb writer, T.E.B. Clarke.

Kind Heart And Coronets featured a tour de force of comic acting by Alec Guinness in eight different parts.

Miss Fritton (Alastair Sim), the headmistress, with some of 'her girls' in a scene from Blue Murder At St Trinians in which Ronald Searle's 'fiends in human shape' are let loose on Europe. Also starring where Terry-Thomas, Joyce Grenfell and George Cole

The 1950s

Ealing and Guinness kept up a stunning standard of output with the satirical *The Man In The White Suit* and *The Lavender Hill Mob* (1951), but as the decade wore on the studio lost its touch, save the occasional hit like 1955's *The Ladykillers*.

Television emerged as an increasingly successful competitor, but there was one 1950s comedy star who was guaranteed to pull crowds into cinemas: Norman Wisdom's first farcical hit was *Trouble In Store* (1953).

Writer/producer Frank Launder specialised in school comedies, varying from the sublime – 1950's *The Happiest Days Of Your Life* – to the less sublime, such as the *St Trinians* films he produced with Sidney Gilliat, beginning with *The Belles Of St Trinians* in 1954.

The above starred the outstanding Alistair Sim, just one of a huge number of richly talented film comedy character actors who populated British films in this period and into the 1960s.

The 1960s

Most conspicuously successful among the British industry's dwindling output were producer Peter Rogers and director Gerald Thomas's *Carry On* films.

John Osborne scripted and Tony Richardson directed a genuine international comedy hit in 1963, *Tom Jones* starring Albert Finney.

However, it was produced by United Artists, and with the end of protectionist quotas for the domestic industry, this was the decade that in cinematic terms sealed Britain's fate.

The 1970s

Television may have kept people away from their local Odeons and Empires, but virtually the only British comedy films made in the late 1960s and 1970s were feature-length versions of top-rating TV sitcoms.

Thus there was: *Till Death Us Do Part* (1968), *Dad's Army* (1971), *Up Pompeii* (1971) (which actually inspired two original sequels, the mediaeval *Up The Chastity Belt* and WWI-based *Up The Front*), *Please Sir* (1971), the curiously popular *On The Buses* (1971), *Steptoe And Son* (1972), *Steptoe And Son Ride Again* (1973), *The Likely Lads* (1976), *Are You Being Served?* (1977), *Porridge* (1979), and so on. Virtually without exception, these films were unable to preserve their strengths as half-hour TV sitcoms.

The 1980s

In the 1980s British film comedy continued to have a parasitic relationship with television: in one case, benefiting from the successful transition of the Monty Python team to cinema, and secondly in the financial support given to the British film industry by Channel 4 following its launch in 1982.

Ex-Pythonites Terry Gilliam and Terry Jones flourished as directors: the former with *Time Bandits* (1981) and *Brazil* (1985), the latter most notably with *Personal Services* (1987). Michael Palin gave excellent leading acting performances in Richard Loncraine's *The Missionary* (1982) and later with Maggie Smith in *A Private Function*, written by Alan Bennett. John Cleese appeared in the movie version of the surreal LWT comedy series *Whoops Apocalypse* (1981), and then his better, self-scripted *Clockwise* before hitting the jackpot with *A Fish Called Wanda* (1988).

Most successful of the Channel 4-supported directors was Bill Forsyth, who directed a trio of beguiling Scottish comedies, *Gregory's Girl* (1981) {actually backed by Scottish television}, *Local Hero* (1983) and *Comfort And Joy* (1984) before losing his way in Hollywood. Other C4 cult comedy hits included *Letter To Brezhnev* (1985), the Comic Strip's *Supergrass* (1987) and Mike Leigh's *High Hopes* (1989).

Director Lewis Gilbert, who with Michael Caine had enjoyed tremendous success in the 1960s with *Alfie*, again gave Caine a career-sustaining comedy role in 1983 with *Educating Rita*, which also confirmed Julie Walters' position as Britain's best comedy actress of the moment.

Otherwise, the attempts of British writers and directors to export successfully British film comedy met with little commercial success through the decade.

Only in 1988 did the picture brighten with *A Fish Called Wanda*, and Jonathan Lynne's *Nuns On The Run* (1990), starring Eric Idle and Robbie Coltrane, both films showing that American audiences were still not entirely impervious to British comedy.

British Radio Comedy

Undoubtedly the most famous radio comedy team, the Goons, (from left to right; Harry Secombe, Michael Bentine, Peter Sellers and Spike Milligan) get ready to charge their glasses – to opticians.

It's a commonly held opinion among British comedy writers that radio can be the most satisfying medium for their work.

This is partly because many of the best TV comedy writers gain an invaluable apprenticeship writing sketches and shows for BBC radio series and seldom lose their affection for radio's immediacy and its respect for (spoken) words.

It's also because there are fewer restrictions on the writer's craft and imagination in radio than in television and film. Douglas Adams' classic 1970s Radio 4 sci-fi series, *The Hitch-Hiker's Guide To The Galaxy* conjured up spectacular aural scenes in outer space that would have been way beyond even Hollywood's most Spielbergian budgets to project as convincingly on the cinema screen (The later BBC TV adaptation of the series seemed an almost amusingly cheapo parody of the original's rich conceptions).

Although British Radio didn't really evolve its own distinctive

kind of comedy until the Second World War, the first important show was one which flourished briefly before the war's outbreak.

Bandwaggon was launched by the BBC in 1938 as an attempt to counter the popularity of dance-band and variety shows broadcast by commercial competitors such as Radio Luxembourg. Its band numbers were interspersed with the antics of two up and coming comedians, Richard 'Stinker" Murdoch and Arthur Askey

Their comedy was fast-moving, replete with catch-phrases (Murdoch's "You silly little man!"; Askey's nasal "I thank you") and early experiments with noisy sound effects. After a shaky start, the show became an enormous hit.

Band Waggon was stopped in its tracks by the war and Murdoch's departure to the RAF. However, its replacement turned out to be the even more popular *It's That Man Again* (ITMA), fronted by Tommy Handley and written by Ted Kavanagh.

ITMA (named after the re-occurring *Daily Express* headline for Hitler's prewar exploits) borrowed from the American, the Jack Benny/Fred Allen-style format of a central star flanked by a gallery of characters. However, Handley and Kavanagh filled the show with a far more numerous and zany assortment of comic creations.

Apart form the the RAF comedy, *Much Binding In The Marsh*, with Richard Murdoch, Kenneth Horne and Sam Costa, ITMA had no competition as the comedy phenomenon of the war; and the show flourished after 1945, transplanted to a mythical tropical island, Tomtopia.

However, it was the American radio shows broadcast to US troops in Europe after 1942 that had the biggest impact on the new generation of raw comedy talent being demobbed in the late '40s. Two big fans of US radio were the young writers, Frank Muir and Denis Norden, who in 1948 were recruited to an ailing show, *Take It From Here*, starring Jimmy Edwards, Dick Bentley, June Whitfield and Alam Cogan.

Muir and Norden injected witty parodies and prototypical sitcom writing for the first time into a BBC radio show, most famously with The Glums, and the show became a sensational hit. Elsewhere, in the early 50s, there were more overt Anglicised versions of US hits: Tedy Ray and Kitty

Bluett were a Burns & Allenish couple in *Ray's A Laugh*; the BBC had its own version of Bergen and McCarthy, with the ventriloquist Peter Brough and his dummy 'son', Archie Andrews, in *Educating Archie*.

However, the most brilliantly imaginative creation of the 1950s could only have come from the exploding synoptic cross-currents of comic genius in the brain of Spike Milligan.

The Goons started out in 1951 as a conventional sketches-and-music show, but an enlightened producer, Peter Eton, let Milligan's free-flowing surrealism (shaped, in part, by his background in jazz and traumatic experiences as a bombardier in the North Africa campaign) have its head, and the show was entirely hijacked by lunatic stories such as *The Dreaded Batter Pudding Hurler*, *Napoleon's Piano* and *I Was Monty's Treble*.

Milligan's bizarre characters – Eccles, Bluebottle, Neddie Seagoon, major Bloodnok, Grytpype-Thynne and Moriarty – were given life by his fellow performers, Harry Secombe and that other neurotic genius of comedy acting, Peter Sellers. The show also took a reckless pleasure in the creation of extended and absurd sound effects, never previously or subsequently rivalled.

Despite frequent accusations of bad taste and attempts by some BBC bureaucrats to suppress it, the show survived for ten years, until Sellers's career (and ego) as an international film star had become unstoppable and Milligan finally had grown too weary of the Corporation's constant resistance to his wilder ideas.

Domestic sitcoms were the staple of 1950s BBC radio comedy: *A Life Of Bliss* with George Cole; *Life With The Lyons* with the real-life American couple, Ben Lyons and Bebe Daniels; and from 1957 the series that ran for 14 years, *The Clitheroe Kid*, starring the dwarfish Mancunian 'schoolboy' comic, Jimmy Clitheroe.

The last few years before British television (revolutionised by the launch of ITV in 1955) usurped radio as the nation's prime entertainment medium were undoubtedly the latter's greatest.

1954 saw the beginning of *Hancock's Half Hour*, written by Ray Galton and Alan Simpson, who in the same period were also scripting radio's top variety show, hosted by Frankie Howerd at the peak of his abilities.

Another popular mid-50s sketches-and-music show, fronted by Kenneth Horne with a team of comic actors including Kenneth Williams, Hugh Paddick and Betty Marsden, was *Beyond Our Ken*. With the addition of a new writing team, Barry Took and Marty Feldman, the show transformed in 1964 into the masterful *Round The Horne*, where innuendo was raised to an art form (chiefly the performances of Horne and Williams).

Through the 1960s and into the 1970s, the genial humour of sitcoms like *The Navy Lark* and *The Men From The Ministry* resisted the changing tides of social values and new comedy around them. But in the late 1960s BBC radio boasted one great show reflecting the new wave of Oxbridge comedy that had flourished since *Beyond The Fringe* and was to have a huge impact on television in the 1970s.

I'm Sorry I'll Read That Again, a gleeful sketch show written and performed by John Cleese, David Hatch (now managing Director of BBC Radio), Tim Brook-Taylor, Graham Garden, Bill Oddie and Jo Kendall, ushered in an era (only recently closed) where it seemed that members of Cambridge University's Footlights club graduated at will to comedy producing and writing jobs at Broadcasting House.

Through the 1970s and into the 1980s radio comedy could still find cult success with young audiences: the topical sketch show, *Weekending*; David Marshall and Andrew Renwick's Pythonesque, *The Burkiss Way*; *The Hitch-Hiker's Guide To The Galaxy*, written by Douglas Adams and produced by Geoffrey Perkins; Perkins, Phil Pope, Angus Deayton, Helen Atkinson-Wood and Michael Fenton-Steven's local radio spoof, *Radio Active* (later transplanted to TV as BBC2's KYTV).

In recent years the British TV channels have come to regard radio as a comedy nursery, and shows, writers, performers and producers are plucked from its grasp at the first sign of promise.

BBC radio has 'given' to Channel 4 the impro comedy panel show, *Whose Line Is it Anyway?* and the crusading journalism send-up *This Is David Lander*; to BBC2 KYTV, *Have I Got News For You*; to BBC1 the sitcom, *An Actor's Life For Me* and to ITV the sitcoms, *After Henry*, *Up The Garden Path* and *Second Thoughts*.

British Sitcom

The 1950s

It was only in the wake of the tinsel-tinged, all-singing, all-dancing launch of commercial ITV in 1955 that sitcoms (or any comedy, come to that) began to appear on TV to rival the radio greats.

ITV's first ratings winner was a farcical army sitcom, *The Army Game*, created by Sid Colin. The show starred Alfie Bass, Bill Fraser and Bernard Bresslaw, whose catch-phrase as gormless Private Popplewell, "I only asked (pronounced arsked)" was a regular feature.

The cast also included, as a gruff sergeant-major, William Hartnell, later to be *Dr Who*. In 1960, Bass and Fraser were 'demobbed' into the far superior, *Bootsie And Snudge*, created by Barry Took and Marty Feldman.

The BBC's best bid for sitcom success to match its new rival's appeal was Ronald Wolfe and Ronald Chesney's *The Rag Trade*. Set among the boisterous women workers in a dressmakers, it starred Miriam Karlin and Sheila Hancock, with strong support from Peter Jones and Reg Varney.

The BBC also transferred one of its most popular domestic sitcoms from radio, *A Life Of Bliss*, to television in 1956. It starred George Cole, playing the kind of shy, muddle-headed middle-class father which was his stock-in-trade, until his triumphant emergence in the late 1970s as the dodgy entrepreneur, Arthur Daley, in *Minder*.

In the wake of *A Life Of Bliss* Tony Hancock, too, crossed to the small screen, shedding Kenneth Williams, Hattie Jacques and Bill Kerr from his radio show in the

The Young Ones on stage with Cliff Richard singing 'Living Doll' – their No1 hit in aid of Comic Relief.

process, but in *Hancock's Half Hour*, with sterling support from Sid James he consistently gave the best performances of his career.

The 1960s

In the early 1960s Tony Hancock, suffering a tragic failure of judgement, finally dumped both his long-standing writers, Ray Galton and Alan Simpson, to make a disappointing series for ITV.

Galton and Simpson bounced back with what was to become, arguably, British television's finest sustained sitcom, *Steptoe And Son*, which ran from 1964 to 1973. The writers brilliantly portrayed the claustrophobic love-hate relationship of two rag-and-bone men – father, Albert and son, Harold.

The show featured some of the best sitcom dialogue ever – sharp, satirical, silly, gutsy, poignant – and Harry H Corbett as Harold and Wilfred Brambell as Albert were actors of enormous comic

skills, equal to all the physical and emotional challenges they were set by the writers.

British films in the early 1960s experienced a 'new wave' vogue of gritty, 'It's grim up North'-style realism, and this sensibility found its comic equivalent in another outstanding BBC sitcom, *The Likely Lads*, written by Dick Clement and Ian LaFrenais between 1965-1969. James Bolam and Rodney Bewes were the two young working class lads. In the 1970s, they returned with an even stronger sequel, *Whatever Happened To The Likely Lads?*

The most controversial sitcom of the 1960s was unquestionably the BBC's *Til Death Us Do Part*. Writer Johnny Speight created a compulsively repugnant comic character in the loud-mouthed, right wing, bigoted, West Ham-supporting Alf Garnett, which Warren Mitchell brought shockingly and hilariously to life. The series ran between 1964-1974, and the character's vivacity was so immense that Speight and Mitchell had to revive him in 1985 in *In Sickness And In Health*.

The model for the most popular form of British sitcom – the ensemble show – was set up in 1968 by Jimmy Perry and David Croft in BBC1's *Dad's Army*. Arthur Lowe was brilliant as the bumptious bank manager, Captain Mainwairing, in command of a Home Guard unit in World War II, and was brilliantly supported by John LeMesurier, Clive Dunn, Ian Lavender, John Laurie and James Beck.

Croft and Perry successfully replicated the formula in the 1970s with *It Ain't Half Hot, Mum*, based around a forces concert party in India at the close of WWII; and in the 1980s with *Hi-De-Hi*, set in a 1950s holiday camp.

With another writing partner, Jeremy Lloyd, Croft also penned, firstly, the more lascivious, hugely popular 1970s sitcom, *Are You Being Served?*, set in the Grace Bros department store; and secondly, the equally broad, but more controversial 1980s hit, *Allo Allo*. Intended as a spoof of the BBC's hit drama series about the French Resistance, *Secret Army*, *Allo Allo* upset many with TV's first prime time portrayal of comic Nazis.

ITV, by comparison, didn't produce many notable sitcoms in the 1960s. Lancastrian, seaside postcard humour was well in evidence in Hylda Baker and Jimmy Jewel's pickle factory sitcom, *Nearest And Dearest*. Writers Vince Powell and Harry Driver created an amiable Jewish/Irish tailoring sitcom, *Never Mind The Quality, Feel The Width*. London Weekend Television enabled John Alderton

to establish himself as a sitcom star in 1968, playing a naive young teacher in *Please Sir*.

The 1970s

LWT sailed into the new decade as the most successful producer of sitcoms for ITV. In 1970 it launched *Doctor In The House*, a popular TV adaptation from Richard Gordon's comic novels and also *On The Buses*, starring Reg Varney.

Thames Television increasingly prospered through the decade with a production-line output of gently smutty sitcoms: *Man About The House*, starring Richard O'Sullivan, and its spin-off, *George And Mildred*, both written by Brian Cooke and Johnny Mortimer. Sid James starred with Diana Coupland in the sitcom, *Bless This House*.

Thames also took unsteady steps in 1971 into the area of racism with Vince Powell and Harry Driver's crass *Love Thy Neighbour*. In 1976 the more conscientious LWT had a misjudged stab at Britain's first all-black sitcom, *The Fosters*.

The BBC's biggest sitcom star of the 1970s was Michael Crawford as the accident-prone, simpering poltroon, Frank Spencer, in *Some Mothers Do 'Ave 'Em*. Leonard Rossiter, fresh from his genius-touched performance as Rigsby in Eric Chappell's Yorkshire Television sitcom, *Rising Damp*, almost eclipsed him in David Nobbs' *The Fall And Rise Of Reginald Perrin*.

Richard Briers and Felicity Kendall were much liked as winsome suburban drop-outs in

The Good Life by Bob Larbey and John Esmonde, from which Penelope Keith also emerged as a formidable comic actress, and was rewarded with her own series, To *The Manor Born*, by Peter Spence.

The latter half of the 1970s saw two successful BBC sitcoms. BBC2 had its first hit show in Carla Lane's series *Butterflies*, starring Wendy Craig. John Sullivan had his first BBC1 hit with *Citizen Smith*, starring Robert Lindsay as Tooting's would-be people's revolutionary, Wolfie Smith.

It was also the decade of John Cleese and Connie Booth's *Fawlty Towers*, 12 episodes so very nearly perfect they demand a superior category all of their own.

The 1980s

The BBC's most polished sitcom success of the 1980s was Anthony Jay and Jonathan Lynn's sophisticated Whitehall satire, *Yes Minister*, while in 1982 the conventions of sitcom were blasted apart by *The Young Ones*, written by Ben Elton, Lise Mayer and Rik Mayall.

Roy Clarke's amiable sitcom about retirement, *Last Of The Summer Wine*, launched by the BBC in the 1970s, emerged a great ratings success in the 1980s. John Sullivan maintained an impressively high writing standard with *Just Good Friends*, *Dear John* and *Only Fools And Horses*, the latter helping David Jason and Nicholas Lyndhurst develop into the country's most popular comedy actors.

Carla Lane's output was far less consistent, but she did create a major hit, *Bread*, based round a Liverpudlian matriarch and her wacky family.

Mel Brooks

"I see him standing bare-chested on top of a mountain shouting – Look at me! – and – Don't let me die! Those are the two things that rule his life." – Gene Wilder on his mental image of Mel Brooks.

Mel Brooks has variously been the writer, performer, producer and director of brilliant, brash American TV and film comedy for over 30 years.

All his work has been characterised by Brooks' boundless energy and unrestrained schizophrenia – his humour is one-half elegant, sophisticated wit and one-half juvenile tastelessness.

In the 1950s he was most notably a script-writer for Sid Caesar; in the 1960s, the creator of a classic comedy character, the *2,000 Year-Old Man*, and of a great sitcom, *Get Smart*; since the 1970s he has been responsible for big-budget Hollywood genre spoofs.

His work

As Woody Allen has progressed as a film-maker the influence of Jewish humour (of the classic, literary kind) in his work has receded into the background. So, Brooks, many would think, is the preeminent populist contemporary proponent of Jewish humour, despite, in his mid-life migration from TV to movies, having swapped some of his Yiddisher verbal dexterity for more visually-oriented comedy.

And although Brooks has said that the "anger, bitterness and frustration" that energises his crazy comedy is based on his outrage at the "many injustices heaped upon the little man", it still ultimately lacks the vulnerability that is a crucial element in traditional Jewish humour.

On the other hand, it evinces buckets of that Yiddish quality, chutzpah ('shameless audacity'): Brooks's films are shamelessly over-loaded with every type of comedic device: one-liners, double takes, double-entendres, parody, slapstick, sight-gags, music, blaspheming, black, scatological, smutty and surreal humour.

His Life

Melvin Kaminsky, the youngest of four children, was born on June 28th 1926 in the heart of Brooklyn's Jewish immigrant community. His family struggled to survive after his father died: Brooks was aged two at the time.

His family moved to Coney island where Brooks got drumming lessons from a budding neighbourhood star, Buddy Rich. At 14 Brooks started to get menial summer jobs in 'Borscht Belt' hotels, finally getting his first professional job there in 1942 as drummer. One night, in the grand tradition, the star comic was sick and the clownish young drummer was sent on in his place – and Brooks was hooked on comedy.

At 17 he was called up into the Army and was sent to France in 1945 as an artillery forward observer.

Once the fighting was over, he stayed on as a corporal, running officers' clubs and variety shows for the troops. Back in America, he resumed his career in the Catskills until in 1949 he met up with an old friend, Sid Caesar.

Caesar had starred in a successful war time Forces revue, *Tars And Spars*, and was thrust into the new medium of television, firstly in *The Admiral Broadway Review* and then from 1950 in NBC's *Your Show Of Shows*. Through Caesar's help Brooks was able to contribute gags to the first show, but then he became established as part of the core writing team.

Brooks stayed with Caesar on the latter's subsequent solo shows

through until 1959 and during that period worked with more up-and-coming writers including Carl Reiner (a performer in *Your Show Of Shows*), Neil Simon, Larry Gelbart and Woody Allen. The crucial friendship Brooks struck up was with Carl Reiner. In 1960 Brooks' fortunes had nose-dived and an eight-year marriage had collapsed; so he decided to try his luck in Hollywood where Reiner was.

In 1961 Brooks and Reiner enjoyed huge success with a series of comedy records, based on a famous party routine they had been doing for years in which

Reiner, posing as a reporter, asked questions about historical figures to which Brooks would superbly improvise answers in the guise of the *2,000-Year-Old-Man*, a world-weary Jewish guy who has literally seen it all.

This set Brooks on a roll through the 1960s which incorporated his co-creating with Buck Henry the espionage-send up sitcom, *Get Smart* (1965-70), starring Don Adams and Barbara Feldon; and then in 1968 his first film as both writer and director, *The Producers*.

Some people regard *The Producers* as Brooks' greatest work but the film wasn't initially liked by audiences or critics, and neither was his second film, based on a 1920s, Soviet novel, *The Twelve Chairs*. Brooks was sinking to another low of frustration and feelings of failure, but bounced back in spectacular style with his hilarious lampooning of cowboy movie cliches, *Blazing Saddles*.

Two more box-office-smash genre spoofs, *Young Frankenstein* (wonderfully evocative of 1930s horror pix and arguably his masterpiece) and *Silent Movie*, followed. By 1976 the 50-year-old Brooks was ranked as America's fifth most bankable movie star. In all his movies Brooks has liked to work with a familiar company of

Key Films

The Producers (1968);
The Twelve Chairs (1970);
Blazing Saddles (1974);
Young Frankenstein (1974);
Silent Movie (1976);
High Anxiety (1977);
History Of The World –
Part One (1981);
To Be Or Not To Be (1983);
Spaceballs (1987);
That's Life (1991).

excellent comedy actors – Harvey Korman, Cloris Leachman, Dom DeLuise, Madeline Kahn and the late Marty Feldman – and co-writers like Ron Clark, Rudy DeLuca and Barry Levinson, with whom he worked on *Silent Movie* and the Hitchcock parody, *High Anxiety*.

Through the 1980s it took Brooks noticeably longer to produce his movies and the end results – like the *Star Wars*-parody *Spaceballs* – have barely proved worth the wait. However, Brooks has not been idle and has built up his own Hollywood production company, Brooksfilms, and produced such notable movies as *The Elephant Man*, *My Favourite Year* and *The Fly*. Since 1964 he has been happily married to the actress Anne Bancroft.

Catchphrase

"I'm out of my mind,
So won't you be kind
And please love Melvin
Brooks?"
(The lyrics to Brooks' own theme song, which he composed, aged 16, during his first season as an entertainer in the "Borscht Belt" – the name given to the predominantly Jewish hotels centred in the Catskill Mountains resort in the state of New York, and in the 1940s and 1950s a celebrated stamping-ground for stand-up comedians)

Performance Extract

From *The 2,000 Year-Old Man*:

Reiner: Sir, could you give us the secret of your longevity?
Brooks: Well the major thing is that I never, ever, touch fried food. I don't eat it, I wouldn't look at it, I don't touch it. And

never run for a bus – there'll always be another. Even if you're late for work... I never ran, I just strolled, jaunty, jolly, walking to the bus stop.
Reiner: But there were no buses in those days. What was the means of transport then?

Brooks: Mostly fear.
Reiner: Fear transported you?
Brooks: Yes. You see, an animal would growl – you'd go two miles in a minute.

Lenny Bruce

"He had a message, a vision, and he wasn't going to be silent. What they really hated about Lenny was that he told the truth. Lenny, despite or perhaps because of his own despair, remained a moralist, a sharp-tongued showbiz Yiddish foul-mouthed evangelist, a free-wheeling poet, a revelation."
– George Melly

Lenny Bruce is without a doubt comedy's premier pop culture icon. He's remembered more for his image, manufactured after his death by the media from the headlines ('Sicko!' 'Junkie!') of his life, and less for the things he said as a passionately satirical comedian on-stage.

The inescapable vision of a darkly dressed comic, spotlit in a

pale corridor of light streaked through with veins of blue cigarette smoke; the outsider hunched over the nightclub microphone muttering acidly funny attacks on society to a hip late-night crowd: this is our lasting romantic image of Lenny Bruce, an image that has dominated stand-up comedy in the past 20 years.

Bruce, perhaps inevitably, died before he could benefit from the 'liberalisation' of society in the mid-1960s that his traumatic confrontations with the authorities had helped bring about. His provocative jokes about sex, religion, politics and racism would hardly start a riot in a comedy club today. But while he may not have left us with many 'classic' routines, every stand-up comedian telling Pope and period jokes today and not deleting their expletives owes him their thanks.

His Work

Bruce was described in 1959 by the *New York Times* as "a sort of abstract-expressionist" comedian. He was primarily a dramatic improviser, starting from a solid base of familiar, well worked-out subjects – religion, morality, the judiciary – and then careering off in whatever direction his mood, his drugs and his audience might take him, though his consistent

philosophy could bring a coherence to his shows.

In San Francisco in 1953 the young Canadian comic, Mort Sahl (born in 1927), began appearing regularly in clubs like The hungry i, casually dressed and delivering stinging satirical political satire with a laid-back, mordant manner that was entirely new.

Woody Allen later said of Sahl: "There was a need for revolution... and Mort was the one. Mort was the vanguard of that group that had an enormous renaissance of nightclub comedy that ended not long after Bill Cosby and I came along. (Sahl) totally restructured comedy. He changed the rhythm of the jokes."

Along with Bruce, in Sahl's wake came the clever sophomore comics like Bob Newhart, Mike Nichols and Elaine May, as well as a new breed of black stand-up comedians like Cosby, Flip Wilson and Dick Gregory.

Bruce was by no means an 'intellectual' comedian like Sahl or Nichols and May. His basic rhythms were rooted in Jewish/Brooklyn wise-cracking that in different and earlier circumstances would have led him straight to the Borscht Belt.

However his 'discovery' by and membership of the burgeoning jazz and drugs underground in New York's Greenwich village made him an easy target for the police to pursue with obscenity and narcotics possession charges.

His Life

Bruce was born Alfred Sneider in 1926 and brought up in the Long Island suburb of New York. He had a difficult, unhappy childhood and ran away from home to join the Navy in 1942.

After the Second World War, he took advantage of the 'G.I. Bill' aimed at reintroducing America's demobbed heroes to their chosen roles in society, by studying acting in New York. He began to perform comedy routines in nightclubs and made his 'showbiz' debut as the Master of Ceremonies at a strip club in Brooklyn.

He even got an early break on television in 1951, winning first prize in the popular *Arthur Godfrey's Talent Scouts Show*. But his subsequent club work didn't go anywhere for several years until he started to be championed by jazz musicians and began appearing in the clubs in Greenwich Village where a whole new underground arts movement, in music, poetry and drama, was taking off.

The influential English theatre critic, Kenneth Tynan, began to sing Bruce's praises after first seeing the still relatively unknown comic in New York's Duane Hotel in 1959. Tynan felt Bruce understood what was happening to his generation better than anyone else. In 1962 Bruce created a minor sensation – of both admiration and prudish disapproval – in London making the first of several visits to Peter Cook's newly opened Establishment Club, further encouraging a flowering of satire in Britain initiated by *Beyond The Fringe* in 1960.

As Bruce's fame began to grow in the early '60s, along with the Establishment's shock and outrage at his language and satirical targets, so did the processes of the law in America, England and Australia begin to repress and oppress him.

In 1962 Bruce was banned in Australia; in 1963 he was banned from entering Britain. Between 1961 and 1965 in America he was prosecuted for possession of narcotics three times and for obscenity four times. In his stage act Bruce retaliated with ever more fiercer criticism of the authorities – he seemed to be caught up in more of a crusade than a career.

In 1964 a number of leading figures in the arts, including Bob Dylan, Saul Bellow, Arthur Miller, Jonathan Miller and Paul Newman, signed a petition protesting at the public persecution of Bruce, stating: "whether we regard Bruce as a moral spokesperson or simply as an entertainer, we believe he should be allowed to perform free from censorship or harassment."

Key Films/etc

The Lenny Bruce Performance Film (1968) – director John Magnuson's simple, black and white, portrait of Bruce in his penultimate live performance.

Lenny (1974) – Bob Fosse's highly praised biographical film, adapted by Julian Barry from his Broadway play, with Dustin Hoffman as Bruce and Valerie Perrine as Bruce's wife, stripper Honey Harlowe.

Also released on video have been a 1972 documentary, Lenny Bruce Without Tears, and Lenny On TV, a collection of his various TV appearances, including The Steve Allen Show and a pilot for a never-produced CBS series.

Nonetheless, the hounding and his debilitating drugs intake saw Bruce declared a bankrupt pauper in San Francisco by the end of 1965. He was found dead in Hollywood, from an apparent overdose of morphine, on August 3rd 1966.

Performance Extract ➤

From *Religions Inc.*:

BRUCE IMAGINES A CONVERSATION IN CHURCH BETWEEN BISHOP SHEEN AND CARDINAL SPELLMAN:

Sheen: Oh, it's terrible, terrible, terrible. They're here!
Spellman: Who's here?

Sheen: You'd better sit down, you're gonna faint. Ready for a shocker? Christ and Moses, schmuck, that's who's here.
Spellman: Oh bullshit. Are you putting me on, now? Where?
Sheen: They're standing in the back – don't look now, you idiot. They can see us.

Spellman: Which ones are they?
Sheen: The ones that're glowing. Hoo! Glowing! Terrible.
Spellman: Are you sure it's them?
Sheen: I've seen 'em in pictures, but I'm pretty sure – Moses is a ringer for Charlton Heston.

Burns and Allen

"First of all you've got to have talent. And then you've got to marry her." George Burns, on the secret of Burns and Allen's success.

George Burns and Gracie Allen are the most famous example of that now seldom-seen comedy phenomenon – the husband and wife act. The tremendous appeal they had for radio audiences in the 1940s and TV audiences in the 1950s lay in the contrast between George's precise sense of timing as a straight man and Gracie's chaotic dizziness as America's Mrs Malaprop. *The George Burns and Gracie Allen Show* was highly innovative, both inventing and dismantling conventions in domestic sitcoms. Burns was breaking through the 'fourth wall' of the TV screen, addressing the viewers directly, stepping out of character and commenting on the plot almost 30 years before comedians like Garry Shandling dreamed of it.

Their Work

George and Gracie teamed up in the middle of the 1920s in vaudeville as a boy-girl double act. Their huge success sprang partly from the basic human chemistry that existed between them and the great natural warmth that they could generate and transmit to an audience.

Catchphrase

Burns and Allen invariably signed-off thus:

Burns: "Say goodnight, Gracie."
Allen: "Goodnight Gracie."

It also sprang from the fact that each of them was distinctively funny in their own right.

George was a deft straight man; he looked dapper in a rumpled sort of way and though Gracie's attitude was usually one of loving pity for what she saw as his hopeless ambition to be a Crosby-style star, he could punctuate her babbling with one deadpan gaze at the audience or a long-suffering draw on his cigar.

Burns and Allen's radio career took off in the 1940s when they remoulded their characters to fit the more life-like setting of the ups-and-downs of a suburban married couple. Gracie would typically get hold of the wrong

Burns (1896-), Allen (1906-1965)

end of the stick or mixed up in some misunderstanding guaranteed to cause maximum embarrassment to George or their neighbours, but they would always stand firm together against the outside world. They kept the plots just as simple for their TV shows, believing that it was as much their relaxed humour and topicality as their famous routines that people tuned in for.

Their Story

George Burns was born Nathan Birnbaum on January 20th 1896, in New York City, one of 12 children. He went into vaudeville in his early teens and first found success as the comedian in a double act with a straight man, Billy Lorraine.

Grace Ethel Cecile Rosalie Allen was born on July 26th 1906, in San Francisco, into a showbiz family. She was initially a dancer, but frustrated with her failure to rise up the billings, became a secretary instead.

Then she was encouraged to approach the better half of a double act about to split – Burns and Lorraine. By mistake, she approached George, but they hit it off anyway and became a team. At first, she was his 'straightman' but got more laughs than he did. Their flirtatious stage relationship

---

Key TV/Films/etc

TV: The George Burns and Gracie Allen Show (CBS 1950-58).

Films: The Big Broadcast (1932); International House (1933); We're Not Dressing (1934); College Swing (1938).

George Burns Films: The Sunshine Boys (1975); Oh God (1977); Oh God Book II (1978); Going in Style (1979); Just You and Me Kid (1979); Oh God You Devil (1984).

Radio: Burns and Allen (NBC 1933-1949; sponsors included Campbell Soups, Grape Nuts, Chesterfield, Hinds Cream, Swan soap and Maxwell House).

---

became the real thing, and they married in 1926.

They visited Britain in 1929, were an instant hit on the BBC, and their lasting legacy was to inspire 20 years of husband-and-wife radio sitcoms here - Ben Lyons and Bebe Daniels in *Life with the Lyons* and Ted Ray and Kitty Bluett in *Ray's A Laugh*.

Back in America, George and Gracie moved from being regular guests on Guy Lombardo's show to hosting their own from 1932. Starting with *The Big Broadcast*, in

---

1932, they made 14 films in the decade. Their radio show claimed audiences of 45 million in the 1940s, especially after they admitted 'on air' that they were really married all along.

Gracie was renowned for publicity stunts: in the 1930s she often popped up in other CBS shows looking for her 'missing brother', and in the 1940 Presidential race, toured the country in her own spoof candidacy on the 'Surprise Party' ticket.

Spotting TV as the force of the future, they transferred the show across for eight successful years from 1950. Though still at the peak of its popularity, Gracie decided to retire in 1958. She died in 1965.

Burns kept going as a stand-up comic, and revived his career in films when Herbert Ross cast him in Neil Simon's *The Sunshine Boys* where he more than held his own against Walter Matthau. It was an Oscar-winning performance he could only top by playing God – which he did in Carl Rainer's 1977 comedy, with John Denver. An unexpectedly big box office hit, it spawned two sequels and fuelled Burns' continuing work well into his 90s as a vastly entertaining chat show guest and (understandably) occasional live performer.

Performance Extract ➤

George: You're brilliant. I'm beginning to think you're a wizard.
Gracie: I'm a what?
George: A wizard. You know what a wizard is.

Gracie: Sure, a snowstorm.
George: Well, if that's a snowstorm, what's a blizzard?
Gracie: Oh, you can't fool me, a blizzard is the inside of a chicken.

George: Did something happen to you when you were a baby?
Gracie: Yes, when I was born I was so surprised I couldn't talk for a year and a half.

Sid Caesar

"Writing for (Sid) Caesar was the highest thing you could aspire to – at least as a TV comedy writer. The Presidency was above that." – Woody Allen.

Sid Caesar was the great 'thinking-person's clown, in the early days of American television. A master of physical and character comedy, possessed of impossibly pliable features that could register a cartoon-like gallery of grimaces, Caesar is more often remembered these days for his 'round table' of writers than for his pioneering work in the 1950s.

His most famous programmes – *Your Show Of Shows*, and *Caesar's Hour* – were ambitious conjunctions of music and comedy. The former was a live 90-minute Saturday night show on NBC that juxtaposed excerpts from opera and ballet with broad comic clowning and madcap mime from Caesar and co-star Imogene Coca. Along with these were included more sophisticated satires about American television and gleeful parodies of Hollywood movies, with Carl Reiner as reporter/ straightman feeding lines to Caesar's crazy characters.

His Work

Larry Gelbart, creator of M*A*S*H, who cut his writing teeth with Caesar, recounted his memories of working with the man.

"The staff crackled with invention and restlessness. In any given hour we would go from satire to mime, to musical jokes, to sketches, to parody. The only audience we tried to please was ourselves... It was a playpen. Sid was generous enough and brave enough to let is do whatever we wanted, and we delivered, delivered like crazy."

Alongside Gelbart on the staff at various times were Mel Tolkin, Neil Simon, Woody Allen and Mel Brooks. Caesar's trademark character was pure Brooks – a Germanic professor claiming to be a great authority on some grand topic, proving himself to be entirely unhinged when cross-examined by a reporter, usually Carl Reiner.

Imogene Coca (born 1909) was a chorus girl turned Broadway performer. Like Caesar, she had an impish and expressive face and flexible, gangly limbs that were ideal for physical comedy, silly dance routines and panto-mime. She was also an accomplished singer, an ideal talent for the Broadway and Hollywood musical spoofs in *Your Show of Shows*.

His Life

Sid Caesar was born on May 8th 1922, the youngest of three sons of Austrian-Polish immigrants. His father was a restaurant owner.

He graduated from high school in 1934 with hopes of becoming a musician, studying saxophone and clarinet while working full-time as a theatre usher. It was in 1942, during National Service in the Coast Guards, that he started to write and perform comedy sketches in revues and to play sax in the Guards orchestra. Max Liebman directed one such revue,

Catchphrase

"Stars over Broadway
See them glow
Get ready to take in
Your Show of Shows."

– from the lyrics to the weekly opening song and dance number of *Your Show of Shows*.

and took it, and Caesar, on a national tour. The show was rewritten as a musical comedy film – *Tars and Spars* – sending up wartime movies. Caesar appeared alongside Jimmy Durante and Danny Kaye and a career was launched.

Post-war, back in New York, Caesar renewed acquaintance with Liebman and took part in his 1948 revue, *Make Mine A Manhattan*, and got a TV breakthrough onto Milton Berle's show. The next year, when Liebman was asked to recreate his Broadway spectaculars as TV shows for NBC, he again recruited Caesar, introducing him to Imogene Coca. A great comedy partnership was born.

Caesar's triumph, *Your Show of Shows*, was notorious for it's star's volatile, even volcanic, temperament. He seemed happily married with three children, but was much given to extreme mood swings. He liked to work in an argumentative atmosphere and sometimes his writers would deliberately goad and upset him knowing that some great comic notion might be sparked off by his explosive rantings.

Your Show of Shows was a big hit in the early days of American TV, when viewers had a higher threshold for 'intellectual' entertainment. As the ownership of TV sets mushroomed in the 1960s, the

Key TV/Films

TV: Admiral Broadway Revue
(NBC 1949);
Your Show of Shows
(NBC 1950-54);
Caesar's Hour (NBC 1954-57);
Sid Caesar Invites You
(ABC 1958);
The Sid Caesar Show
(ABC 1963).

Films: Tars and Spars (1945);
It's A Mad Mad Mad Mad
World (1963);
A Guide for the Married Man
(1967);
Airport '75 (1975);
Silent Movie (1976).

networks seemed a little too ready to drop Caesar's provocative style in favour of 'safer' comedy, even though he still had much to offer. Perhaps they were embarrassed.

In any case Caesar continued to appear in Broadway shows like *Little Me*, and occasionally in movies. He was a memorable, frothing-at-the-mouth studio boss in Mel Brooks' *Silent Movie*, but mostly the story of Caesar's past 20 years has been one of neglect from an industry that ought to know better.

Performance Extract

From *Your Show of Shows*:

DOCTOR RUDOLF VAN RUDDER, AUTHOR OF 'YOU TOO CAN FLY', EXPLAINS HOW AN AIRPLANE GETS OFF THE GROUND.

"Well, it's a simple theory... matter is lighter than air. You see, the motors, they pull the plane forward and they cause a draught and then it taxis faster down the field and the motors go faster and the whole plane vibrates, and then when there's enough of a draught and a vacuum created, the plane rises off the runway and into the air, and from then on, it's a miracle... I don't know what keeps it up."

Cannon and Ball

"The British public love the underdog, so we always have me as the underdog and Tommy as the bossy one. It's as simple as that." – Bobby Ball.

If your taste is for the very traditional style of comedy with its roots deep in the Victorian music hall, then Cannon and Ball fit the bill perfectly. If anything beyond the orthodox is sought, then they won't. Tommy Cannon plays the calm, organised and seriously-minded foil for the irresponsible, overenthusiastic antics of the anxious-to-please, kid-brother figure of Bobby Ball.

The 1980s saw the peak of their popularity on British TV and in the theatres, and many then thought they might assume the mantle of greatness now nobly worn by Britain's best-loved comedy pairing Morecambe and Wise – including Eric Morecambe himself. That they never achieved this status says much about the growing sophistication of audiences and the challenges posed by the advent of much sharper and more irreverent comedy on British television.

Their Life and Work

The town of Oldham in Lancashire is etched deep in both of them: they were both born there, met there, and first performed there. Thomas Derby-shire

(Tommy Cannon) felt like an outsider in his own home as a child. Born on the 27th June 1938, his father left the family when Thomas was six, and when his mother remarried she acquired four other children, all demanding equal attention.

The early days of Robert Harper (Bobby Ball) were equally tough, in a different way. Born 28th January 1944, he grew up in a one-up one-down house with no electricity or hot water.

Both were already performing before they met: Thomas a singer

Cannon (1938-), Ball (1944-)

on amateur nights, and Robert both drumming and singing in a local working men's club; but it was daytime work that brought them into contact, at a factory where both were welders.

After several spontaneous gigs at the factory's social club, they formed a proper partnership – a singing act called The Harper Brothers. Cannon explains: "We used to do six songs with gags in between, but after a while I realised the gags were going far better than the songs." Bobby, convinced his route to fame and fortune lay in singing, took some persuading, but eventually conceded the point and agreed to shift the balance of the act towards the comedy. The recipe worked and within a couple of years they had more club engagements than they could cope with while still working full-time as welders in the day.

The pivotal moment in the transition to full-time showbiz was a week-long booking at a club in Wales – the first time they'd been out of Lancashire. At the conclusion of a highly successful week, both handed in their notice at the factory.

To develop the partnership to a new level of commitment, they decided to adopt new stage names.

Tommy selected 'Cannon', after the American singer Frankie Cannon, and what could be more logical for a traditional double-act than to team that name with 'Ball'? Yet if they hoped for fireworks from the new names, an appearance on *Opportunity Knocks* in 1969 proved to be a devastating damp squid. They scored so badly that the celebrated clapometer barely moved.

Reconstructing their entire act, Ball became ever more the butt of endless insults and put-downs, switching from cock-a-hoop to crushed in an instant, pouting, sulking, twanging his trademark braces – the frantic fool just longing to be loved. The re-jig hit the funnybone and a 1974 spot on the Wheeltappers and Shunters Social Club, run by the lugubrious Colin Crompton, eventually led on to a regular spot on *Bruce Forsyth's Big Night*, in 1978.

Later, came a series of their very own (initially disrupted by an ITV strike) and the mid-'80s saw them winning audiences of around 15 million. They also won joint Variety Club Showbusiness Personalities of the Year awards.

Like many before them, Cannon and Ball tried to transfer their episodic comedy to feature film

length on the big screen, when in 1983 they starred in *Boys in Blue* as a pair of ineffectual village policemen, alongside Roy Kinnear and Arthur English. And like many before them, they found it didn't really work.

Most recently, they have, in a sense, returned home – playing security guards in a northern shopping precinct in the 1991 sitcom, *Plaza Patrol*.

Performance Extract

Cannon will often begin to sing something serious which will be consistently ruined by Ball, who is either jealous of the attention Cannon is getting or is just totally inept.

CANNON SINGS, BALL ACCOMPANIES NICELY ON THE TRUMPET IN THE BACKGROUND.

Cannon: ...and don't overlap into my words – just lay back.

BALL LIES ON THE FLOOR.

Cannon: Not like that you fool – just take it easy.

CANNON CROONS.

Ball: Tommy, I'm going all limp... you're bringing me out in a rash.... I'm sweating on my braces.

Carry On Films

"If on screen you see the front of a house, and someone opens a door and there's a field behind it, that's American humour. If, when the door opens, there's a field with a lavatory in it, that's French humour. But if there's a field with a lavatory, and someone's sitting on it, using it, that's a Carry On film." – Jim Dale, regular Carry On actor.

"We talk a lot about sex in our films. But nothing ever happens.." – Peter Rogers, Carry On producer.

The twin obsessions of toilet humour and unrequited lust have

Catchphrase

"Oooooo Matron." – Kenneth Williams.

made the Carry On series the filmic equivalent of the saucy seaside postcard. Simultaneously, they have made it one of the three most successful British film series, ever, alongside *James Bond* and the *Hammer House of Horror*.

The humour is comprehensive – it is verbal, visual, aural and situational. It is frequently vulgar, but never ever crude. Subtlety is at a premium; no Carry On epic

would be complete without its quota of belching, farting, outraged squealing and attempted romping. The double-entendre was ever the staple ingredient.

It is corny, obvious, sexist, racist, 'age-ist', 'height-ist', 'every-thing-ist'. It is also exceptionally funny, not despite, but precisely because of being so predictable.

The Carry On actors were highly skilled, but the greatest ability required was to deliver the lines without cracking-up. The out-takes are among the funniest around.

Its History

Peter Rogers is the man most responsible for the whole opus. The producer of every single Carry On film began his career as a radio playwright and even worked in a religious films unit. Briefly a journalist, he then produced several children's films before the series began in 1958 with *Carry On Sergeant*. Originally derived from R.F. Delderfield's *The Bull Boys*, a love story about two ballet dancers, one of whom is conscripted, it was rewritten by Norman Hundis as a comedy – without the ballet sequences. Starring Hattie Jacques, Terry Scott, Kenneth Williams, Kenneth Connor and Charles Hawtrey, it was shot in 1957 for £74,000 and

was the third most popular film of its release year.

Perhaps the key to the whole two-decade success story is the accessibility of the humour. There was no 'clever-clever' satire, no razor-sharp witticisms. This was comedy with a broad brush and daubed on liberally. Even then, one could safely laugh before the gag.

Carry On Nurse followed six months later and Rogers announced the titles of four more: *Carry On Teacher*; *Constable*; *Regardless*; and *What A Carry On*. Joan Sims, Sid James and Barbara Windsor all joined the fun.

By the early '60s, the recipe was so familiar that the actors seemed to be playing clichés of their own caricatures; Hattie Jacques, the buxom matronly type often volcanically lovelorn; Williams, all flaring nostrils and outraged denial; Hawtrey, invariably cross-dressing; Sid James, with the most utterly lascivious laugh ever heard; and Babs Windsor, always with more front than Brighton.

The films themselves turned to sending-up others; *Carry On Spying*, a spoof of *The Third Man*; *Carry On Cleo* with Amanda Barrie in the Liz Taylor title role; *Carry On Cowboy* mocked the whole Western genre and, last in the original series, *Carry On Emanuel...*'nuff said. The absolute epitome was, of course, *Carry On*

At Your Convenience – set in a toilet factory.

The Carry On dialogue was a collaborative effort, but the bulk of the early scripts were penned by Norman Hundis, with Talbot Rothwell providing 20. Carry On films have always been suggestive, never explicit, but it is argued that as permissiveness increased, and the films began to suggest less and show more, they lost the vital ingredient of innuendo.

In 1992 the series was revived after 14 fallow years, with the least serious production commemorating the 500th anniversary of the discovery of America by the white man – *Carry On Columbus*. Rogers and director Gerald Thomas were involved as ever, but with many of the former actors now in that great Green Room in the sky, a new generation of talent was (keel) hauled on board. Julian Clary was a natural choice, never knowingly having missed a tacky double-entendre. Rik Mayall, Alexei Sayle, and Nigel Planer also got their chance alongside the old stalwarts like Jim Dale and Bernard Cribbins.

Performance Extract ⟶

From *Carry On Cleo*:

Cleopatra: (AMANDA BARRIE) So you are the great Caesar.
Caesar: (KENNETH WILLIAMS) You recognised me.

Cleopatra: I have seen your bust.
Caesar: I wish I could say the same.

LATER, CAESAR RETURNS FROM ABROAD TO BE JEERED BY THE

ENTIRE SENATE AND SAYS:
"Infamy, infamy, they've all got it in for me."

Charlie Chaplin

"The only authentic genius the movies ever produced." – George Bernard Shaw.

The description 'great' has been rendered virtually meaningless by careless and inappropriate use, but without question is entirely merited in Chaplin's case. The first international superstar (another ruined term) brought joy and laughter to millions with his diffident, charismatic portrayals of the little man overcoming everything wretched fate could hurl at him.

His sense of timing was immaculate – both on film and in reality. Born 1889, he was at his most productive and creative precisely in the era when the cinema took off as a medium of mass entertainment and crowds were flocking to try the new experience.

The Chaplin trademarks as the tramp were the unmistakable baggy trousers, bowler hat, mini-moustache and wonky cane, but he also excelled in many other guises – the upper-crust drunk, a boxing referee, a waiter and once, even as a wife.

His Life and Work

Chaplin's literal rags to riches story – from the workhouses of Lambeth to millionaire status, retirement in Switzerland and a Knighthood – is of course recounted in infinite detail in whole books, but the bare precis begins with Charlie and brother Sydney being brought up in Walworth and Lambeth. Both parents were entertainers, but in the 1890s, Chaplin's father deserted the family and his

(1889-1977)

mother's failing health, mental and physical, prevented her caring for the boys. While they were in the squalor of the workhouse, their father died aged 37, in 1901, and their mother was committed to a lunatic asylum.

By the age of ten Charlie was working in music halls, having already sung at smoking concerts and in public houses. He was a competent clog dancer and learning to be a mimic. Two minor stage roles and a short career as 'Sam Cohen – the Jewish Comedian' preceded a 12-month job in Casey's Circus which led to him joining brother Sydney in 1908 as a member of Fred Karno's comedy company (famed for the 'no-hopers football match' sketch) on the princely sum of £3 10s a week. By 1910 Karno had Chaplin on a three-year contract and the show toured first America and, in 1912, France. On a second visit to America, tour manager Alf Reeves received a telegram: "Is there a man named Chaffin in your company or something like that? If so, will he communicate with Kessel and Bauman."

Chaplin met the owners of the Keystone Comedy Film Company, and took Mack Sennet's offer of a year's contract, making his debut as a reporter in *Making A Living*, but it was *Tillie's Punctured Romance* which established Chaplin as a major figure. In a year with Keystone, Chaplin appeared in 35 films produced at the rate of about one a week, save for *Tillie's* which took 14 weeks and was well over an hour in length. After 14 more for Essanay, on a wage of 1,250 dollars a week, Chaplin moved again, to Mutual, where he was promised more editorial control. While he had not forgotten the custard pies, the drunken stumbling, the chases and revolving doors, he was maturing both in style and accomplishment.

The era at Mutual is considered by many to be his golden period in which he starred in and produced such classics as *The Pawnshop* in which he dismantles a watch, handing it to the appalled shopkeeper complaining it is broken, and also *Easy Street* where he plays a vagabond recruited in to the police, successfully taming a tough, slum neighbourhood. In 1918 he gained total production control, and his own studios at First National. Of his films made there, the best two are *It's A Dog's Life*, with Edna Purviance who was to become a regular leading lady, and an absolute classic, *The Kid*, with a cast of over 100, in 1921.

Chaplin founded United Artists with Mary Pickford, Douglas Fairbanks and D.W. Griffith, and produced two of his finest films, *The Gold Rush* and *City Lights*, but Chaplin's silent genius was about to be challenged head-on. The 'talkies' were looming.

Chaplin's opinion was clear: "Talkies? You can say I detest them. They come to ruin the world's most ancient art, the art of pantomime. They annihilate the great beauty of silence."

If *City Lights*, four years in the making and opening in 1930, was Chaplin's last classic then his last good film is considered by many to be *The Great Dictator*. A satire on Hitler and Mussolini, it could be said the topic was too serious to treat in this way, opening as it did during the war (but before

Key Films

Kid Auto Races at Venice,
The Knockout
(with Fatty Arbuckle),
Tillie's Punctured Romance
(all 1914);
The Pawnshop, The Tramp
(both 1916);
East Street (1917);
A Dog's Life (1919);
The Kid
(with Jackie Coogan, 1921);
The Gold Rush (1925);
City Lights (1930).

America's entry) although defenders rightly argue ridicule is a powerful tool.

One measure of greatness is whether an artist's work outlives the artist. Sir Charles Chaplin (knighted 1975) died on Christmas Day 1977 yet he remains the most instantly recognisable figure in film history. That is greatness. Let the last word come from Chaplin himself: "All I need to make comedy is a park, a policeman, and a pretty girl."

Chevy Chase

"Chevy's very inspirational; sometimes he submits a whole script to me that is just one page with the words 'me being funny'. Fine, the show is built on this; faith and chance." – Lorne Michaels, Producer of *Saturday Night Live.*

Chevy Chase is a prolific movie actor, having appeared in over 20 films, but ever since graduating from college with a degree in audio engineering, he has been at heart a writer. "It seemed natural to me. It still does," he has said.

Saturday Night Live, NBC's snappy satirical TV show from the mid-1970s, first propelled Chase into the American limelight, but he quit after only one year, moving – with nothing at all planned – to Hollywood.

He has a popular niche in the United States but has never quite fired the imagination or entered the hearts of the British public.

His Life and Work

Cornelius Crane Chase was born in New York on the 8th October 1943, the son of a publisher and later editor-in-chief of the *New York Times* books, and a pianist. His parents separated, both later remarrying, and Chase grew up with his mother in a prosperous, middle-class environment. As an adolescent, he played in

several rock bands, including the embryonic *Steely Dan*, though he left before they became famous.

With such a literary and musical background, writing almost

inevitably beckoned the young graduate. His first professional writing was for the *The Great American Dream Machine*, in 1971. This was a poorly-received mishmash of sketches and skits satirising American culture and society, but it led on to a contract to write for *National Lampoon* magazine. He both wrote and performed in an off-Broadway spin-off from the magazine called *Lemmings*, as well as writing for Alan King and the Smothers Brothers.

His screenwriting debut came in the 1974 movie *The Groove Tubes*, a series of parodies mocking such traditional targets as TV networks, politics and big business.

You could describe 1975 and '76 as the 'butterfly-years' of his career. Emerging from a dull cocoon, he dazzled briefly, only to vanish as quickly as he'd arrived. Lorne Michaels (soon to be the producer of *Saturday Night Live*) asked him to join the SNL team in 1975 – but strictly as a writer. Initially, Chase refused, saying "I want the option to perform some of what I write," only to be told by Michaels: "No, you're an unknown acting quantity to me." The deal struck was that Chase could be present at auditions and help select the actors. Of course, he wangled a screen test and got to perform as well.

On October 11th 1975, SNL began the monumental task of broadcasting a live, two-hour show spanning midnight. Amid a cast list of America's top satirists including John Belushi, Dan Ayk-

---

Key TV/Films

TV: Saturday Night Live

Films: The Groove Tube (1974);
Foul Play (1978);
Seems Like Old Times (1980);
National Lampoon's Vacation (1981);
Fletch (1985);
The Three Amigos (1986);
The Couch Trip (1988);
Memoirs of an Invisible Man (1992).

---

royd, Bill Murray, Jane Curtin and Gilda Radner, Chevy Chase comfortably held his own with brilliant comic performances, especially the self-satisfied newsreader and a superb caricature of President Gerry Ford.

Chevy Chase's bravura portrayals and acid scripts earned him a coveted Emmy award only a year after launching the show, and still at the peak of his and its popularity, he quit.

Amazingly, he later confessed he'd simply got bored of it. A failed marriage in California and a couple of films that bombed, preceded a modest revival in his fortunes starting with *Foul Play* (as a policeman detailed to guard a murder witness, Goldie Hawn) then *Caddyshack*, *Heavenly Do* and

---

Seems Like Old Times, in 1980. "Those weren't my best years," he later said. "I was living an unhealthy life, drinking and other things. I was unfocused, with no career goals."

National Lampoon's Vacation marked a second modest upturn in the Chase career, followed in 1985 by a joint effort with former SNL pal Dan Aykroyd in the John Landis picture *Spies Like Us*. That year also saw *Fletch*, his first major success in films. Playing a reporter on an L.A. newspaper investigating drug-trafficking was his first real opportunity to act, other than acting the clown. The sequel, *Fletch Lives*, released in 1989, however, was a far inferior product.

The enduring mystery about Chevy Chase is why, given that his laconic, deadpan and slightly detached style is so well suited to the satire genre, he walked away from it on *Saturday Night Live* so conclusively.

Catchphrase

As the smug newsreader signing-off on Saturday Night Live

"I'm Chevy Chase... and you're not."

Performance Extract ━━━━━━━━━━━▶

As the newsreader on *Saturday Night Live*:

...This bulletin just in from Madrid, Spain, comes the word that Generalissimo Francisco Franco is still dead...

...elsewhere, in Africa, it was announced that the small nation of Chad has changed its name to Brian. In a spirit of Third World solidarity, the nation of Tanzania has changed its name to Debbie...

...the Post Office announced today that it is going to issue a stamp commemorating prostitution in the United States. It's a ten cents stamp – but if you lick it, it's a quarter...

Cheech and Chong

The partnership of Cheech and Chong is largely, and deliberately, oblivious to the laws of society. They are affected far more by events utterly outside their control – violence and above all the Bomb.

As comedy performers, they are very much 'children of their time', the time being the 1960s and '70s. Their humour derives from the drug culture of that era and appeals above all to the generation it created. Drugs, drugs, street-life and drugs form the basis of their comedy. Bodily functions, often it seems the more tasteless the better, were not exempt either.

Their Life and Work

Cheech is Richard Marin, born in the impoverished Watts district of Los Angeles, in 1946. Of Mexican descent, his father was a policeman. The nickname Cheech was

Cheech (1946-), Chong (1940-)

given him in childhood after the Chicano snack, cheecharone, or 'crackling'. At school, despite being a renowned clown, he was also a straight A student and went on to earn a BA degree in English. His interests are said to range from pottery to rock music and he sang with a band who enjoyed the charming name of Captain Shagnasty and His Loch Ness Pickles. To avoid the draft for the Vietnam War, Marin absconded to Canada in 1968, where he met Thomas Chong.

Chong has a Chinese father and a Scottish-Irish mother and was born in Alberta, Canada, in 1940. He too was a music lover and quit school in the tenth grade to take a succession of jobs, mainly in the music business. He played too, in a group called The Vancouvers, co-writing a hit for them called *Does Your Mama Know About Me?* Diversifying into comedy and theatre work for several years, he founded an improvisation group (City Works) which was based in his brother's Vancouver club.

Cheech Marin turned up there looking for work, joined City Works and struck up a good rapport with Chong, which led to them playing the nightclub circuit as a double act. Aiming at the youth audience, they moved to America and started touring with rock bands as support group and gained a significant following. After a particularly excellent gig in Los Angeles, they landed a record

deal with producer Lou Adler. He became the director for their first film, *Up In Smoke*, which also featured Strother Martin, Stacy Keach, Edie Adams and Tom Skerritt. The movie was a depiction of an addict's conception of heaven and hell. Heaven was driving around in a van made out of 100% 'fibreweed' and finding a plateful of coke in the chaotic aftermath of a party. Hell is finding a woman with a nose wide and powerful enough to take it all. Thoroughly 'spaced-out', the movie cost two million dollars to make and grassed – **grossed**, 47 million dollars.

Their next movie they called *Next Movie* (in the UK it was retitled *High Encounters of the Ultimate Kind*). They co-wrote the script and Thomas Chong made his directorial debut in this film which sees the twosome living in an independent time-warped California. Cheech chats up glamorous women, while Chong is a dead hippy dealing dope to himself awaiting the legalisation of grass. Here, as in other films, they include roles for street-wise improvisational performers.

Breaking new ground, they cast themselves in dual roles in the movie *Things Are Tough All Over*. They play themselves and also a pair of Arabs who hire them to drive a car, stuffed with hidden cash, from Chicago to Las Vegas.

Chong once explained to *Playboy* magazine how he felt

Key Films

Up In Smoke (1978); Cheech and Chong's Next Movie (1980); Cheech and Chong's Nice Dreams; Things Are Tough All Over; Cheech and Chong's The Corsican Brothers.

they'd achieved success in their films: "We've managed to incorporate the basic humour of poverty into our appeal, which makes it universal – the underdogs against the world; we give people hope."

A token appearance in a compilation picture, *It Came From Hollywood*, then followed, and they also showed up in one of the great movie disasters – *Yellowbeard*. Its cast list included top names like David Bowie, half the Monty Python team, Spike Milligan and Peter Cook – but it bombed, possibly because the humour was in exceptionally poor taste. (eg. sheep shagging, cowpats and big boobs).

Another flop followed, *Still Smokin'*, but they got back on track with *The Corsican Brothers*, a send-up of Alexandre Dumas' Louis XIV era tale of twins sharing each other's physical feelings.

Performance Extract

Cheech: My four-year-old tells me I dress like a fag. I fixed her though – I took away her lid (dope).

Chong: So what did she do?
Cheech: Now she chases cars like a dog. Gets stoned on the exhaust.

John Cleese

"The funniest man alive". – Biographer, Jonathan Margolis.

"I don't like being a public person. It has brought me lot, but I would much rather not be recognised on the street." – John Cleese.

One of the few comedy greats who not only writes and performs but directs and produces as well, John Cleese achieved fame as one of *Monty Python's Flying Circus*, which he left early to make the much revered *Fawlty Towers*. He has since concentrated on film, having notable success with *A Fish Called Wanda*.

His Life and Work

Born 27th October 1939 in Weston-super-Mare, then in Somerset, John Marwood Cleese was the son of an insurance salesman who had changed his surname from Cheese. Privately educated at prep school and as a day boy at Clifton College (probably where he developed his dislike of the English class system), he suffered from bullying, being something of an obvious target since he stood 6ft 4ins tall by the age of 12. Recording a family first, he sat and passed his university entrance exams, going to Downing College, Cambridge, where he finally plucked up the courage to audition for the celebrated Footlights club and was elected. He performed in a revue called *A Clump of Plinths* which was so successful it transferred, under the new name of *Cambridge Circus*, to the West End, and via a successful run in New Zealand, to Broadway. A cultural gap as wide as the Atlantic saw the show flop in the USA, but it was there Cleese first met both his wife-to-be,

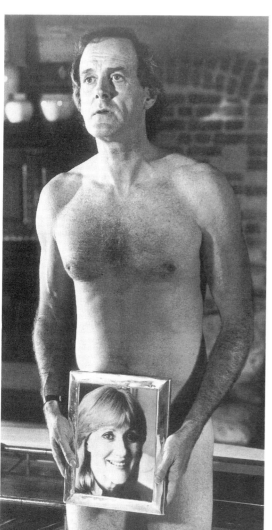

Connie Booth, and Terry Gilliam, then working on the magazine *Help*, who, in a hint of what was to come, used Cleese in a surreal photo-love story about a businessman having an illicit affair with a Cindy doll.

Returning to England, Cleese joined the talented team on the Frost Report, and though Cleese later resented David Frost's taking the only writing credit on the show (dubbing him 'the bubonic plagiarist') he has always acknowledged the impetus it gave his burgeoning career. "Since then I've never had a day out of work."

Cleese also wrote and appeared in fellow Footlights colleague Humphrey Barclay's legendary radio show, *I'm Sorry, I'll Read That Again*. Cleese came to dislike the dreadful puns and forced groans and cheers from the audience and Bill Oddie, who describes him as "endearingly arrogant", notes Cleese "had it written into his contract that he didn't have to come into the rehearsal."

In 1968, he married Connie Booth, settling in Ladbroke Grove, West London. He then began to develop the surrealistic style which was to find its full flowering in Python, with *At Last the 1948 Show* (Graham Chapman, Tim Brooke-Taylor and Marty Feldman also starred).

Monty Python's Flying Circus was iconoclastic. Its impact on television cannot be overstated. It was to comedy what *The Beatles* were to pop music. Thirteen shows were initially commissioned from the six-strong team – Cleese, Graham Chapman, Eric Idle, Michael Palin, Terry Gilliam and Terry Jones – without a pilot.

(1939-)

Catchphrase

"And now for something completely different..." Monty Python's Flying Circus.

They concocted some of TV's most sublime moments, and over 20 years later millions of fans can still recite their favourite sketches, word-perfect. The seamless structure of the show – one sketch running directly into the next – was inspired by Gilliam's animations and allowed them to escape the stifling tyranny of the punchline. Python justly won a BAFTA Best Light Entertainment award in 1972.

Yet Cleese, even in the comic triumph that was Python, disliked standing still and grew weary of "being told be to turn up at 8 a.m. on Monday morning at Wakefield railway station, dressed as a penguin." Though he would rejoin the team for the Python films and a US tour, Cleese left them to make a final series without him.

In seclusion, he and Connie wrote *Fawlty Towers*, a farce disguised as a sitcom. Only 12 were ever recorded; each one a gem. A towering performance from Cleese was its lynchpin but the contributions from Connie, Andrew Sachs as the hapless waiter Manuel, and Prunella Scales as Sybil Fawlty cannot be overlooked. Sybil's piercing call of "Bas-il" became a hallmark, as was the general malevolence between the screen couple. Complaining of feeling a bit unwell, Sybil announces that she is going to have a lie-down. Basil's instant response: "Yes, carry on dear. Let's hope it's nothing trivial." *Fawlty Towers* collected two BAFTA awards, 1975 and '79.

The further fame generated by the persona of the manic hotelier brought yet more stress for Cleese however, and he and Connie split up, Cleese suffering bouts of severe depression, ultimately seeking help in psychotherapy.

Cleese has written several successful books, including *Families and How to Survive Them*. He also founded Video Arts, making training films for businesses with the same meticulous care as he wrote his comedy; evidenced by the price-tag when it was sold – £10 million.

Key TV/Films

TV: The Frost Report; At Last the 1948 Show; Monty Python's Flying Circus; Fawlty Towers; The Taming of the Shrew; also the subject of a South Bank Show Special.

Films: The Statue (1970); And Now For Something Completely Different (1971); Monty Python and the Holy Grail (1975); Monty Python's Life of Brian, Privates on Parade (both 1983); Monty Python's The Meaning of Life (1983); Clockwise (1985); A Fish Called Wanda (1987).

In 1987, Cleese released *A Fish Called Wanda* which he wrote, starred in, produced and co-directed. It was a genuine tour de force, drawing rich comedy from Cleese's continuing fascination with 'class' and the Anglo-American relationship.

Performance Extract

From *Fawlty Towers* (Gourmet Night):

BASIL IS ATTEMPTING TO TYPE IN A FLURRY OF OATHS.
Basil: We've got to change the menu.
Sybil: Why? Why? Why???
Basil: Listen, he's in there, he's out, flat out, so Andre's..
Sybil: Who is?
Basil: What?

Sybil: Who is out?'
Basil: Kurt. Kurt. Who do you think – Henry Kissinger?

HE ATTACKS THE TYPEWRITER AGAIN.

Sybil: What do you mean "out"?
Basil: He's drunk.
Sybil: Drunk?
Basil: Inebriated. Soused. Potted. Got it?

Sybil: I don't believe it.
Basil: I don't believe it either. Perhaps it's a dream.

HE STOPS AND BANGS HIS HEAD ON THE DESK.

Basil: No, it's not a dream, we're stuck with it.

The Comic Strip

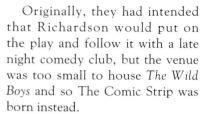

"The Comic Strip series is wry, funny, atmospheric, humoured comedy pieces; and it's a pity there was so much pressure on it to be like *The Young Ones*..." – Ade Edmondson.

The Comic Strip began a new era of television comedy in the eighties, parodying well-known genres from Enid Blyton to Clint Eastwood. At their best, they were irreverent, outrageous and provocative, but the quality sometimes varied.

Springing from an alternative comedy venue of the same name, The Comic Strip was nonetheless a hothouse of talent, attracting and promoting names such as Peter Richardson, Alexei Sayle, Rik Mayall, Ade Edmondson, Nigel Planer, Robbie Coltrane, Dawn French and Jennifer Saunders *(pictured below)*.

Its History

Boom Boom Out Go The Lights was a TV show transmitted by the BBC in October, 1980. It originally involved Alexei Sayle, Keith Allen, Tony Allen, Rik Mayall, Ade Edmondson, Nigel Planer and Peter Richardson. Richardson was later excluded due to differences with producer Paul Jackson.

Following the show, Planer, Mayall, Edmondson and Richardson decided they needed a regular venue, where they could all develop their acts.

Above Raymond's Revue Bar, in the heart of London's Soho, was a small theatre – the Boulevard Theatre – that Richardson and the leading theatrical producer Michael White – who had previously presented the first West End appearances of some of the Python and Goodies' teams – had come across while trying to find a suitable place to stage *The Wild Boys*, a play based on the William Burroughs book.

Originally, they had intended that Richardson would put on the play and follow it with a late night comedy club, but the venue was too small to house *The Wild Boys* and so The Comic Strip was born instead.

The Comic Strip opened in October, 1980, with Rik Mayall, Ade Edmondson, Alexei Sayle, Arnold Brown (an ex-accountant from Scotland), Dawn French and Jennifer Saunders as the regular performers. While Alexei Sayle compered, Peter Richardson was the behind-the-scenes man.

Alexei Sayle attracted the most media attention because of the cruelty of his act. He performed in a suit that was too tight, saying he bought his clothes from a shop for the fuller figure, "Mr Fat Bastard". He was a violent performer, ranting and raving and sparing nobody. He had previously worked as the compere at The Comedy Store, in nearby Leicester Square, where he would allow comics to perform for as long as he felt like and then bang the gong to get them off.

As The Comic Strip established itself as an alternative to the 'death-by-gong' type show at The Comedy Store, so it became the place for television producers to find new talent. It ran until July 1981 and then went on tour including Australia in 1982. Ade Edmondson said "It was good fun – it was like pretending to be a rock band because it was in a bus.... I remember most of the Comic Strip history as a social event rather than a professional event...."

Jeremy Isaacs, the moving force behind Channel 4, had been to see The Comic Strip and Richardson

set up a meeting for him with the main members of the group (excluding Sayle). Six films were commissioned and planned for Channel 4's opening season in 1982. The sixth, *An Evening with Eddie Monsoon*, was later abandoned because it presented a chat show host which Channel 4 felt to be libelous.

Shot on film rather than video, *Five Go Mad in Dorset*, a spoof on the Enid Blyton *Famous Five* stories, was chosen for Channel 4's opening night on the 2nd November, 1982. Dawn French played tomboy George, Saunders was girly Anne, Ade Edmondson was earnest Dick and Peter Richardson the terribly mature Julian. (Timmy, the dog, made it five.) Robbie Coltrane made a highly memorable sweetshop proprietress.

The series began in earnest on 3rd January, 1983, with a re-run of *Five Go Mad*. *The Beat Generation* parodied trendy '60s films; *Summer School* told the story of a university field course; *War* dealt with an invasion of Britain by the Russians and *Bad News Tour* was a parody of a touring rock band.

Dependent on atmosphere and characterisation rather than one-liners and straight-forward gags

and produced by Michael White, the series was a great success.

In 1983/84, the second series of half-hour films – which took on average two weeks to film and two weeks to write, saw the Enid Blyton caricature developed further. In *Five Go Mad on Mescaline*, the Blyton characters were hardened and corrupted. *Dirty Movie; Susie* – the story of a randy school teacher; *Slags; Eddie Monsoon – A Life*, about a violent and nasty South African TV host was a remake of the cancelled original; *Gino – Full Story and Pics*, starred Keith Allen as a man on the run from the police; and *A Fistful of Travellers' Cheques*, parodying Clint Eastwood's *A Fistful of Dollars*, completed the series.

Three Comic Strip specials were made. *The Bullshitters*, a spoof on *The Professionals*, wasn't officially a Comic Strip production because Keith Allen, Richardson's co-star and co-writer, didn't want to be associated with The Comic Strip. Officially under The Comic Strip tag were *Consuela*, a parody of *Rebecca*, and *Private Enterprise*, the story of a van driver on parole.

In November, 1985, Comic Strip's first feature film, *The Supergrass*, was released. Produced

in association with Channel 4, it is about a nerd who invents a fanciful story about drug smuggling to impress his girlfriend. He is overheard by a policeman and arrested. Alexei Sayle and Robbie Coltrane co-starred.

Eat The Rich was released in 1987 and marked a departure from the usual format. This time, the team took only cameo roles while the major performances were by actors.

The third series began in February, 1988. The series of six include *Strike* – the story of an attempt to make a film about the miner's strike and *Didn't you Kill My Brother*, written by Alexei Sayle, Pauline Melville and David Stafford.

The Comic Strip continues as a film production company and is still largely run by Peter Richardson. It has nurtured many film actors including Robbie Coltrane, Alexei Sayle and Keith Allen.

Performance Extract ➤

From *Five Go Mad In Dorset*:

Dick: I say, this is a jolly wizard lunch, Anne. You really are going to make someone a great little wife some day.

Julian: Ummmm, my favourite. Ham and turkey sandwiches, fresh lettuce, heaps of tomatoes and lashings of ginger beer.

(IN THE BACKGROUND, TWO MEN ARE SEEN CARRYING A BOX ACROSS FIELD. THEY STOP AND START DIGGING. A CAR PULLS UP AND A BLACK-GLOVED HAND THROWS OUT A PIECE OF MEAT FOR THE DOG...THE GROUP HAVE SINCE NOTICED THE TWO STRANGE MEN...)

George: Do you think they're

escaped convicts?

Dick: Yes or traitors to our country. We'd better call the police.

Anne: Look, Timmy's fallen over.

George: Oh crikey, he's been poisoned.

Julian: Never mind George, we'll get another – come on everybody, let's find a telephone...

Billy Connolly

"A breath of fetid air, the gangling Glaswegian doyen of bad taste." – John Coldstream, *The Daily Telegraph*.

Billy Connolly, colloquially known as 'The Big Yin', was originally a folk singer who added colourful language and anarchic humour to his act, and was fiercely anti-Establishment. An imposing figure with wild hair, scraggy beard and cheese-grater accent, he remained a club and theatre performer for some time since TV executives found his material infinitely too outrageous for broadcasting and he refused to accept editing. "I react to an audience. It takes all the energy out of a performance when they cut it about," he argued. Yet despite this claim, he has shown himself quite capable of reaching a wider, mainstream audience through television by toning down his act a touch, and can weave an intricate comic web for over two hours of monologue.

His Life and Work

Born 24th November 1942 in Anderston, the son of a post office technician, he and sister Flo and brother Michael were brought up mainly by their aunts after his mother left the family when he was five years old. He left school at 15, was a bookshop messenger boy

and delivered bread, before becoming an apprentice at Stephens' shipyard on the Clyde. He learned to parachute in the Territorial Army and worked on an oil rig in Biafra, his banjo and guitar accompanying him everywhere. Encouraged by friends, he began a solo act, then joined several groups, most notably teaming up with Gerry Rafferty in the Humblebums.

When Rafferty went on to set up Stealer's Wheel, Connolly again went solo. Having noticed he

(1942-)

got more audience response from his patter than the songs, he refocused on the humour aspect of his act. He became a hero in the folk clubs of Scotland, especially among the CND and anti-apartheid supporters. Controversy wasn't long in arriving. On a BBC Religious Affairs programme he gave a Glaswegian translation of the story of Moses, beginning "Nip hame and get yer peepil..." A crowd demonstrated outside the Kelvin Hall studios, and there were further protests from the church when he 'relocated' the Last Supper to Gallowgate, from Galilee. Two records of his stand-up shows launched him, one of them – *Solo Concert* – selling over a quarter of a million so far. Politically active, he made a broadcast for the Labour Party in 1974 and continued to build a loyal following, in Scotland at any rate. *The Great Northern Boot Show*, for example, an act all about wellies, was a big success at the Edinburgh Festival, but it was the release of the album *Cop Yer Whack For This*, a *Sunday Times* profile and an appearance on the Michael Parkinson chat show that started to make inroads into the English audience. Unfortunately for Connolly, that particular show is

best remembered for Rod Hull's Emu proving that the unflappable Parkinson could be rattled.

Connolly's 1975 tour really established him as a national figure. Known as 'Scot of the Anarchic', he was reviled by Scottish pastors for his blasphemous routines and loathed by Conservatives for his vitriolic attacks on Margaret Thatcher. The humour had a raw edge – willies, sanitary towels, haemorrhoids and vomiting figured regularly, along with assaults on racism, bigotry and the Royal Family.

A notorious heavy drinker at that time, Connolly left his first wife in Scotland, moved to England and fell in love with Pamela Stephenson – famous for her appearances on *Not The Nine O'Clock News*. His career dipped in the mid-'80s when his often abusive behaviour and dishevelled appearance won him an unwanted title in 1983: the Scruffiest Man in Britain.

Connolly, largely due to Pamela's influence it is suggested, appears to have mended fences with the Royals, and his career began to revive when he was one of the frontmen for Comic Relief in 1989. In the USA, he had long been able to fill venues for his

one-man show, but found TV or film parts harder to come by. In 1990, however, he won the lead role in *Head of the Class*, in which he plays a Scottish teacher who enters into a marriage of convenience in order to work in the States. The ABC network commissioned him in his own sitcom, *Billy*, but this was axed in 1992. His next project is acting in the film *Naked Cyborg*, with Arnold Schwarzenegger, a spoof on the *Terminator* films.

Performance Extracts ➤

"This friend of mine came round and said – you've got to help me, I've just done the old woman in. I said – you haven't. He said – I can prove it, come round. So we went round to his back garden and there she was, dead, naked under the soil with just her bum sticking up. I said – why did you leave her bum uncovered? He said – well, I

had to have somewhere to park my bike..."

"A Glasgow sheriff asked a woman why she shot her husband with a bow and arrow. She said – I didnae want tae wake the kids..."

"Ian Paisley's wife went to the dentist the other week. The

dentist said – How's the mouth? And she said – he's still in bed."

"I never know why people bother about my soul when I tell blasphemous jokes – after all, it's me that goes to hell. That's where you get sent if you tell jokes like: what's blue and fucks old ladies? Hypothermia."

Peter Cook & Dudley Moore

"Though they did have much in common, especially a brand of surreal humour, their relationship was founded on a certain unease – that of class." – Ronald Berger in *Beyond The Fringe.*

"Peter Cook was the best; unbelievably quick-witted, moving lizard-like to the best line and then onwards to complex, mad improvisations of daredevil skill. There seems to be some immutable rule about comedy; the truly talented stumble and founder while the ruthless self-promoters and self-advertisers – the Dudleys and the Frosties – go forever onward and upward." – Alexei Sayle, *Time Out.*

he found the Oxford University environment a terrible strain, but his talents as a musician spoke for themselves. He became accomplished in jazz, and a first-rate classical pianist. In a neat reversal, the official Edinburgh Festival organisers asked him to assist with a revue to counter that being prepared by the Fringe festival. Moore proposed Alan Bennett as collaborator and suggested a Cambridge pair should also be represented. Over lunch with Cook and Jonathan Miller, the team for *Beyond The Fringe* was assembled. The show was a hit in Edinburgh's Lyceum Theatre in August 1960, and an even bigger

success in London when it transferred the following May.

After the success of *Beyond The Fringe* Cook set about finding a suitable London venue as a home for the embryonic satire boom. The entrepreneurial Cook also planned to set up a magazine, but was beaten to it by *Private Eye*. When the mag was foundering in 1962 Cook stepped in as a major shareholder and suggested the trademark cover format of news photo with bubble captions.

Cook reunited with Moore for *Offbeat*, a comedy show on the infant BBC2. Here they developed the famous 'Dagenham Dialogues' where two cloth-capped cretins

Their Lives and Work

Peter Cook's writing career, began modestly, while still at school. Born 17th November 1937, he had items published in *Punch* and wrote material performed on the school stage, although he readily confesses; "It was really quite appalling." Having skipped National Service by claiming an allergy to feather pillows, he went up to Cambridge in 1957 and joined the Footlights in his second year. By the time he left Cambridge, he had acquired an agent and was a professional writer.

Dudley Moore (born 19th April, 1935) on his own admission was a very pompous child who spent the first seven years of his life "siphoned off in hospital beds and wheelchairs with a club foot." Being so diminutive, frail and conscious of his Dagenham working-class origins, it is no wonder

Cook (1937-), Moore (1935-)

discuss world affairs in a uniquely uninformed monotone. From this came their own series, the classic *Not Only But Also* beginning in January 1965. Successful and successive series established them as comic institutions. Moore's musical talents were well utilised – the theme tune, *Goodbye-ee*, stayed in the top 20 for ten weeks. They found the film format overstretched their material and neither *The Wrong Box* nor *Bedazzled* was the right vehicle. Feeling overpowered by the talents of Cook, Moore relished the chance to make a film on his own, starring in *Thirty is a Dangerous Age, Cynthia*, but its failure was all the more painful as he wanted to prove his independence from his comedy partner.

Back in their natural milieu, the theatre, they reunited for *Behind The Fridge*, a pun on the title of the show that first propelled them to fame. This ran for four years, including a year on Broadway where it was given the anodyne title, *Good Evening*. Moore had settled in America, but worked again with Cook on the notorious *Derek and Clive* records – an exercise in calculated obscenity.

Given the run of cinema failures, it is a wonder Moore ever got another screen role, but a cameo in *Foul Play* plus sheer chance brought him the real breakthrough. While undergoing psychotherapy, Moore's group included director Blake Edwards. When George Segal walked of the set of "10" he summoned Moore to star opposite Bo Derek. The picture made him into the most unlikely of international sex symbols and won him a Golden Globe Best Actor award in 1979. *Arthur*, a film about an immensely rich and infantile drunk was another triumph earning Dudley an Oscar nomination.

Peter Cook's later career has been patchy, to say the least. He appears occasionally on chat shows, takes the odd cameo role in comedy films and manages *Private Eye*. He has been accused of laziness by some, but counters by saying he had achieved all of his ambitions by the age of 30. "Ambition can lead people to take pretty desperate measures at times," he has said, "and I am not that desperate."

Key Films

The Wrong Box (1966);
Bedazzled (1967);
Monte Carlo or Bust (1969);
The Bed Sitting Room (1969);
The Hound of the
Baskervilles (1977).

Peter Cook, alone:
The Adventures of Barry
McKenzie (1972);
Yellowbeard (1983);
Supergirl (1984);
Whoops Apocalypse (1986).

Dudley Moore, alone:
Thirty is a Dangerous Age,
Cynthia (1967);
Alice's Adventures in
Wonderland (1972);
Foul Play (1978);
"10" (1979);
Wholly Moses (1980);
Arthur (1981);
Six Weeks (1982);
Unfaithfully Yours (1983);
Santa Claus (1985);
Like Father Like Son (1987);
Arthur 2 (1988);
On the Rocks (1988).

Performance Extract

From *Bedazzled*, 1967:
THE DEVIL HAS TAKEN ON THE UNLIKELY SHAPE OF TRAFFIC WARDEN, GEORGE SPIGGOT (COOK). IN THIS SCENE, SPIGGOT IS IN A GPO VAN WITH STANLEY MOON (MOORE) AT THE WHEEL.

Spiggot: Pass me over my breeches, there's a good chap.

Moon: 'Pass me my breeches', huh! The Prince of Darkness changing his breeches in a GPO van! What's the matter with you? Where's your style? Use your magic powers.

Spiggot: I daren't waste those. I've got to save all that up for my struggle with Him. (POINTS IN THE AIR)

Moon: I thought you were supposed to be His equal.

Spiggot: Huh! That'll be the day! For a start, He's omnipresent.

Moon: What do you mean?

Spiggot: I only mean He's everywhere, all over the world at the same time, that's what I mean. I'm just highly manoeuvrable.

Moon: So, He's in here right now, then?

Spiggot: Of course He is. He's in the van, He's in the can, He's up the trees, He's in the breeze, He's in your hair, He's everywhere. Spying on you, peering at you, listening to everything you say. There's no privacy for anyone. Get out of here while I'm changing can't you!

Tommy Cooper

Tommy Cooper was a comedy magician, and a magical comedian. His was a rare gift – merely by walking on stage he could provoke howls of laughter. Highly-skilled in the technical arts of magic, he was much revered by fellow professionals, but made his best comedy out of the tricks that went disastrously wrong. Like Les Dawson's ability to play the piano just slightly off-key while sticking to a recognisable melody, Cooper's deliberate bungling was a sure sign of absolute mastery of the ancient craft.

Trademark fez perched above the craggy visage, his one-liners were also legendary: "A man walked into a bar the other day.

(1922-1984)

Ouch, he said. It was an iron bar." "I backed a horse at twenty to one the other day. Still running at half past eight..."

His Life and Work

It is Tommy Cooper's aunt we should all thank for setting him on his way at the age of nine with a present of some magic tricks. The genial giant was born in Caerphilly, South Wales, on 19th March 1922 but grew up in Exeter and Southampton. He joined the Horse Guards (poor horse) in 1940 and rising to the rank of Colour Sergeant, he became part of the entertainments unit. His stage headgear was originally a pith helmet, but one night in Cairo it went missing, so, improvising, he grabbed a fez from a passing waiter and an image was born. Demobbed in 1947, he decided to try his hand as a professional, touring the clubs. Auditioning for a TV show, he was so nervous that all his tricks went hopelessly wrong but the agent thought this was all intentional, and richly comic, and took

him on. Club and theatre success came quickly with the bumbling fool act and he made his debut at the London Palladium in 1952. That same year saw his first TV series – *It's Magic* – on the BBC. The Americans liked him too when he appeared at the Flamingo Hotel in Las Vegas in 1954. "The press said I was the high spot of the show. No wonder, I'm six feet four and the rest were three foot six."

His inspired mixture of mayhem and manic laughter virtually guaranteed TV series and theatre tours for decades, and the signature tune – *The Sheikh of Araby* – became another trademark. He appeared with Eric Sykes in the 1967 film, *The Plank*, and rightly won the Variety Club's ITV Personality of the Year award in 1969 following his series, *Life With Cooper*. The genius of his beautifully honed act was its apparent chaos – starting with

serene confidence it would gradually disintegrate around him as props failed to work, and rabbits were always in the wrong hat. The comic counterpoint was Cooper's face, registering increasingly desperate bewilderment as one catastrophe followed another. It seemed as if the magic was playing tricks with him, rather than the reverse.

A famous routine involves a string of hats as characterisation prompts: proclaiming a ridiculous poem, Cooper would switch hats, faster and faster, invariably losing his way in the middle. Starting over, he'd reprise the first section at double or treble speed – only to get mixed up again and again. Tommy appeared before Royalty at private shows at Buckingham Palace and Windsor Castle as well as starring in several Royal Variety Shows.

Cowboys are supposed to die with their boots on. Tommy Cooper died with his fez on. During a televised theatre show, *Live at Her Majesty's*, Tommy collapsed on stage. True to form, most of the audience believed this was just another trick.

Performance Extracts ➡

(AS HAMLET) To die, to sleep, perchance to dream. I had a funny dream last night. I dreamt I was eating a ten pound marshmallow. I woke up this morning and the pillow was gone.... But soft you now. The fair Ophelia! There's a girl for you, pretty as a picture and not a bad frame either. I mean, she's not like the wife. I'm not saying the wife's ugly, I'm not saying that. When I was walking down the street with her, a police-

man said to me, 'Excuse me, sir, have you reported that accident?'

I've always been unlucky. I had rocking horse once. It died... I've got a cigarette lighter that won't go out...

I had a meal last night. I ordered everything in French to surprise everybody. It was a Chinese restaurant. I said to this Chinese waiter, I said, 'Look this chicken

I've got here's cold.' He said, 'It should be – it's been dead two weeks.' I said, 'Not only that... he's got one leg shorter than the other.' He said, 'What do you want to do? Eat it or dance with it?' I said, 'Forget the chicken... give me a lobster. So he brought the lobster. I looked at it. I said, 'Just a minute... he's only got one claw.' He says, 'Well, he's been in a fight.' 'So give me the winner.'

Bill Cosby

During a quarter of a century as a comedian, Bill Cosby has become recognised as the dominant comic force of black America. He is not a 'racial performer', in the sense that he doesn't talk about being black, but about his childhood, everyday experiences, beliefs and superstitions. As Cosby himself put it: "I don't think you can bring the races together by joking about the differences between them. I'd rather talk about the similarities, about what's universal in their experiences." It is argued that *The Cosby Show* broke the mould of American television in that it showed a successful black family with a level of humour and characterisation which radically differed from the stereotypical, traditional image of blacks. Critics, however, protest that the Huxtable family's position represents tokenism on TV and that it bears very little relation to reality.

(1937-)

His Life and Work

The son of a United States Navy mess steward, William Henry Cosby Jnr was born in a poor neighbourhood of Philadelphia on July 12th 1937. His mother, a domestic maid, would read to the young Cosby and his brothers, Russell and Robert, from the *Bible* and *Mark Twain* in a bid to steer them away from the seedier side of their local environment. He went to a special school for gifted children at Germantown. His academic performance was below the standards set, but he excelled at sports, becoming captain of the track athletics and (American) football teams, and also played baseball and basketball. When told he would have to retake his tenth grade exams, he dropped out – and took a job as a show repairman, before following his father into the Navy in 1956. During four years in the services, he studied physical therapy and gained the equivalent of a high school diploma through a correspondence course. On leaving the Navy, Cosby went to Temple University, in his home city, to specialise in physical education. His footballing skills were such that a scout for the Green Bay Packers suggested he had a real future in the game.

As a child, Cosby had been inspired by the comedy of Sid Caesar and had long been a good mimic. In his second year at Temple, he was hired as occasional joke teller and stand-in for the resident comedian at the nightspot called The Underground. In 1962, he moved on to the Gaslight Club where the young Woody Allen was also appearing as an unknown. Cosby went down well and in 1965 got a big break following an appearance on *Tonight* with Johnny Carson, the TV producer Sheldon Leonard offered Cosby a screen test for the upcoming NBC adventure series, *I Spy*. Cosby starred and won three Emmys as the first black actor in a serious dramatic TV role. As Alexander Scott, he set new limits, portraying a black man aware of his own identity but assimilated into white society. One writer (J Fred MacDonald in *Blacks and White TV*) has said "making a national hero out of a mature black secret agent defending the US (was) one of the most significant roles in the history of blacks on TV."

From 1969 to 1971 Cosby switched to sitcoms, running his own show not only as the star, but also as executive producer, co-director and co-creator. These multi-talents were utilised again in the 1972 TV drama, *To All My Friends On Shore*, which he wrote, scored and produced.

Cosby's film work in the 1970s was prodigious, several times linking up with Sidney Poitier, and also Raquel Welch, Harvey Keitel, and, in *California Suite*, Alan Alda, Jane Fonda and Walter Matthau. The early '80s was a low-profile era, until the fantastic success of *The Cosby Show*, in 1984, skyrocketed him to very peak of the earnings scale.

The Cosby Show lifted NBC from last place to first in the all-important ratings game. It was watched by more people than any other sitcom ever. Cosby was the star, executive consultant and creator. The revolutionary aspect was that it concerned a black family that had really made it. They weren't upwardly mobile – they had arrived. Cosby plays Dr Heathcliff Huxtable, a wealthy obstetrician whose wife, Claire, is an attorney. They and their five children may suffer the standard family dramas, but in their charmed existence we always know it will be all right on the night.

Cosby also has five children in reality, and as if to blur the fact-fantasy distinction even more, all their names begin with "E for Excellence."

Key TV/Films

TV: I Spy; The Cosby Show.

Film: Hickey and Buggs; Uptown Saturday Night; Let's Do It Again; A Piece of Action; California Suite; Leonard the IV.

Performance Extract

Cliff: He's coming.
Denise's date: Who?
Cliff: Elvin.

Denise's date: Who's Elvin?
Cliff: He's the fellow Denise likes.
Date: Then why am I here?

Cliff: Because you're the fellow I like.

The Crazy Gang

The Crazy Gang were the closest British equivalent to the Marx Brothers. Together for 21 years spanning World War II, they specialised in practical jokes – usually on each other – and performed countless shows employing a bawdy knock-about style that focused on the peculiarly British obsession with lavatorial humour. The precise roll-call varied over time, but the regular stalwarts were Teddy Knox, Charlie Naughton, Bud Flanagan, Chesney Allen, Jimmy Gold, and Jimmy Nervo.

Their Life and Work

The origins of the Crazy Gang's house style can be traced back to Fred Karno's 'Krazy Komics' which nurtured many a star, including Charlie Chaplin and Stan Laurel. In Britain, Nervo and Knox had been presenting a show around the provinces in which they'd wangle themselves into all the other acts, with predictably chaotic consequences. In 1932, they came together with Naughton and Gold, Caryll and Mundy and Eddie Gray for a new venture – a revue at the Palladium called *Crazy Week*, under the guiding hand of George Black. A *Crazy Month* followed, in 1933, when Black brought in Flanagan and Allen to augment the already large group, but it was the third *Crazy Month* (but the first with a proper title – *March Hares*) that really marked the beginning of their collaborative work.

All the members brought their distinctive talents to the venture: having initially teamed up in 1919, Nervo and Knox, both highly competent acrobats, were famed for their slow-motion wrestling routine and a parody of two Russian ballet dancers one of whom would be beautifully poised while the other would be clumsy and out of step; Naughton and Gold, who first worked together in 1908, were slapstick artists, experts with the whitewash, flour and soapsuds; Eddie Gray was the busy, red-nosed comic who wove juggling and outbursts of French into his act; and Flanagan and Allen were the epitome of music hall. Unusually, there was no competition between them on stage, each having equal stature although Ches was normally the classy debonair type with Bud playing the layabout labourer. Their classic song was *Underneath the Arches*.

Following the *March Hares* show, the Gang dominated the Palladium stage until the outbreak of war with a long series of revues – *Round About Regent Street*, *London Rhapsody*, *These Foolish Things*, and *The Little Dog Laughed*. The practical jokery became their hallmark, and it wasn't always kept within the team.... Like an early *Candid Camera*, they once conned a theatre fire officer into pointing out to an animal supplier that his beasts had to be fire-proofed.

By the end of the war, Chesney Allen's health had deteriorated to the point that he retired from performing, but later became the Gang's agent and manager. Performing without Ches, the Gang began an extraordinary run at the Victoria Palace in March 1947, in *Together Again*. It ran for 1566 performances, and was followed by other shows: *Knights of Madness*, *Ring of the Bells*, *Jokers Wild*, *These Foolish Kings*, *Clown Jewels* and *Young In Heart*. Throughout they retained the themes of youth and court jesters along with the decidedly unsubtle 'bottoms and bedpans' style. Their humour never really broached the subject of sex, but continually alluded to it indirectly – they would forever be losing their trousers or donning bras and dresses. Pricking the egos of the self-important and pretentious gave them an earth popularity with the many who had suffered at the hands of the pompous. Flanagan came to be recognised as the overall leader, and was awarded an OBE in 1959. Receiving it at the Palace, he glanced at the chamber full of courtiers, turned to Prince Philip and said: "That's a smashing house you've got for a matinee."

Typical of the Crazy Gang's antics were sketches like 'Pre-

Key Films

OK For Sound (1937);
Alf's Button Afloat (1938);
The Frozen Limits (1939);
Gasbags (1940);
Life Is A Circus (1954).

historic Regent Street' with Bud and Ches as two old bookmakers dealing in stone money, and the scene from *These Foolish Things* where Naughton is the baby and Bud the parson coming out with the classic line: "Let's give 'im a nice biblical name, like Isaiah. One eye's 'igher than the other."

Officially, the Crazy Gang retired in 1962. Gold died in 1967, Flanagan in 1968, Gray in 1969, Knox in 1974, Nervo in 1975, Naughton in 1976, and Allen in 1983.

Performance Extracts

"If a bomb fell in a field and a bull ate it, what would it be? Abominable."

"Have you heard? They don't want London Bridge any longer."
"Why not?"
"It's long enough."

Ches: It's a 2:30 race. You start off at 10 to 1.
Bud: What about the other horses?
Ches: They start off an 5 to 4.
Bud: I'll have it won before they get there.

Billy Crystal

"I'm comfortable being old... being black... being Jewish, and I look very, very good in dresses. I like twisting my face and my voice and my mind into different characters." – Billy Crystal.

"What sets the Crystal brand of humour apart from much that has gone before is that it is built from real characters, usually people Crystal knew. He often has the lighter, more poignantly comic flair that arises out of pure human impulse." Daniel Wood, Christian Science Monitor.

Billy Crystal smacked the American Public right between the eyeballs with his portrayal of the gay son in the smash-hit, sitcom spoof *Soap*. More a comic actor than an out-and-out comedian, his performances are deliberately theatrical in style; rather than telling jokes, he invents and becomes complete alter egos. A famed mimic, Whoopi Goldberg says of Crystal: "There's no character he can't do. He does me better than I do me."

His Life and Work

Whatever else he may do in his career, Billy Crystal is destined to be remembered as the man who sat opposite Meg Ryan when she enjoyed an absolutely earth-shattering fake orgasm at a restaurant table in *When Harry Met Sally*. It was one of most brilliant moments of modern cinema, and Rob Reiner's 1989 smash followed that scene with a magnificent pay-off line from the frumpy middle-aged lady at a nearby table: "I'll have a double of whatever she's having."

Crystal was born into a showbiz family in Manhattan, New York on March 14th, 1948, but grew up in the Bronx for two years before they moved to Long Beach, Long Island. With a father who produced jazz concerts in Central Plaza, music was naturally a large element in his childhood, but together with his brothers there was nothing he liked doing more than imitating the comic greats

Mel Brooks, Carl Reiner and Sid Caesar in his living room. At school, he was a good student although he enjoyed both baseball and comedy. Indeed, but for his size (he stands a mere 5ft 6ins) he could probably have made a career in the sport. On the comedy side, he was MC of the school's annual variety show in 1964 and his contribution was a fine take-off of Bill Cosby's 'Noah' routine. Crystal went to Marshall University in West Virginia on a baseball scholarship, but as he arrived the college abandoned the course for lack of funds. Using the blank year productively however, he hosted a phone-in show on the campus radio station.

Transferring to Nassau College on Long Island, he met his wife to be, Janice Goldfinger, and majored in theatre studies before moving on to New York University to study film and TV direction under Martin Scorsese. After four years in an improvisational group, his managers encouraged him to go solo and he nearly got in at the inception of *Saturday Night Live*, NBC's mould-breaking satire show. He prepared a seven-minute monologue, but departed in that lofty vehicle, high dudgeon, when ordered to cut it to two.

Washing his hands of New York, Crystal moved to L.A. and was discovered by *Soap* producer Norman Lear, who cast him as Jodie, the first openly homosexual character on American TV. *Soap*, the magnificent sitcom/soap opera spoof, took the rise out of much of contemporary US culture as well, as seen in the celebrated remark from Jodie's mother when she finds him trying on her clothes – again. "I've told you a hundred times; that dress fastens at the back."

In 1944, nearly a decade after he'd flounced out of *Saturday Night Live*, he was invited back to 'guest-host' the show, which was then on a slide. Crystal's new series of impersonations and impressions revived its fortunes but he stayed less than two years, moving on to take more film work and to co-host, in 1986, the HBO special, Comic Relief in aid of the

homeless with Whoopi Goldberg and Robin Williams. The same year he won high praise for an hour-long HBO show – *Don't Get Me Started*. A *New York Times* critic said this put Crystal in "the serious comedy territory occupied by Lily Tomlin, Woody Allen and only a handful of others."

Key TV/Films

TV: Soap;
The Billy Crystal Comedy Hour;
Saturday Night Live;
A Comedy Salute to Baseball.

Films: Death Flight (1977);
Rabbit Test (1978);
Human Feelings (1978);
Breaking Up Is Hard To
Do (1979);
Enola Gay (1980);
Running Scared (1986);
Throw Momma From the
Train (1987);
When Harry Met Sally (1989);
City Slickers (1991).

Performance Extract

From *When Harry Met Sally*:

HARRY AND SALLY, RECENTLY ACQUAINTED, ARE SHARING A CAR ON A JOURNEY TO NEW YORK.

Harry: You realise, of course, that we could never be friends.
Sally: Why not?
Harry: What I'm saying is – and this is not a 'come-on' in any way shape or form – is that men and women can't be friends because the sex part always gets in the way.

Sally: That's not true. I have a number of men friends and there's no sex involved.
Harry: No you don't.
Sally: Yes I do.
Harry: No you don't. You only think you do.
Sally: You're saying that I'm having sex with these men without my knowledge?
Harry: No, what I'm saying is, they all want to have sex with you.
Sally: No they don't.
Harry: Do too.

Sally: How do you know?
Harry: Because no man can be friends with a woman he finds attractive. He always wants to have sex with her.
Sally: So you're saying that a man can be friends with a woman he finds unattractive?
Harry: No, you pretty much want to nail them too.

Les Dawson

Les Dawson is best known as the morose comic with an endless fund of mother-in-law jokes which generally begin: "I'm not saying she's ugly, but..." Yet like many comedians, he yearns to be taken seriously. "There's a Hamlet in all of us," he says.

Dawson is one of the great pantomime dames, but really can act and indeed The Royal Shakespeare Company actually invited him to play Falstaff in 1989, but he reluctantly turned it down because it meant an 18-month commitment.

A fine pianist, Dawson is also a novelist, having produced over a dozen books. He has been criticised for being anti-women, but derides the notion. "That's absolute rubbish... Whatever I do I talk about family life; death, marriage, children, wife, mother-in-law. They are the basis of all humour and everything I do is done with affection. Most people condemn things they actually like."

His Life and Work

Dawson's origins were about as far from the world of showbiz as could be imagined. He was the son of a labourer, born in Manchester on 2nd February, 1933, boxed for

(1933-)

a local youth club and left school at 14. He had a series of mundane jobs, did his National Service in the Army, short-circuited a career as an electrician, and then went to Paris to try to make it as a writer. This too came to naught and returning home he took up as an insurance salesman. At that time his great talent was the piano which he played to professional standard in the clubs and pubs. He introduced singing and joined a jazz band, the *Cotton City Slickers.*

Working next as a vacuum cleaner salesman for Hoover came one of those chance moments that begin many a career. While travelling, he spotted a poster inviting people to audition for Max Wall. Dawson went in, played the piano and sang. Three days later a letter arrived saying he'd passed and for him to move to London so Wall could promote him. Dawson moved.

Wall couldn't initially place him, and sent Dawson for professional singing lessons, eventually getting him the understudy's job for the lead role in *Pyjama Game.* He was never required. Wall's business ventures collapsed, but Dawson got the break – a one-week booking at a club in Hull in 1956. His first night as singer/musician was a shambles. On his second night, he went on drunk, abused the audiences – and got

Key TV

Sez Les;
Dawson Watch;
Blankety Blank;
Opportunity Knocks: Dawson;
Nona.

laughs. It was a turning point. He began to get some radio work and married his beloved Meg in 1960. She would be with him for 25 years until her death, which devastated Dawson, in 1986.

A regionally broadcast TV show, *Comedy Bandbox,* followed in 1963 and the next year he appeared on *Opportunity Knocks.* Though he didn't win on a national level, he scored the highest number of votes with the studio audience. Soon, the lugubrious Dawson was a TV regular, popping up on shows like *Blackpool Night, Billy Cotton's Bandshow,* and guesting for Cilla Black and Val Doonican. A series of his own – *Sez Les* – launched him as compere/comic and throughout the 1970s he was almost a permanent fixture on the nation's TV screens. Despite the occasional hiccup (*Dawson's Weekly* in 1975 for example, was meant to establish him as the new Tony Hancock, but the Press

panned it) he remained popular and in 1984 took over the reins from Terry Wogan on the ailing game show, *Blankety Blank.* Dawson's approach was to send it up, and the critics and the ratings both appeared to approve. A later stint fronting *Opportunity Knocks* wasn't such a success because he wasn't allowed to be critical but kept him in the public eye.

Dawson's shows could not generally be described as innovative, but a fine idea completely in character with his self-mocking style, was to feature the Roly-Polys, a dance troupe of what can only be called well-upholstered ladies of a certain age. Hill's Angels they were not.

No sylph-like figure himself, Dawson can act for real, and has appeared in several dramas, including *Nona,* a 1991 black comedy about life in Argentina after the Falklands War in which he played a 100-year old woman. In his comedy, he often appears in drag and with fine observation has perfectly captured the persona of the stout frumpy housewife, arms folded across ample bosom, pinny pulled too tight, right down to the habit of mouthing silently the ends of sentences about "personal parts"... In a very orthodox fashion, he is actually very good at what he does.

Performance Extracts

"We often come to see the wife's mother here. She lives in Birmingham, but she looks better from Blackpool."

"The wife's mother is outside in the car. I would have brought her in, but I've lost the key to the

boot. To add to my trough of woe, she came to live with us three months ago. As soon as I heard the knock on the door I knew it was her because the mice were throwing themselves on the traps..."

"I've brought the wife with me again, well it saves kissing her goodbye. Don't get me wrong, I'm not saying she's ugly, but I keep her photograph on the mantelpiece – it keeps the kids away from the fire."

Ken Dodd

"I think he's fantastic. He's a master of a certain type of comedy that is hard to categorise – you go in, get high, laugh your head off and come out wondering just what happened." Griff Rhys Jones.

"Comedians have always been a vital part of my life. I once proposed that there should be a chair of comedy at a university – maybe I'll endow one before I pop off... A professor of giggle-ology." Ken Dodd.

They call Ken Dodd the comedians' comedian. His is a brilliant and eccentric variety of stand-up comedy, bolstered both by his daft accessories like the tickling stick and, previously, the Diddymen, and his own startling appearance – buck teeth from a childhood cycling accident and that fingers-in-the-socket hairstyle. He is also a lifelong student of the theories of comedy. His home in Knotty Ash, Liverpool, is lined with over 10,000 books on comedy and showbusiness. Dodd is serious about funding research into humour, and has for years been compiling a 'Giggle Map of Britain' based on the detailed notes he has kept from every single performance in his career. Correlating these notes with different regions, he has claimed "to know what brand goes best in what place. And gradually I built up a grand piece of intelligence: about where irony is most liked, where to do one-liners."

His Life and Work

Kenneth Arthur Dodd was born 8th November 1927 in the Knotty Ash suburb of Liverpool, son of Arthur, a coal merchant who invested most of the proceeds with the local bookmakers. The remainder was kept in a box under the mattress, not in a bank – a point not lost on the young Kenneth, but one that years later would bring him much unwanted publicity. On leaving High Holt Grammar School aged 14, Ken went into the family business but also performed at the occasional concert party with a ventriloquist's doll called Charlie Brown. By the age of 21 he was a regular on the clubs circuit as 'Professor Yaffle Chuckabutty, Operatic Tenor and Sausage-Knotter'.

Urged on by his then girlfriend, Anita, and his mother, he went

(1927-)

Catchphrases

"How tickled I am..."
"Hello missus"
"Tatty-bye"
"What a lovely day for ..."
"Discumknockerated"

Key Theatre/TV

Theatre: Ken Dodd's Laughter Show.

TV: The Ken Dodd Show;
Doddy's Music Box;
The Good Old Days;
Super Troupers;
Funny You Should Say That;
Ken Dodd's World of Laughter.

full-time into showbiz aged 27 and got his first important engagement at the Nottingham Playhouse in September 1954. From here onwards, until her death in 1977, it was Anita's job to take meticulous notes at every show. She gave up her job as a nurse to be with him, and though they never married, she was his constant companion. The notes recorded every conceivable detail, right down to the weather. It is from these records that the Giggle Map derives.

Dodd's most famous act took shape the mid and late-50s when he developed the concept of the Diddymen (variously described as being from the broken-biscuit factory or the jam butty mine) and integrated the tickling-stick routines. Though favouring the stage, he has worked extensively in radio, with numerous series of *Ken Dodd's World of Laughter*, but the crucial breakthrough into the seriously big time came in 1965

with a show at the London Palladium that ran for 42 weeks and broke all the previous box office records.

In this phase, Dodd also struck gold with his excellent singing. *Happiness*, later to become his theme tune, was a hit in 1964, *Tears* was a number one hit in '65, and *Promises* also sold well the next year.

Dodd continued to make successful TV shows and series, but always seemed more at home in the theatre where the greater timespan allowed him to toy with the audience more, timing his peaks and often stretching his shows to well over two hours. Indeed, he gained a place in the *Guinness Book Of Records* when told an incredible 1500 jokes non-stop in a three-and-a-half hour marathon.

Ken Dodd gives his all when performing. Offstage, he is a deeply private man. He has never married and regards all questions about his personal life as insults: "It's as if somebody said 'Can I have a look at your bank account?'" Dodd's private low-point was Anita's death, after 24 years together, but his public low point came in 1989 when he was taken to court by the Inland Revenue for unpaid taxes. It appeared performance records

were not the only notes Dodd was hoarding – the court heard he had stashed £336,000 in cash in his attic. Though the sums were different, it was like father, like son. Dodd's explanation betrayed some of his personal insecurities: he said he hoarded the money because it meant to him that he was a star.

Performance Extracts ➡

"What a thrill, ladies and gentlemen, to stand here this evening, here in this magnificent...(GLANCES AROUND)...shed – no, no, this theatre of the imagination. Of course, you have to use a lot of imagination... I have to – I have to imagine that you are enjoying

yourselves. You have to imagine that I am a comedian..."

"I woke up this morning – I was up at the crack of noon. This morning I thought, what a beautiful day – what a beautiful day for going up to Lady Smith and saying

I hear you've been relieved... what a beautiful day for going up to Count Zeppelin and saying you'll never sell a sausage that size..."

"It's 15 years since I went out of my mind – I'd never go back."

Ben Elton

"I'm not a smug git in a shiny suit, I ain't smug, I'm just a git in a shiny suit." – Ben Elton.

"Top of the whole class... he was phenomenally prolific, capable of writing a whole spot in half a day." – Geoff Posner, director of *The Young Ones* and *Saturday Live*.

Ben Elton was one of the most popular stand-up comedians in Britain in the 1980s. His rapid, machine-gun fire delivery – apparently perfected to stop hecklers from gaining a foothold – earned him the nickname 'motormouth'.

The tabloid press branded him a 'red' comic after his attacks on

Catchphrase

(very fast) "My name's Ben Elton, thank you, goodnight."

the Government of the day and particularly 'Mrs Thatch' and also because he eschewed traditional sexist and racist targets.

His Life and Work

Born May 3rd 1959, the youngest of four, in Catford, south-east London, Benjamin Charles Elton had very intellectual antecedents. His father, Lewis, was a Professor at Surrey University, his mother, a teacher. His uncle, Sir Geoffrey Elton, was Regius Professor Emeritus of Modern History at Cambridge University and his grandfather was the late Professor Leopold Ehrenberg – the family later changed their name – who escaped from Czechoslovakia and the Nazis in the 1930s.

When Elton was ten, the family moved to Guildford, in Surrey,

and he attended Godalming Grammar School. After gaining 'A' levels in English, History and Theatre Studies at South Warwickshire College of Further Education, he went to Manchester University in 1977, graduating with a 2.1 in Drama. Whilst there, Elton wrote comic plays, which were put on by fellow students.

In London, Elton's first appearances at the Comedy Store and the Comic Strip were badly received. "My actual reason for becoming a comedian was because I wanted to get my writing around; it has to be said that everybody said 'don't'." But as he began to do more and more observational material, so Elton improved and he went on to compere the Comedy Store, before the original venue closed down in 1982.

Rik Mayall and Lise Mayer provided the launch-pad for

Elton's scriptwriting talents. They called him in to help with a sit-com based on a group of students living in digs. At the BBC, Paul Jackson read the script. "I was just knocked out by it – it was the single funniest script I'd ever read. It was so different from what I'd expected it to be..." The four original actors in *The Young Ones* were Mayall as Rik, the pseudo right-on sociology student, Nigel Planer as Neil, the hippy, Ade Edmondson as Vivian, the mad punk, and Peter Richardson as Mike, the bossy poser. When Richardson was dropped due to differences between him and Jackson, Ben Elton wanted to make up the four, but it was felt that his acting ability wasn't up to it. He later made a few cameo appearances. Chris Ryan was chosen instead. *The Young Ones* became a hugely funny, anarchic sit-com, with a big cult following.

Elton's first solo TV credit was for writing *Happy Families*, a complicated serial involving the search for the four far-flung girls of the Fuddle family, all played by Jennifer Saunders. He also became involved in writing the second series of *Blackadder* with Richard Curtis and Rowan Atkinson. When Atkinson dropped out, Elton took over. *Blackadder II* took place in the court of Queen

Elizabeth I – played by Miranda Richardson – and starred Rowan Atkinson. Elton also co-wrote *Blackadder III* in 1987 and *Blackadder Goes Forth*; set in World War I it was the last series.

Saturday Live was another Paul Jackson project, this time for LWT. It was an attempt to mix cabaret with music and the pilot was shown in January, 1985. Presented by Lenny Henry, the show also featured Andy De La Tour, Chris Barrie, French and Saunders and the Dangerous Brothers (Mayall and Edmondson). A series of ten later ran from January to March 1986, with a new compere each week. Ben Elton was initially asked just to write for the show, but ended up performing six minutes at the end.

In February, 1987, *Saturday Live* returned with Elton as the regular compere. He became the star of the series, performing two sets each show, of which one was always political. Also in 1987, Mayall and Elton attempted a follow-up to *The Young Ones* with *Filthy, Rich and Catflap*. It had nowhere near the success of its predecessor.

Friday Night Live went out a year later on Channel 4. The last of the series was broadcast in April, 1988. Elton returned to the

BBC in 1989/90 with the series *The Man From Auntie*, which he both wrote and performed. This featured the hilarious Fartie's Guides to sex and other potentially awkward situations.

Elton has since written two novels, *Stark*, 1989, (to be dramatised for TV) – a novel about saving the world and *Gridlock*, 1991, in which the world ground to a halt because there were too many cars on the roads. Both were best-sellers. He has also written two plays, *Gasping* (1990) about the privatisation of air, starring Hugh Laurie and Bernard Hill, and *Silly Cow* (1991) in which Dawn French appeared as a tabloid journalist. Both ran in the West End.

Key TV/etc

TV: Saturday Live;
The Young Ones;
Blackadder;
Happy Families;
Filthy, Rich and Catflap;
The Man From Auntie.

Books: Stark; Gridlock.

Plays: Gasping; Silly Cow.

Performance Extract ➤

From *Saturday Live*: Topical Monologue from 1987 about privatisation of BA and Leyland: "Ladies and gentlemen, a week in politics when the party that has been in power for eight years chose to spend the entire week telling the opposition they're not

fit to govern – well, it hasn't worried them for a while, has it?... They've sold off British Leyland, they've sold off British Leyland Trucks... of course they say we haven't sold it – oh no we haven't sold it – we've merged. So next time you're down the butcher's

picking up half a pound of sausages for your tea, just remember you're not buying them you're merging with 'em – for the mutual good of you and the sausages... bit of a political image there, I've been to university, I don't mind showing off.

Marty Feldman

Feldman's comedy was very much in the classic clowning tradition, and given his distinctive and unforgettable features, tended to the visual rather than the verbal. The slightly manic expression sprang mainly from the rolling, bulging eyeballs – the result of a thyroid condition brought on initially by a boating accident – and the crooked nose, which was acquired courtesy of a boxing match.

Although his face became his fortune, Feldman was also a talented comedy writer with a keen insight into the absurdities of life. Much as he loved writing, considering it the more important stage, he always felt performance was an integral element of the creative whole. Something of his nature can be deduced from the fact that when performing his own work, he generally took the role of victim rather than aggressor. That said, Mel Brooks' comment that "he was heaven, and hell, to work with", suggests another side co-existed with the sympathetic.

His Life and Work

Marty Feldman was born the son of Polish-Russian-Jewish immigrants, in London's Canning Town on July 8th 1934. His father was a pushcart peddler, and later a clothing manufacturer. Leaving school at 15, he had a string of jobs – messenger boy, jazz trumpeter, assistant to a sideshow act, racecourse tipster, an artist's model, and a book thief. He visited France, but was thrown out for vagrancy. On returning home, he put together a sort of primitive Marx Brothers act, appearing in the music halls as Morris, Marty and Mitch.

His career really took off when he joined the BBC as a staff writer in 1957, beginning a long and fruitful relationship with Barry Took. Their collaborations included *Take It From Here*, the opening and closing spots on *The Glums*, contributions to Frankie Howerd's *Bandbox* and *Round The Horne*, which won them the Writers' Guild award in 1967. From 1965, Feldman became head writer on the successful TV show *The Frost Report*, where each programme was centred around a

Freshly Dead   6 Months Dead

broad theme – youth, women, crime, children, etc. Here, Feldman's ideas, in crossfertilisation with those of the bulk of the future Python team (Cleese, Chapman, Palin, Jones and Idle), were among his most influential and dynamic. Feldman was normally responsible for one of the two main sketches each week, and greatly prized the honour when the show won the 1967 Golden Rose of Montreux. This success led on to *At Last The 1948 Show* in which Cleese recommended that Feldman should perform as well as write.

On the back of this success, Feldman got his own show on BBC2, called simply *Marty*. Less structured than *The Frost Report*, it was nevertheless sufficiently zany in its own right to run for two series with regular audiences around the 15 million mark. Again, the chief writers were Feldman and Took with the embryonic Python team making strong use of Feldman's gifts for bizarre expressions and anarchic characterisations.

Further TV work followed, but in 1974, Feldman left to pursue his dream of being a Hollywood writer/performer. Joining the Mel Brooks entourage, along with Gene Wilder, Madeleine Kahn and Peter Boyle, Feldman got the roles of Eye-Gore the cheerful hunchback in the spoof *Young Frankenstein*, Sergeant Sacker in Wilder's *Adventures of Sherlock Holmes' Smarter Brother* and Marty Eggs in Brooks' *Silent Movie*. His own film, *The Last Remake of Beau Geste* was poor, but his next – *In God We Trust*, which he starred in, co-wrote, directed and edited, with his wife as one of the producers – was abysmal. Savaged by the critics, it ran for one single week after its US premiere and the remainder of his contract with Universal was scrapped.

However, Cleese, Chapman, Idle, Cook and Milligan were in Mexico making the buccaneers spoof, *Yellowbeard*, and invited

> # Films
>
> Every Home Should Have One (1969);
> Young Frankenstein (1973);
> The Adventures of Sherlock Holmes' Smarter Brother (1975);
> Silent Movie (1976);
> The Last Remake of Beau Geste (1977);
> In God We Trust (1980);
> Yellowbeard (1983);
> Slapstick (1983).

Marty to star. Though the movie itself was a catastrophic flop, the making of it was an oasis of joy for Feldman after his Hollywood experiences. With immaculate timing, Feldman died the day filming was completed – December 2nd 1982. Barry Took's poignant comment about his friend was that Marty "had a craving for stardom which, when it came, didn't satisfy him, and when it left him, destroyed him."

Performance Extract →

From *At Last The 1948 Show*:

FELDMAN IS A HARMLESS MAN WAITING AT A BUS STOP WHO GETS DRAWN INTO CONVERSATION WITH A MANIAC (JOHN CLEESE) FASCINATED BY ANTS, AND WANTING TO DEMONSTRATE THEIR MATING CALLS.

Cleese: All right – guess what it is then... (WAVES ARMS)
Feldman: An ant.
Cleese: Good, good. It's an ant. What's he doing?
Feldman: I don't know what it's doing.
Cleese: It's signalling. It's sig-

nalling. It's saying – give us a hand with this small vole.
Feldman: Wait a minute. How do you know it's saying – give us a hand with this small vole? I mean, it's so specific.
Cleese: ...Well, I don't know – it might be anything.
Feldman: You what?
Cleese: It might be anything. I'm not a bloody ant, am I? How should I know what a bloody ant says? Who cares what a bloody ant says.
Feldman: Well, you brought it up in the first place.
Cleese: Shut up or I'll eat you.

(SCREAMS) That is the death cry of a worker ant. Now – you do it...
Feldman: No.
Cleese: Go on – you do it.
Feldman: (PATHETIC SCREAM)
Cleese: Rotten. What a rotten death cry of a worker ant. Rotten. (VERY LOUD SCREAM) Whereas a queen ant, which is a thousand times larger, goes (VERY LOUD SCREAM) You do it.
(FELDMAN RUSHES OFF. OFF SCREEN SQUEAL OF BRAKES AND VERY LOUD SCREAM)
Cleese: That's it. That's it. That's quite good...

W. C. Fields

Fields created a profoundly put upon character, the hapless victim of both misfortune and all the institutions of American society. He was the master of the comic aside, spoken slyly under his breath, saying what many were afraid to say and well knowing that the underdog always got the laugh. These qualities, together with the bulbous nose, round body, skinny legs and coarse voice, captured the hearts of American audiences over four decades.

Allied to the underdog persona, however, was that of a cantankerous misogynist and misanthrope with the underlying notion that only the nasty people thrive. Fields used character names to symbolise this: Filthy McNasty; J Pinkerton Snoopington, the bank manager; and Eustace McGargle, for example.

His Life and Work

W.C. Fields was born William Claude Dukinfield on January 29th 1880, in Philadelphia – a town for which he evidently had little regard. He later said: "Last weekend I went to Philadelphia but it was closed," and his famous remark about preferring his home

Catchphrases

On being asked what he'd want on his tombstone: "On the whole, I'd rather be in Philadelphia."

"I don't drink water. Fishes fuck in it."

town to death, but only just, illustrates his scathing attitude.

He ran away from home aged 11 and lived on the streets, sometimes selling newspapers. He taught himself to juggle, worked at an amusement park and having perfected the skill, toured the United States for two decades and went on to be the first American to headline at the Paris club, the Folies-Bergeres. In 1900, he married Harriet (known as Hattie) Hughes in San Francisco and she joined him in his act until their baby boy was born in 1904, after which he continued to tour alone.

Developing a vaudeville act, he created the famous golf lesson sketch in which the ball is never hit (later to be utilised in more than one film), a game of pool with trick balls and the trademark muttered asides. He was a big hit at the Ziegfeld Follies, with a distinctive style – impromptu juggling and a contemptuous neglect of the audience. The irritable, hater-of-all-mankind character first found real expression in the musical, *Poppy*, in a two-year run from 1923, later turned into a movie, *Sally of the Sawdust*, directed by the great D.W.

Griffith who also worked extensively with Chaplin. Unlike the silent genius Chaplin, Fields transferred successfully when the 'talkies' arrived, making his first sound shorts in 1932-33: *The Dentist* (featuring the golf session), *The Fatal Glass of Beer*, *The Pharmacist* and *The Barber Shop*.

Writing the majority of his own scripts, Fields used pen-names regularly – Otis J Criblecoblis, Charles Bogle and Mahatma Kane Jeeves: this last was derived, he said, from the umpteen boring English high society plays he had sat through in which someone always came on and said to the butler or footman, "M'hat, M'cane, Jeeves."

It's A Gift, in 1934, is considered by many to be Fields' greatest film. With a screen wife to carp at, a screen baby to moan about, this was the perfect vehicle for the misanthropic, loathe-everyone character that by now was Fields' hallmark. Illness – he was an alcoholic – robbed him of several years work in the mid-1930s, but moving from Paramount to Universal in 1938, he was revitalised. *Never Give A Sucker An Even Break* (1941) is considered his

Key Films

Pool Sharks (1915);
David Copperfield (1935);
You Can't Cheat an Honest Man (1939);
My Little Chickadee (1940);
Never Give A Sucker An Even Break (1941).

last important work and legend has it he wrote the story-line on the back of an envelope while seated on the toilet. The surrealistic plot concerns the making of a film by Fields, playing himself, and takes a broad swipe at a range of Hollywood movie cliches, capturing his own sour outlook on life and expressing it outlandishly.

Fields died on Christmas Day in 1946.

Performance Extract

From *My Little Chickadee*:

Fields: I was tending a bar on the lower East Side. A tough paloma by the name of Chicago Molly comes in. We had lunch on the bar that day consisting of succotash, asparagus with mayonnaise and Philadelphia cream cheese. She dips her mit into this melange, I was yawning at the time and she hits me right in the mouth with it. Well, I jumps over the bar and knocks her down.

Bartender: You knocked her down? I was the one who knocked her down.

Fields: On yeah, yeah... You knocked her down... but I was the one started kicking her. (TO BYSTANDER) Ever kicked a woman in the midriff with corsets on?

Bystander: No, I can't recall any such incident.

Fields: Nearly broke my big toe. Never had such a painful experience.

Bystander: Did you ever see her again?

Bartender: Yeah, she came back the next night and beat up the both of us.

Fields: Yeah, but she had another woman with her.

French and Saunders

For a comedy double-act that really did start out just for a laugh, Dawn French and Jennifer Saunders must be among the most successful 'jokers' in the business.

"We started when there were a lot of pro-feminist, hard-hitting acts about, but we didn't do that – which was to our advantage," said Jennifer Saunders.

Developing their own interpretation of the traditional comic formula, Saunders appeared to be the star while French played the down-trodden side-kick. Their strength lay in sharp characterisations of modern-day female stereotypes.

Their Life and Work

Dawn French and Jennifer Saunders were born on 11th October, 1957, and 5th July, 1958, respectively. They led strangely parallel lives before finally meeting at the Central School of Speech and Drama on a teaching course in 1977. Both had fathers in the RAF and as children, they shared the same best friend, one after another.

After 'A' levels, French studied in New York on a year's scholarship from the English Speaking Union, while Jennifer Saunders spent 12 months in Italy.

At college, a state of mutual hatred existed until they simultaneously moved into the same flat and discovered a shared sense of humour. They began improvising and committing the best bits to memory, performing for their flatmates and at the end of term

cabaret as a joke, and it was in the same spirit that they carried off their first performance at the newly-opened Comic Strip in London.

Peter Richardson immediately spotted their potential and after an initial fortnightly guest spot, they joined the regular team, appearing up to five times a week. "We didn't really have a double-act then; all we did was sketches, and then we'd stop and be slightly embarrassed and bow and say thank-you", said Jennifer Saunders.

French, who had also been teaching throughout this period, left to go on tour with the Comic

Strip in 1981. Cameos in the anarchic sitcom *The Young Ones* followed, as did the first series of *The Comic Strip*, commissioned by Jeremy Isaacs for Channel 4's opening season. *Five Go Mad in Dorset*, a spoof on Enid Blyton's Famous Five series, went out on the station's opening night.

In the mid-80s, French and Saunders were in great demand. They had, by now, built up a stage act consisting of solid characterisation. On October 6th, 1983, their first TV show was transmitted. A second series of *The Comic Strip Presents*, consisting of seven half-hour films, went out in 1984. In 1985 Jennifer Saunders achieved recognition as a solo performer in *Happy Families*, written by Ben Elton, where she played a mother and her four daughters.

Girls on Top (Central, 1985), written by French and Saunders, with Tracey Ullman and Ruby Wax, began as a reaction to the lack of decent female roles in *The Young Ones*. The foursome played outlandish lodgers in a Chelsea flat owned by an eccentric novelist (Joan Greenwood). Produced and directed by Paul Jackson, a further series was made in 1986.

Of the two *Comic Strip Specials* made in 1986, French and Saunders wrote *Consuela*. At this same time, the duo also performed on Channel 4's *Saturday Live* and they began their involvement with Comic Relief, the comedy charity.

National recognition arrived with their own series, *French and Saunders*. The first, beginning in March, 1987, on BBC2, packaged

sketches in a fake, tatty TV variety show. *Raw Sex* provided the music, Dawn was the YOP helper and Jennifer, the star. The show also had a team of incompetent dancers, *Hot Hoofers*. There were good spoofs, including *The Avengers*, ridiculous fashion shows and synchronised swimming routines. The second series, in March, 1988, had a much looser format. It included their now legendary contraception sketch, plus a memorable documentary on ballet dancers. By the time the third series was launched, the duo were established as one of the most popular acts on British TV.

Dawn French went on to perform in the West End play, *When I Was A Girl I Used To Scream And Shout*, and Ben Elton's comedy *Silly Cow*. She also had her own series on BBC2 about the joys of eating, *Scoff*. In 1991, she starred in the series *Murder Most*

Key TV/Film

TV: The Comic Strip (1982-3, 1984-6); Girls on Top (1985); Happy Families (1985); French and Saunders.

Film: Supergrass

Horrid, a bizarre collection of spoof murder mysteries, in which she played a huge array of characters and earned critical success. French has also produced a book, *French Knits*, which are jumpers for the larger woman. She is married to comic Lenny Henry.

Jennifer Saunders is married to Ade Edmondson, of *The Young Ones* and *Comic Strip* fame. They have three children. Her most recent project is a new solo series, *Absolutely Fabulous*, for the BBC.

Performance Extract

Dawn: What are you going to the doctor for – have you got a fungus or a thrush or what?

Jennifer: No.

Dawn: Well that's a shame, because if you did have, I could cure it. All you get is some raw lemon rind and Deep Heat and rub it on, that's all you do. Well what are you going to the doctor for then?

Jennifer: Well I'm not supposed to say. I'm going to get a contraception.

Dawn: (SUPERIOR) Ooo-er.

Jennifer: You know, the pill.

Dawn: Yes.

Jennifer: What is it then?

Dawn: Do you know about contraception or not?

Jennifer: Not.

Dawn: Right. The first most important thing about contraception is to choose the right contraceptive utensil – like, for instance I personally would not choose the pill.

Jennifer: Why not?

Dawn: Because all it does is block your philippine tubes and makes your bosoms five times as big, which in your case is unnecessary and careless, frankly.

Jennifer: Well I might not go on the pill then, I might go on something else.

Dawn: Like what? Like what? They're all as bad. If you told the doctor you don't want to go

on the pill, you know what he'll do?

Jennifer: What?

Dawn: He'll insert a UFO inside you. Do you know what one of those is or not?

Jennifer: Not.

Dawn: Right. Other name, coil. Do you know what a slinky looks like?

Jennifer: Yes.

Dawn: Well it's like a huge slinky, and it's got barbed wire on it, and they squish it all up and stuff it up inside your bladder and it hooks on, and stops babies. The only drawback is, you can get out of control going up and down stairs that's all.

Stephen Fry & Hugh Laurie

"Hugh and I often become like adolescents... being funny is a compulsion, really. Showbusiness legitimises that compulsion... which is delightful." – Stephen Fry.

Stephen Fry and Hugh Laurie do not appear to know the meaning of the word 'relax', being almost indecently prolific writers. They are frequent performers of their own material on a wide range of TV and radio shows and if that were not enough, both may also be heard and/or seen in numerous commercials between programmes. Theirs is generally a highly intellectual brand of humour but terrific characterisations and visual slapstick scenes are also commonly interwoven into the rich overall texture.

Their Life and Work

Stephen Fry was born in Norfolk on August 24th 1957. He went to boarding school at the age of seven though he managed to get himself expelled for shoplifting. Though educationally advanced (taking his 'O' levels at 13) Fry was asthmatic and extremely tall, two qualities which set him distinctly apart from his peers. Regularly in trouble at schools for "taking lots of things that I had no business with or need for", at the age of 17, shortly before taking his 'A' levels, he went into a pub and stole an overcoat which had a wallet full of credit cards in the pocket. He went AWOL for three months, on a wild spending spree. When

finally caught, he spent three months on remand at Pucklechurch where he was known as 'The Professor' because he read so

avidly and played the piano. Prison, he later said, "was the making of me." Redeeming himself, he got his 'A' levels and

Fry (1957-), Laurie (1959-)

a scholarship at Queen's College, Cambridge, to read English. There he met Hugh Laurie, the President of Footlights.

Hugh Laurie shares a similar background. Born in 1959 he was the son of a GP and went to public school at Eton where he was a model pupil and in his own words, "a bit of a square." His father won an Olympic gold medal for rowing and Hugh inherited his enthusiasm and prowess. He took time out from performing with the Cambridge Footlights to row with the Cambridge team in the Oxford and Cambridge boat race, in 1980. The race was a memorable one: Cambridge lost by a few feet.

The Footlights Revue of 1981 marked Fry and Laurie's first important work. Together with Tony Slattery and Emma Thompson (a regular guest at pink gin binges in Fry's rooms) they created a show which went on to great success both in Edinburgh's Festival and in Australia.

Returning home, and no longer students, Fry, Laurie and Thompson were immediately signed up by Granada TV to create *Al Fresco*, with other leading lights of their genre, Ben Elton, Robbie Coltrane, and Siobhan Redmond. Supposedly ITV's answer to the Beeb's *Not the Nine O'Clock News*, it never really fired on all cylinders. Fry then appeared in a play at Chichester, and, between performances, updated the old

musical *Me And My Girl* which became a hit again all over the world – London, New York, Tokyo, Budapest and Australia.

Fry and Laurie, by now fully paid-up members of that incessantly incestuous club of 'alternative comedians' began appearing in a whole strings of shows like *The Young Ones*, the anarchic sitcom with Rik Mayall, Ade Edmondson and Nigel Planer; its far inferior successor, *Filthy, Rich and Catflap*; *Happy Families*; *Blackadder*; and *Saturday Live*.

Blackadder, a comedy set in the medieval court, starring Rowan Atkinson, was followed by *Blackadder II* (Elizabethan); *Blackadder III* (Regency). In the final series, Blackadder Goes Forth, Fry and Laurie acted to perfection as the General and the gormless Lieutenant in the World War I trenches. The success of their witty routines on *Saturday Live* led to the first of several of their own series – *A Bit of Fry and Laurie* – which featured mimicry, farce, a bewildering collage of impersonations (Rhodes Boyson, Robert Robinson and God) together with splendid characterisations like Fry as the dirty vicar and Laurie the heartless TV interviewer.

The 1990s also saw them starring in an interpretation of the *Jeeves and Wooster* novels of P.G. Wodehouse for TV. The more extended comedy format allowed both to show their acting

proficiency. Fry fits ideally as Jeeves, and as Bertie Wooster, Laurie has brought the upper-class twit role to a new peak, with excellent facial expressions and a charming, innocent benevolence towards mankind.

Hugh Laurie also starred in Ben Elton's play, *Gasping*, in 1990 in the West End. He teamed up once again with Stephen Fry and Emma Thompson, in *Peter's Friends*, a feature film directed by Kenneth Branagh released in the autumn of 1992.

Fry has an independent career, and also a cause. 1991 saw his first novel – *The Liar* – published to critical acclaim. His cause is the Terence Higgins Trust – the AIDS charity – for which he co-ordinates an annual fund-raising event, *Hysteria*.

Performance Extract

LAURIE: "Now Kenneth Baker, it seems to me, is a perfect argument for why one should always try and kill Kenneth Baker."

FRY: "He just picked me up and slapped me, really hard. I cried and cried, but he wouldn't take any notice. Then he put a plastic tag round my wrist, cut my umbilical cord and put me in a cot. It was awful."

Jackie Gleason

Big and brash, a magnificent 'physical' comedian, very much in the tradition of vaudeville, Jackie Gleason is best remembered for two series in the 1950s: his own eponymous show and *The Honeymooners*, in which he played Ralph Kramden, a grumpy bus driver. The multi-talented Gleason produced, wrote, directed, scored and conducted the music, and starred in the show. Part of the secret of its success was that it coincided with the boom in ownership of TV sets and was the first show to explore the stresses and frustrations of America's blue-collar workers.

His Life and Work

Herbert John Gleason was born the younger son of Herbert and Mae on February 26th 1916, in Brooklyn, New York. His brother died when Jackie, as he was known, was three years old. When he was eight his father disappeared, leaving Mae to scratch a bare living in the change booth of a subway station. Gleason's first showbiz work came aged 16, as MC of Brooklyn's Folly Theatre. He later worked as a barber and in a carnival, returning to the MC role in Pennsylvania and New Jersey resorts. In 1935, he became assistant MC and 'bouncer' at the Miami club in Newark, New Jersey, supplementing his wage with part time work as a DJ on the local WAAT Newark radio station. Two years of cabaret work followed in the New York clubs, Leon and Eddie's, and Club 18. While there, he was spotted by Jack Warner, the movie producer.

Warner gave him a one-year Hollywood contract and he appeared in small comedy or melodramatic roles in several pictures in 1941 and 1942. Returning to New York, Gleason did further stage work, including some six months with Nancy Walker in *Along Fifth Avenue*, and took over from Bob Crosby on NBC's *Old Gold* Sunday night radio show.

Switching to TV in 1949, he found early success with *The Life Of Riley*, originally a radio show itself. Gleason appeared for six months, but quit to join the *Cavalcade of Stars* on the old DuMont network where he first paraded the character of the ineffectual and irascible bus driver, Ralph Kramden. In 1952, *The Jackie Gleason Show* was aired, in which he cultivated a motley crew of characters including Reggie van Gleason, the Poor Soul, Joe the Bartender and Charlie the Loudmouth. It also featured Gleason's greatest character, Ralph, in a recurring sketch called *The Honeymooners*. Such was its popularity, that Gleason became known as 'Mr Saturday Night.'

Several straight acting roles followed and then Gleason signed an agreement to develop *The Honeymooners* from a sketch into a series. He contracted to make 78 episodes, two years worth, in front of a studio audience.

The Honeymooners was set in a tenement apartment in Brooklyn – the home of bus driver Ralph and his wife Alice, played by Audrey Meadows. The delicious irony of the title was that their marriage was as drab and stark as their flat: they'd lived there 14 years before buying a new piece of furniture – a TV set. Ed and Trixie Norton (Art Carney and Joyce Randolph) were their upstairs neighbours. Something of a Walter Mitty character, Ralph was forever dreaming up ludicrous money-making schemes to augment his lousy pay. Naturally, he refused to let his wife work. Ralph was a loner who

Key TV/Films

TV: The Life of Riley; Cavalcade of Stars; The Jackie Gleason Show; The Honeymooners.

Film: 15 in all, including – The Hustler (1961); Requiem for a Heavyweight (1962); Gigot (1963); Smokey and the Bandit (1977).

made many mistakes but never learned from them. But he wasn't a quitter, and if you could get to talk to him you'd find he was actually quite nice. "All of my characters are psychologically constructed... I give each one a saving grace, a touch of sympathy," said Gleason. The interplay between Gleason and Carney has been likened to that between Laurel and Hardy and the contrast of Gleason's physicality with Meadows' deadpan humour as Alice gave the show a double comic pivot. A curiosity of the show was that Gleason rarely, if ever, rehearsed his lines, since he possessed a photographic

memory. The show ran, on and off, until 1970, with frequent changes of the cast between series - Gleason played opposite three different actresses, but 'Ralph' only ever had one wife.

The last black-and-white episode, *The Adoption*, in 1966, was screened as an hour-long special, and in 1976, Gleason, Meadows and Carney from the original foursome were joined by a subsequent Trixie, Jane Kean, for a 21st Anniversary celebration. This they followed up with a Christmas special and the next year, a Valentine's Day show.

As Sheriff Buford T. Justice, Gleason starred alongside Burt Reynolds in the frantic *Smokey and the Bandit* in 1977, following up this box-office success with two sequels in 1980 and 1983.

In 1986, Gleason found over 50 'lost' episodes of *The Honeymooners* in his basement, filmed between 1952-55. When screened, there was a brief Honeymooners revival... a second honeymoon?

Jackie Gleason, once described as "the most celebrated buffoon ever to rise through United States television", was elected to the Television Hall of Fame in 1985. He died two years later.

Performance Extracts

From *The Honeymooners*:

Ralph: I'm ashamed Alice. I'm embarrassed. Of all the guys down at the bus depot, I'm the only one that never has any money at the end of the week. Take tonight for instance – Joe McCloskey had 20 bucks, Pete Crowley had 35 bucks and Frank Willis had even more

than that... Of all the bus drivers, I'm the only one that ain't got a dime."
Alice: Well don't feel too bad, Ralph. You're the only bus driver that's got a uranium mine in Asbury Park.

Trixie: Do you want anything at the store besides milk, Alice?

Alice: You'd better get a pound of margarine, too.
(RALPH ENTERS, WEARING HIS RACCOON LODGE OUTFIT)
Alice: Maybe you won't have to get the margarine – 400 pounds of lard just walked in.
Ralph: You have just said the secret word, Alice. You have just won yourself a trip to the moon.

Whoopi Goldberg

"Whoopi Goldberg is a slight, sprite-like comic actress whose mind and body are inhabited by some of the drollest and most touching characters one is ever likely to encounter.. she has the face and personality of the wise child with ingenuous eyes and a puckish smile. As she tells her tales of misfits and outcasts, and even as she offers wry, satiric comments, she is consistently disarming." – Mel Gussow, *New York Times*.

"One part Elaine May, one part Groucho, one part Ruth Draper, one part Richard Pryor, and five parts never seen before." – Mike Nicholls, Broadway producer/ director.

Prior to *The Colour Purple*, Whoopi Goldberg was famed as a stand-up comic specialising in improvisational monologues, although at heart she was really a character actress performing material she had written herself. Emerging from fringe theatre with a flexible and impressive range of skills including mimicry, facial expression and body gestures, she first hit the national scene in 1984 when her one-woman show took Broadway by storm. Her characters are an eclectic mix of types, united only in not having their problems to seek.

Her Life and Work

Whoopi Goldberg refuses to divulge her real name, will only admit to being born in New York in 1950. She and her younger brother were brought up by their mother alone in a housing project, the father having abandoned them. Initially taught by nuns at a parish school, she first acted at the Helena Rubenstein Children's Theatre at the Hudson Guild, aged eight to ten. Intuitively a mimic, her early influences were Gracie Allen, Carole Lombard, Spencer Tracy and Robert Duvall. "I'm a real sponge in terms of seeing things and absorbing them," she has said, "and with the people I have admired over the years, I've stolen from them and added the things that I know instinctively. It was always the character actors I went for."

She dropped out of high school and became a hippy "like everyone else in the '60s," becoming involved in politics, particularly the civil rights issue. In the late '60s she found work in the chorus line of *Hair* and *Jesus Christ Superstar*. After a failed marriage in the 1970s she and her daughter flew to the West Coast and went to San Diego. Intending to stay a week, she remained six years, becoming a founder member of the city's Rep Theatre and joining Spontaneous Combustion, an improvisational troupe.

It was here she also invented her stage name. Originally, as a joke, she intended it to be Whoopi Cushion, but her mother persuaded her this wasn't adequately serious, so she adopted Goldberg, a name from her family history. She played in a two-hander with Don Victor but when he quit on the eve of one of their shows she went on alone and found she could cope. Throughout her time in fringe theatre she supported herself and her daughter with jobs ranging from beautician to bank teller to bricklayer. She graduated from a beauty college and took a job as a mortuary hairdresser, saying: "I was tired of working on living people who all wanted to look like Farrah Fawcett."

In the early '80s Goldberg began developing a series of unique characterisations: Fontaine, a jive-talking drug addict with a PhD. in literature; a nine-year-old girl who doesn't want to be black any more; a crippled young woman who becomes able-bodied in her dreams; and a 13-year-old Catholic girl who becomes pregnant and gives herself an abortion. Elements of these were based on the real-life experiences of people she'd known. These four charac-

ters formed the basis of *The Spook Show* (also known as *A Broad Abroad* when she took it to Europe) which she performed across the United States. A sell-out series of shows in New York won her critical praise and encouraged producer/director Mike Nicholls to run it on Broadway. In October 1984 she included two new characters with the four regulars when *Whoopi Goldberg* opened at the Lyceum Theatre. The two newcomers were Ugmo, an old black vaudeville star and a Jamaican woman who comes to

the USA as a live-in domestic for a lecherous millionaire. A performance was recorded for transmission on HBO in 1985 and a newspaper critic applauded her "good timing, lively facial expression, considerable flexibility in her impersonations and real skill with accents."

In 1985, Whoopi Goldberg made the often difficult switch from stage to screen with a triumphal performance in Steven Spielberg's *The Colour Purple*, derived from the Alice Walker novel about a black teenage bride in the deep south. The film got ten Oscar nominations – but won none. Her career dipped until the success of *Ghost* in 1990, in which she starred alongside Patrick Swayze and Demi Moore, winning an Oscar for Best Supporting Actress. In the early '90s she was hot property indeed.

Performance Extract

From *Ghost*, 1990:

ODA-MAE (WHHOPI GOLDBERG) IS A MEDIUM WHO HAD FAKED HER SEANCE SESSIONS UNTIL A REAL GHOST, SAM (PATRICK SWAYZE), MURDERED LOVER OF MOLLY (DEMI MOORE), ASKS FOR HER HELP.

Oda-Mae: You now, confidentially, nothing like this has ever happened to me, nothin', and now I can't turn it off... (PICKS UP S PHOTO) Is this him? (TO SAM) Is this you?
Sam: Yeah.
Oda-Mae: White but cute.
Molly: What I don't understand is why did he come back? Why is he

still here?
Oda-Mae: He's stuck, that's what he is, he's in between worlds. You know, it happens sometimes that the spirit gets yanked out so quick that the essence still feels it has work to do here.
Sam: Would you stop rambling?
Oda-Mae: I'm not rambling, I'm answering her questions. (TO MOLLY) He's got an attitude now.
Sam: I don't have an attitude!
Oda-Mae: Yes, you do have an attitude. (TO MOLLY) We're havin' a little discussion. (TO SAM) If you didn't have an attitude, you wouldn't have raised your voice to me just now, would you?
Sam: God damn it, Oda-Mae! I did not...

Oda-Mae: Don't you God damn it me! Don't you take the Lord's name in vain with me, you understand?
Sam: Would you relax?
Oda-Mae: No! You relax, you're the dead guy.

One of her many stage characters, Tonteyn – a junkie:

I'm into books, you know. I got a PhD in literature from Columbia. I know you don't think I was born a junkie. I have an education. I got a PhD I can't do shit with, you know? So I stay high so I don't get mad.

Joyce Grenfell

On the face of it, "Don't do that, Sydney" would not seem to be one of the theatre's most memorable lines, but delivered in the inimitable manner of Joyce Grenfell's nursery school teacher, it is indeed a classic. The secret is in the tone – patience wearing thin... exasperation round the corner..., will the little darlings never sit still?

Grenfell's gift was her delightful ability to point up, with the most delicate touch, the stuffiness and pretension of polite British society. She was a kind of updated, verbal Jane Austen. The nursery school teacher monologue was her crowning achievement, its rather resigned cadences being universally recognisable as the special language adults invariably employ in their dealings with children. A true master of inflection, her material was deceptively gentle, the stiletto sliding in so softly it was barely noticeable... but no less lethally accurate for that. Grenfell often cited Ruth Draper – a relation by marriage – as the inspiration for her monologues.

Her Life and Work

Born Joyce Irene Phipps in well-heeled Montpelier Square, London, on February 10th 1910, she was the daughter of Paul Phipps, an American-born architect, and the former Nora Langhorne of Virginia. Another of the Langhorne sisters became Lady Nancy Astor. As a child, Joyce enjoyed theatre, especially Noel Coward and Ivor Novello, and after schooling in Surrey went to RADA at 17. In December 1928, she married Reginald Grenfell.

Working briefly in commercial art, designing posters and Christmas cards, she began contributing humourous verse to *Punch* in 1935, and following a three-week apprenticeship, she became radio critic for *The Observer* newspaper in March 1937. In November of 1938, the Grenfells attended a dinner party at the home of well-known humourist Stephen Potter

(author of *Gamesmanship* and *One-Upmanship*) where she described a Women's Institute 'talk' she had recently attended, on how to make something out of nothing. Potter was impressed and invited her for dinner again, two months later, to meet Herbert Farjeon, the theatrical producer and author of the revue *Nine Sharp*, just completing a sell-out run at the Adelphi. She

(1910-1979)

parodied the WI talk again, and Farjeon invited her to appear in his next show, *The Little Revue*. Joyce performed the WI skit and another about three different kinds of mothers.

During the war, Grenfell was often on the radio and performed in a further three Farjeon revues designed to divert people's minds from the air-raid blitzes on London. She also worked for the Canadian Red Cross. In 1944, she set off around the world with ENSA (affectionately known by its audiences as Every Night Something Awful) entertaining the troops with her songs and sketches. In 15 months she went to 14 countries.

Post-war, she resumed writing with Stephen Potter, working on the factual *HOW* programmes. Joyce contributed a section on how to apply for a job, and illustrated her points by also showing how not to apply. This witty approach became a success and regular characters emerged: the listener's friend, a compere/guide; Len, the keen technical buff;

Mrs Truebel, a refugee living in Golders Green; Fern Brixton, a vegetarian lover of beauty; and the nursery school teacher. Roy Plomley and Celia Johnson often took part in the shows. Further radio work followed, including *We Beg To Differ*, a light-hearted discussion of issues that divided the sexes, in which somebody decided four women were required to play against two men.

In the late '40s and early '50s, Grenfell played several film roles, including probably her best as a gym mistress in *The Happiest Days of Your Life* with Margaret Rutherford.

Returning to the stage, she starred in *Joyce Grenfell Requests the Pleasure...* Opening in 1954, it ran for a year in London and transferred to New York the next year and toured the States in 1956-57. Among the outstanding personas she created for this show were the gushing young lady at the cocktail party, the mother of a teenage girl about to make an unfortunate marriage, a spinster working for three ungrateful

Key Films

The Happiest Days of Your Life (1939);
A Run For Your Money (1949);
Genevieve (1953);
the St. Trinian's series.

brothers and, of course, the celebrated and long-suffering teacher...

Another show of her own came in 1958, and for many years after that she was a regular on a number of BBC radio shows, especially the panel game *Face The Music*.

Joyce Grenfell died on November 30th, 1979.

Performance Extracts ➡

About a quiet girl called Ethel, whose character is transformed when she goes to football matches;

I don't understand Ethel,
I don't, I don't really.
She's one of my very best friends.
Just about the best nearly.
She's an awfully nice girl, Ethel is,
Dainty and refined.
I mean she'd never do or say
Anything unkind.
But get her inside of a stadium
And she seems to go out of her
   mind

Kill him she yells – knock his
   block off
(at hockey or football or what)
Kill him she yells, turning purple,
Kill the perishing lot.
Sh-sh, I say, Ethel,
Sh-sh, and I die of shame,
Kill him and bash his teeth in his
   face,
She says
And calls him a dirty name.

Nursery school extract.

Grenfell: "No Sydney, silly old fat man isn't a good name for a bunny rabbit... It is not as funny as all that. There's no need to roll about on the floor... Timmy, what have you got in your hand? We haven't had toast and marmalade for two days... George – don't do that..."

Tony Hancock

"The only happiness I could achieve is to perfect the talent I have, however small it may be... if the time came when I found out that I had come to the end of what I could develop out of my own ability, I wouldn't want to do it any more." Tony Hancock.

"One by one he shut the door on all the people he knew; then he shut the door on himself." Spike Milligan.

At their peak, a third of the country tuned in to Tony Hancock's shows. His best performances comfortably stand comparison with other giants of comedy, most famously of all the 'Blood Donor' sketch. A master of timing, he dared to use extended silences, even on the radio, as in the celebrated episode of *Hancock's Half Hour* where very nearly nothing at all happens on a wet Sunday afternoon. To this day, older residents of Cheam and North Cheam, in Surrey, are likely to be asked with a smile if they know Railway Cuttings, Hancock's stage address in the fictional East Cheam.

For all his fame, there wasn't a great deal of fortune – much of his earnings disappearing into drink – and the adjectives that are invariably attached to Hancock's name are enigmatic and genius.

His Life and Work

Born in the Small Heath district of Birmingham on May 12th 1924, Tony Hancock grew up in Bournemouth, where his parents ran The Railway Hotel, a popular lodging with the many music hall artists performing for the south coast holiday crowds. Hancock's father was a showman too, a regular entertainer at masonic evenings and smoking concerts, introducing the young Tony to variety at a very tender age. When Hancock was 11 his father died, and soon afterwards his mother remarried.

(1924-1968)

Hancock went to good schools, but left at 15 and began his own career in the business. Performing at smokers, he went on as the 'Confidential Comic' with a set largely 'borrowed' from Max Miller – the main difference then being that Hancock had absolutely no sense of timing. Whatsoever.

George Fairweather, a professional comic, gave Hancock a spot in his show for the troops. Hancock told dirty jokes – most of which he didn't understand – and was dreadful. He used the same set at a gig in a Catholic church hall with important consequences. The audience walked out in disgust – and he never told another dirty joke. When Fairweather went into the army, Hancock took over the running of the Bournemouth War Services Organisation and began to write his own material. One short example is more than enough: In the township of Toenail City/Lived the Sheriff, a man of good class/ But he drank like a fish did the Sheriff/ Till his breath burned a hole in the glass.

Hancock himself signed up for the RAF and tried to get into ENSA, but nervousness wrecked his attempt. He joined up instead with the Ralph Reader Gang Shows, singing a serious ballad as well as performing comedy sketches. A revue, Wings, born of the show, toured until September 1947. Then came a spell at the Windmill Theatre, ("We never closed" being their famous boast during the war) a strip club in Soho, where Harry Worth and Morecambe and Wise appeared on the same bill. After a show in Bognor Regis, Hancock collected all his best sketches and began to develop a regular act on his own, including some improbable impersonations.

Having first appeared on radio during the war, he returned to it in the 1950s in several shows produced by Duncan Wood, who would later be producer of all the TV *Hancock's Half Hours*, but the meeting with Ray Galton and Alan Simpson was the crucial moment. They were brought in as untried hopefuls when Hancock and co-star Derek Roy couldn't work with the original writers for a 1951 radio show, *Happy Go Lucky*. This talented duo would go on to write much of his finest material, and the outstanding *Steptoe and Son* series, but their first writing specifically for Hancock was on *Calling All Forces*.

The first radio show of *Hancock's Half Hour* was broadcast in October 1954, also starring Moira Lister, Bill Kerr and Sid James. The series dealt with Hancock's vain attempts to carve out a career in showbiz while living with two scroungers in the mythical East Cheam. The innovative aspect was in the degree of character development, the extended theme and the absence of the hitherto traditional musical interludes. Transferring to the TV in 1956, there were eventually six of these classic series screened, with a total of 102 on the radio. The humour came from the smallest of situations, using Hancock's own natural characteristics of melancholic gloominess and misplaced optimism.

In real life, Hancock managed to alienate all his former colleagues and cut the final tie with Galton and Simpson in 1963. After professional suicide, came personal suicide. In Melbourne, Australia, where he had gone to record a TV series, Hancock took his own life in his hotel room on June 24th 1968.

Key TV/Films

TV: Hancock's Half Hour.

Films: The Rebel (1960); The Punch and Judy Man (1962).

Performance Extract ➔

From *The Blood Donor*:

Doctor: I've just taken a small sample to test.
Hancock: A sample? How much do you want, then?
Doctor: A pint of course.
Hancock: A pint. Have you gone raving mad? Oh well, I mean, you must be joking.
Doctor: A pint is a perfectly normal quantity.
Hancock: You don't seriously expect me to believe that. I mean, I came in here in all good faith to help my country. I don't mind giving a reasonable amount, but a pint... that's nearly an armful. I'm sorry, I'm not walking around with an empty arm for anybody... No, I'm sorry, I've been misinformed... I've made a mistake... I'll do something else, I'll be a traffic warden.

Tommy Handley

"Tommy never left the microphone for the entire half hour show, bluffing his way out of awkward situations; suave, serious, light-hearted, allowing others to score off him, distributing the laughs equally between him and his opposite numbers." Ted Kavanagh, ITMA writer.

For a nation at war, *It's That Man Again*, Tommy Handley's phenomenally popular radio show was a fantastic tonic. The weekly half-hour of quick-fire patter, regular-as-clockwork catchphrases and, best of all, the ridiculing of the Nazi propaganda effort was about the only reliable light relief amid the fears and worries.

Tommy Handley was the main-spring of ITMA – as it was colloquially known. He was the voice of calm in a cast of eccentrics constantly interrupting his diligent work as the minister of Aggravations and Mysteries, c/o The Office of Twerps.

His Life and Work

Born in Liverpool in 1894, Handley was in showbiz as a conjuror even as a child, became a good baritone singer during the first World War and discovered he had a talent for comedy. In the 1920s he toured with Leslie Henson and Tom Walls in a sketch written for the troops, called *The Disorderly Room*, in which Handley played the officer in charge. He later played this sketch at a Royal Variety Performance at the London Coliseum in 1923, and used it frequently in his subsequent career as something to fall back on. Handley began to

establish himself as a master of gibberish – speaking a load of old double-dutch while still making himself understood.

The important breakthrough came with a successful audition for the BBC at the Savoy Hill studios in the early 30s. Handley had not yet established a nation-wide following, so was able to

experiment in a series a radio shows (including *Radio Radiance*, *Inaninn*, *Handley's Manoeuvres*, *Tommy' Tours* and *Hot Pot*) using a range of guises in an attempt to discover what worked and what didn't.

In the middle 30s, *Band Wagon*, with Arthur Askey and Richard Murdoch, was a popular radio

show, probably the first comedy show with a recognisable story-line. To follow this, the BBC wanted a George Burns/Gracie Allen type show, but couldn't develop the right scripts so they turned to Handley, producer Francis Worsley and writer Ted Kavanagh for an alternative suggestion. They chose to set the programmes on a ship from which Handley, aided by his secretary Dotty and the mad Russian inventor Vodkin, could broadcast whatever he liked. The title for the show was lifted from a *Daily Express* headline they used each time Hitler staked another territorial claim, and was therefore already on everyone's lips.

The run of four pilot shows in the summer of 1939 were none too successful, but by the time the series proper began in September, war had been declared and the mood of the country had changed. With the advent of war, new ministries had appeared almost overnight and Handley felt ITMA should send this up too – hence the Minister of Aggravations at the Office of Twerps.

Further characters emerged – a fusspot civil servant; the elusive spy Funf, utilised to belittle the Nazis; and after being 'evacuated' to the country there was Farmer Jollop. With the cinemas and theatres closed, ITMA regularly won audiences of 16 million listeners. In 1941, the show was relocated to the seaside and retitled ITSA – *It's That Sand Again...* (ITSA, ITSA, ITSA – Date). Handley played the Mayor of Foaming-at-the-Mouth, and the show included large doses of surrealism, clever verbal puns, lots

Catchphrases

Hello Folks;
TTFN – Ta ta for now;
It's being so cheerful as keeps me going;
Don't forget the diver, Sir, don't forget the diver;
After you, Claude, no, no, after you Cecil;
Can I do you now Sir...? I don't mind if I do...
(and many, many more)

Key Films

It's That Man Again (1942);
Time Flies (1944).

of catchphrases and was all delivered at breakneck speed.

Postwar, Handley acquired a new position – Governor of Never-never Island, Tomtopia and writer Kavanagh produced yet another new set of eccentric characters to mill around him.

Tommy's Handley's warm and friendly voice, beginning each show with "Hello Folks", was much needed reassurance in a time of crisis. How deeply loved he was can be judged from the fact that when he died suddenly, of a brain haemorrhage, in 1949, 10,000 mourners flocked to his funeral.

Performance Extract

Vodkin: Oh Mr. Handmedown, it works, it works.
Handley: What does? Our broadcasting station?
Vodkin: No, the eggs factory. It has exceeded all cackle-ations.
Handley: Tell me about it, old cock.
Vodkin: Every hen she lay two times, once in the morning and once at night.
Handley: What, no matinees?
Vodkin: At night, the hen sleeps - yes?

Handley: Hen-variably.
Vodkin: I switch the light and up she wakes. The cock he crow - the hen she lay and then she sleep again. Again I switch the light and again she lay. Now a million eggs I have.
Handley: I wish I had as many shillings.
Vodkin: What are you going to do?
Handley: I know. We'll sell 'em. Call 'em ITMA eggs – the yolk of the century. Is our radio

station ready?
Vodkin: Oh yes, Mr. Hamandegg.
Handley: We'll get busy – we'll broadcast the ITMA eggs programme right away. Well folks, the next part of the programme comes to you by courtesy of the ITMA egg factory – the eggs with chick appeal.
Announcer: Allo, Ici radio Twerpenburg. Defense de cracher.

Will Hay

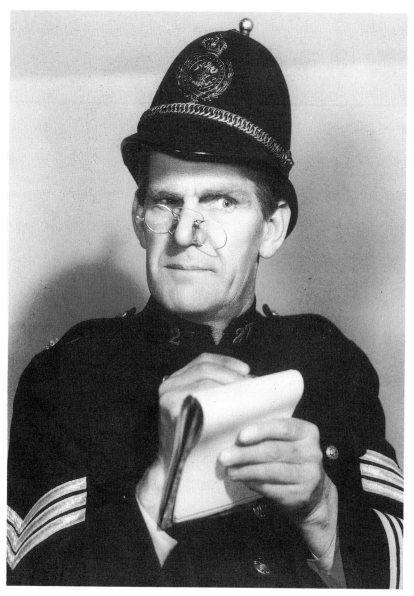

However hilarious the scenario though, Hay's delivery was always completely deadpan. There was never so much as a hint of a smile.

A favourite moment from his sketches has Hay interrupting the fat boy and the old man, another key element in most of his work, when they are playing an illicit game of 'banker'. He reproaches them sternly, but eventually gets lured into the game himself.... A policeman inevitably shows up and the others flee, leaving Hay to take the rap alone. This exchange of roles between Boy and Master was a recurrent theme in Hay's sketches.

His Life and Work

William Thomson Hay was born in Stockton on Tees in December, 1888. Whilst still a boy, the family moved to Lowestoft and later to Hemel Hempstead, then London and finally Manchester just as Hay was finishing school. Hay's father was a strict disciplinarian, vetting everything his children read and ensuring that they become good god-fearing citizens.

Hay left home and married in 1907. He worked at a calico printers and later as an engineer, all the while building up a growing reputation as a stand-up comic at smoking concerts. A number of firms booked him as an after-dinner speaker and to the dismay of his parents, he decided to give the entertainment business a go.

"Modern audiences require a more intellectual type of comedy. In my sketch I portray school life in caricature. It is not burlesque, but an exaggerated portrayal of English character – a particular living type of schoolmaster." – Will Hay.

Will Hay played the famous teacher from St Michael's School. With his wonky mortar-board, tattered gown and the famous pince-nez half way down his nose, he was a much-loved character of the music hall in the '20s and in films in the '30s and early '40s.

Vital to Hay's act was the fat, know-it-all boy who constantly questioned the accuracy of Hay's teaching, causing endless havoc in the classroom and provoking an hysterical tirade of double-speak from Hay.

(1888-1949)

When he needed new material to enter a talent competition at the Palace Theatre in Manchester, his sisters suggested a sketch in which he donned a mortar-board and gown and sang a song of his own. Hay called his musical sketch 'Bend Down', and each verse recounted a prank or disobedience by a pupil, culminating in the chorus "Bend down for six of the best." (The pince-nez, inspired by Hay's father, came later.)

In 1909, when he first performed the character of the schoolmaster, Hay's career as a music hall comic had begun. The sketch was initially based on the schoolmaster and one boy. He performed this and other sketches in one of Fred Karno's touring troupes.

Hay never really looked like a comic. His expression was serious and academic, but with the addition of his mortar-board, fraying gown and the pince-nez, he achieved a somewhat eccentric look.

In the early 1920s, Hay began to expand the St Michael's routine, adding an old man. While the fat, know-it-all boy was always smarter than the schoolmaster, both were smarter than the stupid, devious 80-year-old man. At one stage, Will Hay Junior played the young boy and H Gordon Saunders the old man. However, a more successful duo were Moore Marriott's mad old "Harbottle" and Graham Moffatt's shrieking young "Albert".

Hay's success continued through the '20s and '30s, with his skits centring on the constant battle between the all-too-clever boy and the frankly slipshod master, with his attempts to blind the boy with increasingly frantic and illogical arguments. "The character I play is really a very pathetic fellow," said Hay.

Though the schoolmaster persona is Hay's enduring legacy, he did play other roles – albeit equally authoritarian and pompous. In films in the 1930s for example, he variously played a magistrate, a policeman, a fireman, a prison governor and famously in *Oh Mr Porter*, a stationmaster in rural Ireland where Hay's convoluted logic is seen at its best.

Perhaps the greatest irony of Will Hay's life is that while he made his career from feigning low academic ability, he was in fact an extremely intelligent man. He was almost entirely self-educated, teaching himself German, French and Italian and becoming a serious astronomer. In 1933 he discovered a white spot on the planet Saturn and wrote up his findings in a 1935 book, *Through My Telescope*. For this achievement he was made a Fellow of the Royal Astronomical Society, and such was his specialist knowledge that during the war he temporarily suspended his career to teach astronomy and navigation to the Royal Navy Volunteer Reserve Special Branch.

In 1946, Hay suffered a stroke which forced him into retirement, and he died three years later.

Key Films

Those Were The Days (1934);
Boys Will Be boys (1935);
Good Morning Boys (1937);
Oh Mr Porter (1937);
Go To Blazes (1942).

Performance Extract

Hay: I'll have your name first.
Boy: Wye.
Hay: Why? There's no particular reason why, simply that you came in first. You see it doesn't matter to me whether I have your name first or his, only I'm expecting a bit of bother with him, so I thought I'd settle with yours. Well, come on, what is it?

Boy: Wye.
Hay: Well, when you open a school one of the first things you do, after the school is built and the mortgage arranged, is to buy a register and in it you enter the names of the boys.
Boy: Yes.
Hay: Well, I've bought this and I'm going to use it. Well, come on, what is it?

Boy: Wye.
Hay: Because I want to put it in the book.
Boy: Well, put it in the book.
Hay: I will, when I know it.
Boy: But you do know it.
Hay: No I don't.
Boy: Well you ought to.
Hay: Why??
Boy: Yes.

Lenny Henry

"To see a young black kid doing these conventional, white, impressions was absolutely stunning. We all gave him full marks for everything. He was obviously going to be a star." – Martin Jackson, judge on *New Faces*, 1975.

had fixed the venue – a restaurant in Regent Street. Henry, a renowned lover of curries, was appalled to find the rendezvous was very smart, and French. Two hundred yards down the road stands The Veeraswamy, the oldest and still one of the best Indian restaurants in London.

Walking, or rather bouncing down the street, Henry was far from shy.

Like other members of what has become known as the 'alternative comedy' set, Lenny Henry's work is often deeply political, yet he has also secured a solid base in the mainstream of British humour with more orthodox material. He is quite prepared to examine the issues surrounding race and colour, although, ironically, at the beginning of his career, he served a five year apprenticeship on *The Black and White Minstrel Show*, where he didn't need to 'black up'; and, with a further significant twist of fate in his 1991 Hollywood movie, *True Identity*, he 'whitened up' with suitably comic consequences.

Highly versatile, he is a writer, stand-up comic, impersonator, film actor and singer. Among his notable impersonations are Tina Turner, Michael Jackson and a wonderful David Bellamy. His own creations are also a legend – the best being Delbert Wilkins and Theophilus P. Wildebeeste.

At 6ft 4ins Henry is also highly visible. He was once due to meet a journalist in central London for aninterview over lunch. His agent

He would have been instantly recognisable in any case, but insisted on greeting the fans who mobbed him with bellowed cries of "Katanga, my friends" and "Ooooh-Kaaye". The short walk took nearly 20 minutes, and once in the restaurant, normal service was wholly disrupted as he signed dozens of autographs.

His Life and Work

Lenworth Henry was born in 1958 in Dudley, near Birmingham. His mother had moved to England from Jamaica with some of her children (she was eventually to have seven in all), her husband following soon after. Henry has said he first realised he had a gift for comedy when he did impressions of cartoon characters for his friends at primary school. He can still perform a fine *Top Cat* impression. Comedy was his best

(1958-)

subject at school, which he left at the age of 15 to begin an apprenticeship as an engineer at a local factory, but his working environment changed utterly after his *New Faces* success. He went into the northern clubs circuit and got onto *The Black and White Minstrel Show*, performing often from 1975-81. In this period, he also appeared with *Cannon and Ball* in summer seasons at seaside resorts and in two series of *The Fosters*, an ITV sitcom about a black family. His stage act at this time was liberally laced with racist material, but as he matured he began to discard its blunter elements.

Dawn French (who became Mrs Lenny Henry in 1984) came to see him gig at an RAF base, in Wiltshire, where the audience gave him a hard time, shouting "Where's the sambo?" even before he came on... French befriended him and began to attend his shows regularly, giving him notes after each one suggesting improvements and alternatives to the racist stereotypes. The big break came with a children's Saturday morning show, *Tiswas*, with Chris Tarrant, which became cult viewing even among young adults. Here the "Ooooh-Kaaye" character was born – Algernon, an exuberant Rasta with a vivid vocabulary and even bolder headgear. *Tiswas*

(1978-80) led on to a late-night adult version of the show, *OTT* – meaning Over The Top – in 1981. *Three of A Kind* saw him collaborating successfully with Tracey Ullman and David Copperfield and marked the beginning of a long time liaison with scriptwriter Kim Fuller. In 1984, Henry got his own BBC show, launching a host of new characters, including the outrageous soul singer Theophilus P Wildebeeste, the Reverend Nat West, the elderly Deakus and the street-wise youth Delbert Wilkins. A second series followed in 1986, with a Christmas special in 1987. *The Delbert Wilkins Show* followed, built entirely around the deeply-insecure Brixton hustler running a pirate radio station. Henry has said: "I like Delbert because he's political, because he has a point and because he talks about black people in Britain and the way we're perceived. As Delbert, I can be very political and get away with it."

Saturday Live also provided a political platform, but Henry's appeal spans the spectrum and his work is not easily categorised. His career was critically assessed in a *South Bank Show* programme in 1988, and Henry moved on to serious film-making, appearing in *Alive and Kicking* as smack dealer 'Smudger Smith', and in the

Key TV/Films

TV: Tiswas;
OTT;
Three of a Kind;
The Lenny Henry Show;
The Suicide Club;
Just Like That!;
Bernard and the Genie;
Alive and Kicking.

Film: True Identity

Touchstone Pictures movie, *True Identity*. Henry and Hollywood didn't care for one another, however, and the three-year contract was scrapped. "When I was out there, I felt like this tiny little link in a chain. I really didn't like not having any say..." Back in Britain, he runs his own company, Crucial Films.

Performance Extract

Delbert Wilkins: "I went to this club, right, and the bouncer on the door was typical, you know, big guy – 'hate' tattooed on one fist, and 'fist' tattooed on the other... I walked towards him, I knew no fear, you know 'at I mean – 'cos I'm from the Brixton posse,

right? My hair was slicked back - my hair was so slick there were guys surfin' on it... Yesterday, right, I was stopped by the police 15 times and I keep saying – Look, I was nowhere near the Belgrano, right... The police don't need any more bloody extra powers. That's

like putting a spear on the end of a cruise missile, you just don't need it, know 'at I mean?"

Benny Hill

"**M**y would-be lovers never succeed. A man who succeeds is not funny. A man who fails is funny... if my sketches teach anything it is that, for the male, sex is a snare and a delusion. What's so corrupting about that?" – Benny Hill.

"Benny was one of the great comedians of our age who could make people laugh in America and the Far East, as well as Britain." – Henry McGee, Hill's long-time associate.

Benny Hill's comedy is, in many regards, remarkably similar to that of the *Carry On* films. It differs in that the subject of sex is not merely one of several themes, but the overriding obsession. In practically every sketch, there are sexual undertones, overtones or outright suggestiveness. Yet, as Hill himself rightly points out, there is never consummation – the failure of the quest is the eternal theme. While some of his comic invention was genuinely funny, it relied on recycling the same idea in a thousand guises. With increasing permissiveness the ever-present bevy of busty young women came to be more and more scantily-clad, but as public perceptions moved on, Hill's didn't. In his later years this style came to alienate as many as it previously amused.

Devoting fully 30 years of his life almost exclusively to television work, Hill was indeed a star - and an international one. Based on visual and slapstick comedy, his shows were readily understood anywhere and they were sold to 80 countries around the globe. Late in his career he became a major star in the United States.

His Life and Work

Alfie Hill was born in Southampton on 21st January 1924, the son of a circus entertainer, and later, surgical appliance fitter. Hill's grandfather opened the boy's eyes to showbiz, often taking him to see touring revues. His first ever stage appearance was in a school production as the rabbit in *Alice in Wonderland*. Aged 14, Hill joined a semi-professional group, Bobby's Concert Party, and, leaving school at 15 worked as a Woolworth's stockroom clerk and later as a milkman. He learned to play the drums and worked on his comedy routines before selling the drum kit and moving to

(1924-1992)

London, Dick Whittington-like, with the proceeds, aged 17. Initial failure found him sleeping rough on Streatham Common, but he eventually found work in a theatre in East Ham – as props boy. Joining the Army, he served in the Royal Electrical and Mechanical Engineers (REME) despite apparently knowing next to nothing about vehicles, but used the opportunity to develop his act yet further, signing up with Stars in Battledress as a stand-up comic.

Post-war, Hill auditioned to be Reg Varney's straight man. There was one other candidate – Peter Sellers. Hill got the job for his calypso performance satirising the Attlee government, while Sellers' somewhat tamer offering was a George Formby number on the ukelele. Hill stayed with Varney until 1949 at which time he started to pepper the BBC with unsolicited scripts, eventually winning the occasional appearance on light entertainment shows and finally, his own programme in 1951. His work then included a take-off of the whole *Juke Box Jury* team, simultaneously, and a series of playlets in which he took over 50 separate parts and the embryonic visual jokes, parodies and impressions that were to become his staple fare. Hill always wrote the vast majority of his own material and all the music for his shows. The style was often Chaplin-esque, but already he was developing his trademark speeded-up formats.

Even then, the BBC found some of his material dubious, the more so since there existed strict guidelines as to what could and could not be said on TV. To dance round this problem, Hill began to utilise innuendo extensively, leading his audiences to expect a 'naughty' punchline only to deliver something perfectly respectable. The gormless Fred Scuttle character was a master of this.

He made several films in the '60s, but was lured back into television by Lew Grade's newly-formed Thames Television which screened the enormously successful *Benny Hill Show* that featured his own version of the Goldwyn Girls, known as Hill's Angels. Invariably dressed as stereotype male fantasies (skimpy uniforms, often nurses or policewomen, always in stockings and suspenders) they would chase Hill and others across parks or beaches in the triple-speed closing credits. The nudge-nudge style was effective, but only in small doses.

In 1971, Benny Hill reached number one in the charts with his lewdly suggestive song *Ernie*, who "drove the fastest milk cart in the West" inspired, it is said, by his earlier employment. Also in the 1970s Hill was elected to Television's Hall of Fame and in 1981 came the award of The Funniest Man on TV.

Key Films

Light Up The Sky (1960); Those Magnificent Men in Their Flying Machines (1965); Chitty Chitty Bang Bang (1968); The Italian Job (1969).

As Hill's brand of humour became increasingly scorned in the UK during the 1980s, he became a huge star across the Atlantic. The shows were re-edited, removing the colloquial and specifically British references, while highlighting the slapstick visual and sexual humour which evidently still appealed to the Americans. Several of his hour-long shows, made over a ten-year period, were re-cut to half hour slots and some stations screened these twice a night. In 1989, Thames cancelled his contract. The burgeoning 'alternative' comedy style was now in vogue and many felt Hill's treatment of women was offensively sexist, condescending and even dangerous. Benny Hill was an intensely private man, rarely giving interviews, and seldom appearing anywhere on stage or in public. There was much talk about his reclusive personality: he never married, lived alone, and appeared uninterested in material gain or even personal comfort. He died on April 18th 1992.

Performance Extracts

Hill: "It's my sex drive, Doctor, it's too high. I want you to lower it."

Dr: "At 92? You must be joking. It's all in the mind."

Hill: "That's why I want you to lower it...."

"I'd love to see her in 3D – that's my hotel room..."

Scantily-clad girl: "My boyfriend calls me dimples."

Hill: "I don't see any dimples."

Girl: "You're not my boyfriend."

Bob Hope

To many, he is the absolute epitome of what it is to be an American. Patriotism, Mom's home-made apple pie, the flag, Mr President, drive-in movies, the Star-Spangled Banner and Bob Hope equals the United States. Remarkable really, since he was born in Kent, the Garden of England.

Hope's stage performances rely on developing a dialogue with his audience. They are dry, laid-back and conversational, and he is prepared to wait for the laughs to come. Hope has said: "That's my whole technique. I know how to telegraph to an audience that this is a joke and that if they don't laugh right now, they're not playing the game and nobody has any fun." He has been generous in his praise of other comics even when it was not entirely reciprocated; for instance: "Seldom is the word 'genius' used to describe a comedian, especially by another comedian, but to me (Groucho) Marx was just that." Yet, echoing the criticisms of many, Marx said of him: "Bob Hope is not a comedian. He just translates what others write for him."

His Life and Work

Leslie Townes Hope born Eltham, Kent on May 29th, 1903, was one of seven boys in the family of a master stonemason and builder. The family emigrated to Cleveland, in the US, when the young Hope was four years old. Nicknamed 'Hopelessly' at school, his early hero was Charlie Chaplin. Hope actually carried off first prize in a Chaplin look-alike competition, winning a new

(1903-)

cooker for his family. A competent dancer, Hope entered amateur night competitions, often with considerable success, but on leaving school went to work as a clerk with a motor manufacturer. His first dance routine partner, Lefty Durbin, died in 1925, and Hope then teamed up with George Byrne, calling themselves The Dancing Demons. Hope and Byrne performed on the same bill as Fatty Arbuckle in Cleveland and went on to join a touring show, The Jolly Follies, in which Hope also performed a black-farce act, sang in a quartet and played the saxophone.

Graduating to Broadway in 1932, Hope came to realise that dancing, however good, was not enough on its own, and started an association with the highly regarded joke writer, Al Boasbery. Having married Dolores Reade, a nightclub singer, Hope moved into radio and film work. He joined Frank Parker's radio show, getting his name added to the title, eventually taking it over entirely when Parker quit in 1936. His first picture was *The Big Broadcast* in 1938, but more important in the longer term was *Thanks For The Memory*, the song written for him and Shirley Ross to sing. Hope adopted this as his theme tune, and in a particularly poignant moment he gave a special rendition on board the Queen Mary the night that Britain entered the war.

The 'Road Movies' really made Bob Hope. Constantly in jovial rivalry with Bing Crosby for the affections of the glamorous Dorothy Lamour, the threesome's adventures on the *Road To Singapore* and everywhere else were huge hits. The plots were fairly feeble and repetitive, but that was hardly the point. It was the sharp-witted interplay and Hope's recurring failure to get the girl that made them so famous.

Bob Hope also became a star on TV. His eponymous monthly shows on NBC ran for three years until 1955, and some subsequent special shows pulled audiences not far below that for the Superbowl.

His critics deride him for the absence of a positive style and lack of persona, but in so doing they miss the essential point of his act. It is because he just stands there and chatters away whimsically, that he is so accessible and popular. They also damn him for his renowned meanness, especially where this spills over into failing to credit his scriptwriters. Hope has countered this last by saying, "I think I was among the first to admit openly that I employed writers." He is famed for his passion for golf and, in the glitzy American way of things, has been befriended by successive Presidents. There is a Museum of Hope in Burbank, California.

Performance Extracts

"I'm a little tired tonight. I'm building a new house... You'll like the inside of the house, it's got a really beautiful bathroom. When you want cold water, all you have to do is dig. When you want hot water, you just go deeper... And I've got a new idea in the bedroom – the walls just pull out from a bed. I have a Murphy bed and a Morris chair in my room. The room is so small the other morning Murphy woke up with an accent."

"The proposed US wheat deal to Russia nearly fell through. Khrushchev agreed to $375 million but tried to back out when he discovered we didn't give Green Stamps... two more books and he can get Stalin into Forest Lawn." (1963)

On his 82nd birthday, Hope said: "I think it's wonderful you could all be here for the 43rd anniversary of my 39th birthday. We decided not to light the candles this year... we were afraid Pan Am would mistake it for a runway..."

Frankie Howerd

Many comedians plead with their audiences. Only Frankie Howerd pleaded them, no, begged them – "No, no, don't laugh..." Invariably, they'd laugh all the louder.

Howerd turned his dire personal insecurities and chronic hypochondria to his own ends in his magnificent routines, assuming a look of wounded indignation whenever his lascivious double-entendres were taken at anything other than their face value. He acted with his whole body, that moon face, bushy eyebrows and

pursed lips contorting inside the baggy, rumpled suit to give purely innocent material a scandalous second meaning. He well understood Ronnie Barker's dictum about the relationship between

innuendo and age – "If you understand it, you're old enough." Howerd's best exposition of this was his rendition of *My Way*, sung absolutely word for word with the Sinatra version, but positively filthy in its implications.

Neither his life nor his career was straightforward. Indeed they seemed locked together in a roller-coaster ride of triumphs and disasters. On stage, he appeared entirely spontaneous, yet, as a documentary profile on TV made plain, he depended totally on an exact script. The most telling shot was of him walking on a beach, repeating the same few lines over and over, to get the pauses and inflections just right. He said himself: "People are fooled into thinking I'm funny offstage. I'm not. I wish I was. I wish I was a Harry Secombe, but I rely on writers to be funny."

His Life and Work

Francis Alex Howard was born in York, on March 6th 1922, but moved soon after to Eltham, in Kent. (He later changed his surname to Howerd to be sure it would at least be noticed as a misprint.) His father, who was in the Army, died when Francis was just three, leaving his mother to bring up the three children.

His first stage role was in a local church production of *Tilly of Bloomsbury*, in which, at the age of 13, he played Tilly's father. Encouraged, he later went to audition at RADA but he was so badly affected by nerves that he stammered and stuttered his way to a swift rejection. Howerd served as a Sergeant in the Royal Artillery

Funny Business   109

(1922-1992)

in the war but met failure again when turned down by the Forces' own company, Stars in Battledress, though he did entertain unofficially.

After the war, he toured the provincial venues accompanied by a silent stooge in the shape of pianist Madame Blanchie Moore, "known to me as Flossie, known to Southend as Dockyard Dora... no, don't laugh, poor old soul, it's not funny... it might be one of our own." The first big break came when he became resident comic on the BBC's *Variety Bandbox* series, the forerunner of *Saturday Night At The London Palladium*. Here he developed some of the hallmark catchphrases he was to use down the decades – "I was am-aaaazed"; "Ladies and gentle—men" and "Not on your nelly." Here too, he perfected the knack of working an audience, talking to them directly or throwing caustic asides, using that mournful visage to convey more than mere words ever could.

Work became hard to come by however, in the middle and late '50s, and despite some acting roles (*Charley's Aunt* and *A Midsummer Night's Dream*) his career was on the slide. In 1961, for example, he was unemployed for nine months. In his personal life there was also crisis: his beloved mother, a constant source of inspiration, died, and Howerd himself suffered a nervous breakdown. So low was his morale at this stage that he seriously contemplated quitting showbiz altogether and running a pub instead, but, supported by friends like Eric Sykes, Barry Took, Marty Feldman and Johnny Speight (who was writing for Howerd for nothing), he decided to soldier on.

Redemption was at hand, with a booking on *That Was The Week That Was* satirising chancellor Reginald Maudling's 1963 Budget. This he followed with the big success of *A Funny Thing Happened To Me On The Way To The Forum* – a musical adaptation of the plays of Plautus. Howerd played the slave Pseudolus and the show ran for 762 performances from October 1963, restoring Howerd to the status of star. Film work swiftly came in: *The Great St Trinian's Train Robbery* and a number of *Carry On* films – *Carry*

Key Films

The Runaway Bus (1954); Further Up The Creek (1959); several Carry On films.

On Doctor, Up the Jungle, Up The Chastity Belt, Up The Front.

Another bite at the Ancient Roman cherry was the outrageously funny *Up Pompeii*, with Howerd as the narrator-cum-slave Lurcio. "I'm absolutely indispensable. That's why they've made me Major Domo. I said Domo. Let us have no misunderstandings at the commencement." Lasting and consistent success yet again eluded him however, and there was a second trough in his career until the mid-80s when the emergent 'alternative' comedy set him up as their darling. In the early '90s he re-emerged with a further series of stand-up routines in front of audiences as widely varied as university students and coal miners. He died in the middle of recording the series, on 19th April, 1992.

Performance Extracts

"It was my turn in the surgery but the nurse said, do you mind if this lady goes in before you, she's in terrible trouble, her legs are stuck together. And there she was, poor dear, hobbling along, joined above the knee. So what could I do? I let her go in. She wasn't in there a minute, and came out right as rain. I was amazed. So when I went in, I said how did you cure that woman so quickly, the one with her legs stuck together? He

said, legs stuck together? She just had two legs down one knicker... So when I went out there she was waiting for her bus. All right now? I said. She said yes – I must be off home to my children. I said how many have you got? Sixteen, she said. I said 16, that's an awful lot, you don't want to have any more than that. She said don't worry, I won't, not now I've got my hearing aid. I said what's your hearing aid got to do with it? She said well,

I've always been deaf and at night in bed my husband would say, are you going to sleep or what? And I'd say – what? And that's how I came to have 16 children..."

"Today I'm going to tell you what happened to me in the Sahara desert. In the Sahara-ha-ra desert. And oooh, no... it was hot. Oooh, it was real hot. Even the Sphinx had sunglasses on..."

Barry Humphries

Barry Humphries could reasonably be described as a 'professional Australian'. Speaking about Dame Edna Everage, his finest creation, Humphries say: "I must say I try to incorporate in her... all the paradoxes of my old homeland. The sentimentality, the harsh extremes, the galloping cultural paranoia, the leaping at the second-hand and taking it to excess, the transcendental vulgarity..."

Humphries is a man of many talents: comedian, writer, impresario, artist and art collector, and also deeply reluctant to appear anywhere in public out of character. Since he borders on the reclusive himself, it is difficult to assess just how much of him comes through in his stage personas, which are themselves equally many and varied. Dame Edna Everage, Housewife Superstar, and Sir Les Patterson, cultural attaché to the Court of St James are the two best known, but others in his extensive repertoire have included over the years Buster Thomson, an ex-public schoolboy, Neil Singleton, the lefty intellectual, Morrie O'Connor, a used picture salesman, Lance Boyle, trade unionist, and Sandy stone, the profoundly boring suburban man.

Catchphrases

Dame Edna: "Spooky, darlings"
"Hello possums"
"Call me old fashioned,
darlings, but..."

McKenzie: "... my one-eyed
trouser snake."

Referring to his entire stable of creations, Humphries has said they are "accurately based on real people who never lived". They are caricatures, rather than characters.

His Life and Work

Barry Humphries was born in the Kew district of Melbourne, Australia in 1934. His father was an affluent construction manager, but as a child Humphries spurned the outdoor, sporting life so beloved of many Aussies in favour of reading. A highly intelligent boy, he attended Grammar School and in 1952 went up to Melbourne University to read law, Philosophy and Fine Art. Here he began to appear in revues, impersonating Hitler and creating the persona of a mad scientist, Dr

Humphries. He also enjoyed the surrealistic and shocking school of Dada art, once staging an exhibition featuring a work called Pus in Boots (sic) – a pair of wellingtons filled with custard.... Saying that he was "entertained by the idea of slightly fictionalising myself" he staged various practical jokes: an accomplice, John Perry, would feign blindness and climb into a non-smoking compartment of a train. Enter Humphries, who begins to smoke. The 'blind man' objects, whereupon Les Patterson, to the horror of the other passengers, beats him up... Even so, he says he was never challenged. The idea was to "turn life into a minispectacle with me as the audience" able to observe the reactions of those not in the know.

Abandoning his studies in the mid-50s, Humphries moved into rep theatre, introducing the char-

(1934-)

acter of Mrs Norm Everage, a housewife offering to billet a foreign athlete for the Melbourne Olympics of 1956. After three years of one-man shows, he moved to London and sought work as a serious actor, winning the part as understudy to Ron Moody's Fagin, in the musical *Oliver*. Peter Cook invited him to perform at the Establishment Club, but Everage was less well received than the drunken, foul-mouthed, sex-starved ex-pat Barry McKenzie, later famed for the airline sick-bag and Russian salad joke... Work it out for yourselves.

His first TV show in Britain came in 1968 – *The Barry Humphries Scandals*. Experimental pieces in the main, they featured Edna Everage visiting London tourist-sites and describing them idiosyncratically to camera. Sir Les Patterson, the vomit-stained and abusive unofficial "cultural attache to the Court of St James" was introduced in Sydney, in 1974, but the real breakthrough

Key Films

Bedazzled (1965);
The Adventures of Barry McKenzie (1972);
Barry McKenzie Holds His Own (1974);
Shock Treatment (1981);
Les Patterson Saves The World (1987).

came in the UK four years later when *An Audience with Dame Edna Everage* (now promoted to the titled classes) saw Humphries roundly abusing a theatre full of invited guests – or rather victims. *Another Audience with Dame Edna*, in 1984, featured one of television's most glorious moments. Addressing Judy Steel, wife of the Liberal Party leader David Steel, Dame Edna began politely enough: "What a charming frock that is, Judy". Only to follow up: "Do tell us its history. Was it a pair of curtains?"

The Dame Edna Experience commenced in 1987, as the chat show to end all chat shows. Celebrity guests, including some remarkably major stars (Sean Connery, Larry Hagman and many more) wearing name-tags in case she forgot who they were, would be ridiculed and humiliated. Some never made it past the video-link at the bottom of the liftshaft to Edna's penthouse.

NBC brought Edna's show to American viewers in 1991 to great acclaim. In her 1992 series, *Neighbourhood Watch*, she startled guests on the show by letting herself into their homes and having an outrageous snoop.

Edna's career was triumphal. From mere Mrs Norm Everage (Norm, her husband, was very big in dried fruit) she progressed through disapproving observer of the swinging '60s to the 'Put Australia First' matronly figure, to world traveller, friend of the stars, Housewife Superstar and finally – Megastar.

Performance Extracts

Sir Les Patterson: "Anyway, Les Patterson's the name and a bit of background on old Les won't go too far astray. At the moment I am holding down an enormous encumbency, ladies and gentlemen. I think I can say without fear of contradiction it is one of the biggest encumbencies I have ever held down in my political career. I am an Australian cultural attache to the Court of St James... I'm sort of Australian Henry Kissinger and I'm here on another whistle-stop tour at the moment. Just back from New Zealand as a matter of fact, fronting up a Royal

Commission there into these sightings, these saucers, these UFOs, Unidentified Fuckin' Objects... why, I'm sorry, please forgive me ladies, that just slipped out..."

Dame Edna: "Chances are the honeymoon night still holds its horrors for most young couples and this is largely because we cannot be always be sure what our partner is going to do after he's shaken the confetti out of his shoes and checked the room service menu a couple of times. I well remember a queer phrase of

my wonderful mother's that came back to me on my honeymoon night: "some men don't like it plain and simple," she croaked... I followed my mother's eyes to the top of the wardrobe where my father always kept a mysterious little black suitcase that we were never allowed to look in... I never did see the contents of Daddy's box... I've been forced to admit that the odd thing goes on behind locked bedroom doors that would make my old Daddy's portmanteau look as innocent as a Masonic apron. Spookily enough, my father was a Mason incidentally..."

Danny Kaye

"Those who may have supposed that Kaye was something of a one-man vaudeville act will be surprised to discover that he is a very accomplished actor."
– Critic, Howard Barnes.

As much an all-round entertainer as a comic, Danny Kaye's vast range gave him an entrée into showbusiness, in all its forms, in the '40s and '50s. An accomplished singer, dancer and actor, as well as a comedian, his was a mercurial talent. Not surprisingly, he became one of the then highest paid comics in the world.

His Life and Work

Almost from birth, in Brooklyn on January 18th, 1913, David Daniel Kaminski wanted to entertain. The youngest child of two Russian emigres, Jacob and Clara, he would perform for anyone who was sitting still long enough to watch.

At the New York City Public School 149, he appeared in a minstrel show, but on moving to The Thomas Jefferson High School, his enthusiasm temporarily switched to athletics.

After three-and-a-half years of high school, Kaye ran away to Hollywood. He found work first as a soda fountain boy, then as a clerk in an insurance company. But the lure of showbusiness proved too strong to be denied and he soon turned his talents to entertaining at private parties. As one half of Red and Blackie, a double-act, he performed a song and dance routine, complete with comic patter. The act was broadcast on station WBBC Brooklyn, which led to employment as entertainers in the Borscht Circuit hotels and camps in the Catskill Mountains for four successive summers. During the winters, Kaye tried to interest a Broadway producer in his act.

In 1933, he was booked by the dancing act Dave Harvey and Kathleen Young. One night, in mid-routine, he lost his balance much to the audience's great amusement. Building on this, he subsequently got billing in his own right, as Danny Kaye – short for Kaminski. When the team moved to Detroit, A.B. Marcus, producer of an annual revue, wanted to book just Harvey and Young, but they refused unless Kaye was booked as well.

The revue, La Vie Parée, toured the United States for five months, then moved on to the Orient. Kaye was by now singing, dancing, performing monologues, doing rapid costume changes and learning to work without props. Faced with non-English speaking audiences in the Far East, he developed both his face-making technique and the peculiar ability to sing in gibberish, occasionally emphasising a word to make a point.

Back in the States, he became part of the Borscht Circuit, where he met pianist-composer Sylvia Fine. Some of her songs were included in *The Straw Hat Revue*, with Imogene Coca, in which Kaye scored a small hit on Broadway in 1939. Kaye and Fine married in 1940. Fine was responsible for much of Kaye's success, later acting as his writer (in collaboration with Max Liebman), personal director, coach, critic and occasionally, accompanist.

In 1940, Kaye appeared at the New York nightclub, La Martinique. Moss Hart saw his performance and wrote a part for him in *Lady In The Dark* with Gertrude Lawrence. By the end of 1940, Kaye was the star of the show; his ability to reel off the names of 57 Russian composers in 38 seconds was legendary.

The following year, Kaye took the lead in *Let's Face It*, a musical comedy in which he sang a number of songs written especially for him by Cole Porter.

Rejected by the army because of a back problem, Kaye spent World War Two entertaining the troops.

Kaye accepted Sam Goldwyn's offer of a film career and made his first film, *Up In Arms*, in 1944. In the post-war years, Kaye was a big success, and the best examples of his work are considered to be *Wonder Man* (1945), *The Secret Life of Walter Mitty* (1947), *The Inspector General* (1949) and *Hans Christian Anderson* (1952). Generally taking on a number of roles or characters with several personalities, these films gave Kaye the chance to showcase his clowning, dancing and nonsense patter.

Kaye was not only a star in his native America. In 1948, he showed he could do it on this side of the water, at the London Palladium, and in 1950, he sold out the 24,000-seater Canadian National Exhibition Grandstand for 14 successive performances.

Kaye and his wife formed their own production company, Dena Productions in 1953. *The Court*

Key Films

Up In Arms (1944);
The Secret Life of Walter Mitty (1947);
The Inspector General (1949);
Hans Christian Andersen (1952);
White Christmas (1954);
The Court Jester (1956);
The Five Pennies (1959).

Jester is generally believed to be the best of the films they made.

Kaye proved he could also make the transition to television with his one-man TV show, *The Danny Kaye Show*, which ran for four seasons from 1963-67.

There was more to Kaye than his public persona however. During the '50s, he devoted much of his time to UNICEF and was appointed an Ambassador-at-large. He travelled around the world, campaigning and giving fund-raising performances. One of his trips was recorded in the documentary film, *Assignment Children*.

In 1967, Kaye was due to appear at the Chichester Festival in his first classic play, *The Servant of Two Masters*, but at short notice, he broke his contract to embark on a trip to Israel during the Six-Day War and he suddenly became an outspoken champion of Israel.

He returned to Broadway in 1970, playing Noah in the musical *Two By Two*. His later TV appearances included *Peter Pan* in 1975, *Skokie* in 1981, in which he played a holocaust survivor, and a cameo role in 1986 in *The Cosby Show*. Towards the end of his life, working for UNICEF became his prime concern. He died March 3rd 1987.

Performance Extract ➡

From *The Court Jester*:

KAYE PLAYS A HAPLESS FOREST OUTLAW, HAWKINS. HE IS FORCED INTO A JOUSTING COMBAT WITH THE MIGHTY GRISWOLD. HE THINKS HE WILL CERTAINLY DIE, BUT...

Griselda: Griswold dies as he drinks the toast.
Hawkins: What?
Griselda: Listen, I've put a pellet of poison in one of the vessels.
Hawkins: Which one?
Griselda: The one with a figure of a pestle.
Hawkins: The vessel with the pestle.
Griselda: Yes, but you don't want the vessel with the pestle, you want the chalice from the palace.
Hawkins: I... I don't want the vessel with the pestle, I want the chalice from the... what?
May Jean: The chalice from the palace.
Hawkins: Mmm?
Griselda: It's a little crystal chalice with the figure of a palace.
Hawkins: Does the chalice from the palace have the pellet with the poison?
Griselda: No. The pellet with the poison's in the vessel with the pestle.
Hawkins: Oh, the pestle with the vessel.

May Jean: *The vessel with the pestle.*
Hawkins: What about the palace from the chalice?
Griselda: Not the palace from the chalice, the *chalice from the palace.*
Hawkins: Where's the pellet with the poison?
Griselda: In the vessel with the pestle.
May Jean: Don't you see? The pellet with the poison's in the vessel with the pestle.
Griselda: The chalice from the palace has the brew that is true.
May Jean: So easy, I can say it.
Hawkins: Well, then you fight him.

Buster Keaton

"The best way to get a laugh is to create a genuine thrill and then relieve the tension with comedy. Getting laughs depends on the element of surprise, and surprises are harder and harder to get as audiences, seeing more pictures, become more and more comedy wise. But when you take a genuine thrill, build up to it and then turn it into a ridiculous situation, you always get that surprise element." – Buster Keaton.

Buster Keaton was one of the greatest comics of the silent movie era, who, like Chaplin, found the advent of the talkies brought down the curtain on his finest work. His hallmark was the blank expressionless face, utterly devoid

of emotion no matter what the danger, or hilarity, of the situation. Yet if his face was becalmed, his body was hyperactive. With staggering courage, he performed all his own stunts, save one where he hired a pole vaulter to plummet in through a second floor window. True, Keaton was a brilliant and fearless acrobat, but the slightest error could well have cost him his life. One memorable dive was a full 85 feet from a suspension bridge into a safety net in *The Paleface*. His biographer J.P. Lebel wrote: "He gives proof, in the leap ,of a dazzling elasticity."

Keaton's career embraced Hollywood's best and worst – the fame and fortune, the great houses, yachts and flamboyant parties, and also financial and personal ruin. Yet in his twilight years, the film of his life story renewed his fame, and as belated recognition for his personal bravery, professional dedication and technical expertise on both sides of the camera, Hollywood gave him a Special Academy Award for "his unique talents which brought immortal comedies to the screen."

His Life and Work

Born Joseph Frank Keaton on 4th October 1895 in Kansas, he was of Scotch-Irish descent, the son of Joe H Keaton, a famous acrobat-comedian. His parents toured the mid-West selling patent medicines and performing music, monologues and playlets in a travelling show, as The Two Keatons. As a baby, Keaton fell down a staircase and came up smiling. Harry Houdini, the great escapologist, then touring with them, was so

impressed at the infant's literal bounce that he nicknamed him Buster, the old vaudeville term for a comic fall. At the tender of three Buster joined his parents on stage, the act becoming The Three Keatons, in a costume mimicking his father's appearance – bald wig and wispy beard. The toddler, already well-versed in the relevant skills and evidently with acrobatics in his genes, was regularly flung around the stage, but was never hurt. However, in the early years of the century Keaton's father was drinking to excess too often, and Buster and his mother, fearing their act was becoming too dangerous, fled. She settled in Detroit, and Buster went on to New York. There he met Fatty Arbuckle who was to be a friend for life. Invited to watch the filming at Arbuckle's studio, Keaton was entranced, and gave up $250 a week in vaudeville for an uncertain $40 a week in films.

From the very start of his film career Keaton remained stone-faced, noticing how the audience laughed when he didn't. He mastered the arts of slapstick and after the First World War, in which Keaton was sent to France but saw no action, he took over Arbuckle's studio. He married Natalie Talmadge in 1923 and was at the peak of his creativity. Together with Chaplin, he dominated movies in the 1920s – *Our Hospitality*, *Sherlock Junior*, *The Navigator* and *The General* are considered his masterpieces. Keaton fully exploited his remarkable skills as an acrobat, but cleverly also stretched the boundaries of slapstick. Keaton's filmic control extended to cover direction and production, but then

Key Films

The Playhouse (1921);
Cops (1922);
Our Hospitality (1923);
Sherlock Junior (1924);
The Navigator (1924);
Go West (1925);
The General (1926);
The Cameraman (1928).

made a decision he later called "the worst mistake of my career" – he gave up his own studio to change the way he made his films. *The Cameraman* was a success, but Keaton later claimed he had to fight for every joke.

With the coming of the talkies, Keaton's star dimmed. He was drinking heavily, as had his father before him, and was discovered, by his wife, drunk in bed with another woman in 1932. Natalie divorced him, and sued him for virtually all he had. The very next year MGM fired him. It wasn't that he was a drunk, divorced and broke – Hollywood can cope with all of that and then some – he just wasn't funny any more. He underwent treatment for his alcoholism in 1935, and married his nurse at the clinic. This relationship foundered rapidly, and Keaton married a third time in 1949, with greater success; they were still together when Buster died.

Charlie Chaplin invited him to appear in *Limelight* in 1952, and the 1957 bio-pic, *The Buster Keaton Story*, starring Donald O'Connor, both won over a new generation to Keaton's talents and allowed him to live out the final years before his death in February 1966 in relative prosperity.

Laurel and Hardy

"They are a constant joy." – John Cleese.

"They form the perfect symmetry of comicality." – Ken Dodd.

"We seemed to sense each other. I loved editing and cutting the pictures, something Ollie wasn't interested in – he preferred to spend his afternoons playing golf. But whatever I did was tops with him. There was never any argument between us, ever," Stan Laurel.

The Laurel and Hardy partnership is arguably the finest double act ever seen on film. Remarkably prolific, they appeared together in 77 shorts and 28 feature-length films and had independent careers prior to teaming up when both were in their thirties. Laurel's tearful whimpering and Hardy's flustered tie-fiddling are as instantly recognisable as Chaplin's busy walk, and became the hallmarks of their silent work. Their film careers together stretched from 1927 to 1952, comfortably crossing the great watershed in films – the advent of talkies – by the simple expedient of largely ignoring it, adding dialogue only where the visual comedy positively required it.

Their humour generally hinged on the comic consequences of loss of dignity. As great friends, they had a tremendous respect for one another, reputedly never arguing. Laurel was the driving creative force, enjoying the technical aspects of film-making as much as the performing.

Their Life and Work

Stan Laurel was born Arthur Stanley Jefferson in Ulverston, Lancashire in 1890. His father was a well-known local theatrical entrepreneur who introduced his

Catchphrases

"Another nice mess you've gotten me into..."
(Now usually quoted as "Another fine mess...")

"Why don't you do something to help me?"

son to the stage at the age of 16. Touring with various groups for seven years, Laurel (who chose the stage name simply because he liked it) played both straight and comic roles, and while in Fred Karno's troupe, was understudy to Charlie Chaplin himself in *The Mumming Birds*. In 1917 he made his first film, *Nuts In May*, which won him a contract with Universal, and later, work with producer Hal Roach.

Oliver Norvell Hardy was born in Harlem, Georgia in 1892. After military college and law studies at the University of Georgia, he ran a movie-theatre for three years then joined a film company in Florida. In 1926 Hardy joined Hal Roach's company and first met Stan Laurel. There has always been slight confusion over which was their first official film together. Roach changed distributors in 1927, which meant films were being released by two different companies at the same time. In whatever order then, their first three were *Putting Pants on Philip*, *The Battle of the Century* and *The Second Hundred Years*. *The Battle of the Century* has become a movie

Key Films

Far too many to list.

classic, featuring the greatest pie throwing sequence ever seen, involving 5,000 pies.

Their comedy style focused on the cataclysmic destruction of property – usually Hardy's – touching naïvety, and nagging wives, all enhanced by Hardy's sly glances to camera. A typical and classic film is *Leave 'em Laughing*, (1928) in which Stan goes to the dentist, but Ollie ends up in the chair, and both get a hefty dose of nitrous oxide (better known as every comedian's favourite substance, laughing gas) and cause a monster traffic jam. Another gem is *The Finishing Touch*, a hysterical lesson in D-DIY – Don't Do It Yourself.

By the end of 1929, most studios had moved on from silent movies, and *Berth Marks* was their first all-talking short, although they hadn't truly mastered the new medium – it was simultaneously released as a silent film. *The*

Music Box (1932), in which they delivered a piano, won them an Oscar. *Pardon Us* in 193! was their first full-length film and *Sons Of The Desert* (1934) was a pastiche of their best shorts material, and *Blockheads* (1938) is another fine picture in which Stan goes on guarding a trench for 20 years after World War I has finished.

After *Saps at Sea*, they split with Roach and signed to MGM, but didn't enjoy the experience. It was Hollywood at its most authoritarian. They were forced to perform with scripts by writers they did not know and without Laurel's immaculate and sensitive editorial control, the finished products were tame and tired. In the 1940s and 50s they toured abroad and made live appearances. Oliver Hardy died in 1957, and three years later Laurel was awarded a Special Oscar 'for his creative pioneering in the field of cinema comedy.' Refusing all offers of TV, Stan Laurel died in 1964. Today, the Sons Of The Desert organisation keeps their blessed memory alive.

Performance Extracts

From *The Fixer Uppers*, 1935:

STAN AND OLLIE ARE IN A BAR, EXPECTING A CALL, WHEN THE PHONE RINGS.

Ollie: See who that is. It might be him.
Stan: (ON PHONE) Hello... It sure is. (HANGS UP)
Ollie: Who was it?
Stan: Oh, some fella having a joke.

Ollie: Well, what did he say?
Stan: I said, 'Hello,' and the fella said, 'It's a long distance from Atlanta, Georgia,' and I said, 'It sure is.' Silliest thing I ever heard.

From *A Chump At Oxford*, 1940:

STAN AND OLLIE ARRIVE AT COLLEGE DRESSED IN UNIFORM AND

ARE APPROACHED BY A STUDENT IN A DIFFERENT UNIFORM.

Student: Pardon me, but haven't you come to the wrong college?
Ollie: Well, this is Oxford, isn't it?
Student: Yes, but you're dressed for Eton.
Stan: That's swell, we haven't eaten since breakfast!

Jay Leno

"I like to write jokes, tell them, and go home." – Jay Leno.

"It is great fun, but in many ways it's not unlike working in an office. The joy is in not doing the same jokes over and over, like not doing the same typing each day." – Jay Leno.

Jay Leno entered the mega-bucks league when he took over full-time from Johnny Carson on the *Tonight* show in 1992, having been the regular holiday relief for five years. Yet before that, he had established himself as a fine stand-up comic with an expressive and unforgettable face and legendary stamina. He would tour the United States, by road, clocking up thousands of miles and over 300 gigs a year. Scorning dirty jokes and shock tactics, his material derives above all from news topicality, but also politics in general, showbusiness and popular culture.

His Life and Work

James Douglas Muir Leno was born in New Rochelle, New York, in 1950 and grew up in Andover, Massachusetts. His background is seriously non-showbiz – father was an insurance salesman, his mother a housewife. Reputedly, one of his earliest jokes was an off-the-cuff response at school when a teacher said: "People were very cruel in the days of Robin Hood. They used to boil people in oil." To which Leno retorted: "But they couldn't boil Tuck. He was a Friar."

After a degree in speech therapy at Emerson College, Boston, Leno set out to be a stand-up comic.

(1950-)

Working by day as a mechanic at the Rolls-Royce plant in Boston, he would drive five nights a week to New York just on the off-chance of getting a spot at the Improv club. He had previously been one half of a double act with Gene Braunstein, but they broke up when both auditioned for a local Boston improvisation group, Fresh Fruit Cocktail, and only Leno was accepted.

Before his monumental odyssey on the road, Leno played in what he has called Boston's 'combat zone' – nursing homes, college halls of residence, brothels; anywhere in fact that he could get an audience and get paid for working. As the club scene boomed, like *Tommy* in Roger Daltrey's rock opera, he must have played 'em all. Like all comics, he studied the opposition and critically analysed their techniques. Leno became friends with David Letterman and was also earning extra money writing gags for Jimmie Walker.

Leno's career was on an upswing through the 1970s, as he began to open for a range of entertainers including Perry Como, Johnny Mathis, John Denver, Henry Mancini, James Brown and Tom Jones, and a 1977 appearance on *Tonight* with Johnny Carson gave him yet wider exposure. Film work began to come in from 1977 onwards: *Fun With Dick And Jane*, and *Silver Bears* was followed by *American Hot Wax* and *Americathon*, with Larry Miller in 1979, as did guest slots on TV like *Saturday Night Live*, *The Merv Griffin Show* and *The Mike Douglas Show*.

When David Letterman got his own show in the 1980s, Leno became a regular guest, appearing over 30 times. This was the turning point. "Dave's show did everything. It is geared well to what I do, in the sense that a lot of jokes I do there wouldn't work on other shows, because the host wouldn't have the rapport I have with David and wouldn't know what I'm talking about." In 1986, Leno played to a sold-out Carnegie Hall and made two TV specials, but standing in for Carson each Monday night and for eight full weeks a year brought instant national acclaim.

Leno's style when doing his live shows is unusual, in that he prefers to have the house lights on to enable him to see the faces of his audience. Believing that comedy has to be relevant to be effective, at the beginning of a show he will generally fix his stare on one member of the audience and stay with him until he begins to laugh,

Key Films

Silver Bears (1977);
Collision Course (1987).

acting as catalyst for all the rest. Leno writes all his own material for his live shows, and when standing in on *Tonight* he used his own team of writers, including a rabbi from New Jersey, rather than Carson's regular scriptwriters. Strongly news-oriented, if the audience doesn't recognise the story he is referring to, he will smack his wrist in mock reproach. In his private life, Leno lives in Beverly Hills with his wife and has a private collection of cars and motorcycles.

Performance Extracts

"I see in *People* magazine that Nancy Reagan was just in Beverly Hills accepting a humanitarian-of-the-year award. Yeah, I'm glad she beat out that conniving bitch Mother Teresa. Yeah, I guess Mrs Reagan won that award for her anti-drug programme. I don't use drugs, I never use drugs. But every time I see Nancy Reagan, I want to shoot up and die in the street."

On college dorms: "You could have girls in your room and liquor in your room and drugs in your room. There was only one thing you couldn't have in your room – and that was a hotplate."

"It's tough enough finding out you're adopted. Now you find out you're defrosted. A Tennessee couple are divorcing and they're arguing over who gets the frozen embryos. And you thought dividing up the record albums would be tough...."

Harold Lloyd

Regarding his glasses: "With them I am Harold Lloyd; without them, a private citizen. At a cost of 75 cents, they provided a trademark recognised instantly wherever pictures are shown." – Harold Lloyd.

All comedians have a defining characteristic, whether it is costume like Dame Edna, delivery like Ben Elton, a 'look' – George Burns, or a prop – Ken Dodd. A pair of horn-rimmed spectacles gave Harold Lloyd his definition: innocent and vulnerable, swept up

by forces beyond his control. Almost anonymous without them, he believed the glasses would "suggest the character – quiet, normal, boyish, clean, sympathetic, not impossible to romance... The comedy should be better for not depending upon a putty nose or its equivalent."

Lloyd, along with Chaplin, Keaton and Langdon, dominated the silent movie era. Like Keaton, he performed most of his own stunts and was a master of physical, slapstick comedy. Stage-struck "as far back as memory serves and to the exclusion of all else", Lloyd was brave in another way, too. Incredibly, given the excellence of much of his work, he said: "We never knew from day to day, or hour to hour, what we would do to bring the laughs. Most of our humour was spontaneous and without written scripts."

He was also among the first to use trick photography in his work.

His Life and Work

Harold Clayton Lloyd was born April 20th 1894, in Nebraska, the younger of two boys. The family had a peripatetic existence during his childhood, moving to seven different towns in his home state and in Colorado. Ambition already burning in him as a youngster, he got work in theatres and opera houses as usher, sweet seller, call boy, electrician and grip. Aged 12, he made his stage debut as Little Abe in *Tess of the D'Urbevilles* and went on, in 1912, to join John Lane Connor's Grand Theatre Stock Company, using his make-up skills to play a range of parts from old men to Indians.

That same year he made his film debut – as a bit-part extra.

He conned his way into Universal Studios by putting on make-up, having previously noticed that the gatekeeper didn't stop anyone in greasepaint, and managed to secure more work as an extra and obtain the occasional small role. Hal Roach, then an extra himself, inherited some money and invited Lloyd to join him in setting up a company, in 1914. Lloyd was then trying out two characters – Lonesome Luke, who wore his clothes far too tight, and Willie Work, a lazy loafer. Pathe Pictures offered Roach a contract for films, with Lloyd as the lead. Basically improvising through the film, Lloyd said later that whatever the plot, it always ended with a chase.

It was in 1917 that Lloyd developed the hallmark 'glasses character' and for the next five years made a film every single week, often directing as well as playing the lead. In 1919, he suffered serious injury to his hands when a trick bomb exploded, and it was feared he may not work again. The year 1922 saw his first feature length comedy – *Grandma's Boy* – which came about by chance. He discovered he hadn't used up all the film stock, so he carried on until he had. Audiences, and Pathe, loved it and commissioned him for a further six films of five reels or more.

He began to use trick photography to good effect, appearing to dangle over precipices, to walk narrow girders, and to balance on the hands of a huge clock on the side of a building.

Lloyd's partnership with Hal Roach ended with *Why Worry*, in

Key Films

Grandma's Boy (1922);
Doctor Jack (1923);
Why Worry (1923);
The Freshman (1925);
Movie Crazy (1932);
The Sin Of Harold Diddlebock (1948, renamed Mad Wednesday);
Lloyd's World of Comedy (1962).

which he played a rich hypochondriac. While making this picture he married his leading lady, Mildred Davies. Setting up his own studio, the Harold Lloyd Corporation, he produced an eight-reel comedy, *Girl Shy*, in 1924, and in the same year, *Hot Water*. In 1925 came probably his finest opus – *The Freshman*. More followed, including, in 1929, his first talking movie, *Welcome Danger*. He made films for Paramount, Pathe and Fox in the '30s, but after the failure of *Professor Beware* in 1938, he effectively retired from the screen, but continued to work in production and search for good scripts. He is said to have appeared in over 500 movies, among the last being his sequel to *The Freshman*, *The Sin of Harold Diddlebock*. A new generation got the chance to see his rare talents in the 1940s and '50s when some early material was re-released, and he went on to produce a compilation of the best clips from his own pictures, in 1962. Having been one of the highest paid stars of the silent and early talkies eras, Harold Lloyd died on March 8th, 1971.

Dean Martin & Jerry Lewis

"Dean was my catcher – the greatest straight-man in the history of showbusiness. His sense of timing was flawless, so infinite and so fragile it almost looked as if he didn't do anything at all. The truth is, I would never have done so well with anyone else." – Jerry Lewis.

For ten years, Dean Martin and Jerry Lewis were a hugely successful double act. They made 17 films together and in the 1950s, they were the industry's greatest money-spinners. Dean Martin was the suave one, who sang songs and rode off with the girl; Jerry Lewis was the buffoon, the best man who forgot the ring and stepped on the bride's dress. But the partnership foundered when Martin grew bored of playing the straight man to Lewis's endless jokes and after an acrimonious split in 1956, the two barely spoke. Both went on, however, to forge successful solo careers.

"Two of the greatest turning points in my career: first, meetin' Jerry Lewis; second, leavin' Jerry Lewis." – Dean Martin.

Their Life and Work

Dean Martin was born Dino Crocetti in Ohio, in 1917. After leaving school in the 11th grade, he took on a variety of jobs. He delivered bootleg alcohol during prohibition and worked as a petrol station attendant before turning to boxing. He became something of a local sporting hero until a serious injury to his nose, which he had corrected with plas-

tic surgery, put him off. After stints as a dealer and croupier in a number of gambling halls, his love of singing led to work with some local bands. He stayed with Sammy Watkins' band for three years before beginning to make a name for himself as a solo performer in the '40s.

Jerry Lewis, the younger of the pair, was born Joseph Levitch in Newark, New Jersey, in 1926. His was a showbusiness background. While his parents were on the road performing, the young Jerry stayed with relatives. Every summer, he joined them at the Catskills resort in upstate New York, where they were resident entertainers. Lewis left high school after the first year to

become an usher at the Paramount Theatre in New York. By the time he was 18, Jerry Lewis was touring with his own act. He would mimic singers on stage whilst their records were being played in the wings.

Legend has it that Martin and Lewis were introduced on a New York street corner in 1946. Certainly, they began appearing on the same bill at local clubs over the next few months. At the 500 Club in Atlantic City, they appeared on stage in an impromptu double act. Martin sang while Lewis jumped around on stage, doing handstands, conducting the band with his shoes, dropping dishes and other crazy antics. The audience's delighted response con-

Martin (1917-), Lewis (1926-)

firmed their own instinct that they should continue performing together.

By the late 1940s, Martin and Lewis were headlining on cabaret bills and had secured a large following. In 1949, they went to Hollywood for their first film, My Friend Irma, with Marie Wilson and Diana Lynn. To coincide with the film's release, Martin and Lewis also headlined a stage show to accompany it. A sequel, My Friend Irma Goes West, was made 18 months later.

A spot on Bob Hope's radio show was not successful, however. The duo had to be seen to be understood.

In 1950, Dean Martin and Jerry Lewis made their debut on The Colgate Comedy Show with an hour of material taken directly from their stage show.

Their heyday was the early 1950s. The double act was at its best in films such as At War With The Army, Sailor Beware and Living It Up, in which Jerry Lewis believes that he is dying of radiation poisoning and Martin is the doctor who tries to convince him that he isn't. Because their contract at Paramount required them to make two films a year, their output was prodigious. But the public was not prepared to countenance their experiment of switching roles, as in The Stooge

(1953), where Dean Martin played the conceited vaudeville star to Lewis's straight man. Between films, the duo continued to appear on TV, tour and make records.

Both Martin and Lewis were volatile characters with explosive tempers, and in 1954 rumours started to circulate that a particularly bad row had split up the partnership. They carried on despite their differences, but Partners (1956) was made amid further rumours concerning the stability of the act. Nonetheless, an extended season at the Copaca-bana nightclub immediately afterwards was a tremendous success, proving once again that their very best work was always done in front of a live audience.

Hollywood Or Bust was to be their last film together. By now, Martin felt himself to be just a singing prop to Lewis's madcap antics and complained throughout filming. He also considered that Lewis took himself much too seriously, even believing that he was the next Chaplin.

There was never any formal announcement of a split, but in The Delicate Delinquent, Jerry Lewis appeared with Darren McGavin in the role originally intended for Martin, and in April 1957, Martin sold his interests in their production company.

Key Films

My Friend Irma (1949);
Sailor Beware (1951);
Jumping Jacks (1952);
Money From Home (1953);
You're Never Too Young (1955).

Apart, the pair have experienced both spectacular highs and crushing lows. Lewis's first solo appearance in films was not unsuccessful and he continued his association with Paramount. It took Martin time to find his feet, however. A couple of good dramatic roles in Some Came Running and Career eventually provided the lift he needed. His records remained popular throughout, and later, he had a nine-year run on television with a weekly variety show. Lewis's film career faltered in the '70s and his prime-time TV show lasted just two years, but he had later success playing opposite Robert De Niro in The King Of Comedy. He also won at least eight best director awards internationally, and became a cult figure in France, but in 1980 filed for bankruptcy. In the US, Lewis was also well-known for the telethons which raised millions for children suffering from muscular dystrophy.

Performance Extract

Jerry: Our nightclub will be a smash. And before I forget it – we'd better get a big neon sign outside. We want folks to be able to find us, you know.

Dean: You mean – our name up in lights?

Jerry: Sure – I've got the whole

thing worked out. As you drive up to the club at night, the first thing you see is the big neon sign: "Now appearing – Jerry Lewis, the world's youngest comedian."

Dean: (DISAPPOINTED) That's all the sign says?

Jerry: Oh yes – your singing. Well, right below where this big neon sign says, "Now appearing, Jerry Lewis, the world's youngest comedian...."

Dean: (ANXIOUSLY) Yeah?

Jerry: It says: "Also the world's oldest, Dean Martin."

Steve Martin

"There's got to be order for my comedy to work, because chaos in the midst of chaos is not funny, but chaos in the midst of order is funny." – Steve Martin.

"He basically has one joke, and he's it." – David Felton, *Rolling Stone* magazine.

Steve Martin's style of humour is like a magnet: it attracts some and repels others. Latterly best known for his film work, he was previously an experimental stand-up comic seeking to present "little personal, private observations of the world in general and to show how you have to become com-pletely crazy to survive." This notion of one man, alone, in a mad world is a leitmotif running through his whole canon.

His stand-up act was an extraordinary conception; it contained no gags as such – indeed he made the telling of a joke into a joke itself – but served up a surrealistic mix of failed magic and straight nonsense. In a strange jumble of material, he would often perform routines with no punchline, or alternatively provide the pay-off line and let the audience work out the gag for themselves.

His Life and Work

Appropriately enough, Steve Martin was born in the town of Waco, in Texas, on 14th August 1945, but into a conservative, middle-class family. When he was five, the family moved to California, eventually settling near Anaheim, home to Disneyland. From the age of ten, the young Martin had a succession of summer vacation and after-school-hours jobs there; firstly selling guide books, trick ropes and novelty devices in the joke shop, and, aged 15, getting the job of his dreams in Merlin's Magic Shop on Main Street. He learnt to play the banjo, but was obsessed by magic and became so proficient, the owners let him perform for the customers. After leaving school,

Catchphrases

"Well excuuuuuuse me..."

"A wild and crazy guy."

(1945-)

he attended Long Beach State College, studying philosophy, but dropped his studies after three years without graduating. Having enroled on a TV writing course at UCLA, he sent ideas to Mason Williams, then chief writer on *The Smothers Brothers Comedy Hour* and was hired, becoming one of the ten-strong team that won a collective Emmy in 1968.

Later, Steve Martin also wrote for Glen Campbell, Ray Stevens, Pat Paulsen, John Denver and Sonny and Cher, who invited him onto their show as a background character. Though earning well from writing, Martin also wanted to perform, and having trimmed his hair, lost the beard and generally smartened up, he went to be warm-up man for both Sonny and Cher and Helen Reddy. He made the first of what would be many appearances on Johnny Carson's show in 1973, but even in 1975, he was so frustrated at his under-achievement that he seriously considered quitting the business altogether.

Radically reforming his routine in a last-ditch bid for success, he went full-throttle for the bizarre and outrageous. Two coruscating weeks of sell-out shows at the San Francisco Boarding House proved the turning point. He was then showcased on *Saturday Night Live* and in 1977 embarked on a spectacularly successful short tour in which he made over $1,000,000, and performed in front of an esti-mated 500,000 people. His act was weird, including characters like the repulsive man who is aghast when his 102-year old mother asks for $10 for food, and the man who shoots his girlfriend because he can't be bothered to drive her home. Martin also explained how he'd met Jackie Onassis in the launderette, and how he'd been giving the cat a bath but the fur was sticking to his tongue.

In a prolific creative blitz in the late 1970s, he released three comedy albums – two of which went platinum and the third, gold – was also nominated for an Academy Award for the eight-minute short *The Absent Minded Waiter*, and published a best-selling book of short stories, *Cruel Shoes*. Collaborating with Carl Reiner as director, Martin made three films – *The Jerk*, *Dead Men Don't Wear Plaid* and *The Man With Two Brains* – all of which were less than ecstatically received at the time, only becoming successful later.

The 1984 picture, *All Of Me*, also directed by Reiner, was vitally important to Martin in two ways. First, he met the woman who was to become his wife, English actress Victoria Tennant, and second, it breathed new life into his flagging film career. As Roger Cobb, the successful lawyer who has to share the same body as Lily Tomlin, Martin won critical acclaim and Best Actor awards from both the New York Film Critics and the National Board of Review. Martin himself considers *Roxanne* his most crucial movie, however – had it flopped, he felt, his career could well have ended too. He needn't have worried.

Steve Martin would probably be delighted to be described as an enigma. Certainly, inter-view-ers have variously called him 'thoughtful', 'precise', 'dead-pan' and 'a masked man' who is highly protective of both his work and his personal life. He remains a true son of Waco, in more than one sense.

Key Films

The Absent Minded Waiter (short, 1978);
The Jerk (1979);
The Man With Two Brains (1983);
All Of Me (1984);
Roxanne (1987);
Parenthood (1989);
Father Of The Bride (1992).

Performance Extract

"I wanted to buy some carpeting - d'you know what they want for carpeting? $15 a square yard. I am not going pay that for carpeting... so what I did, I bought two square yards and when I go home I strap them to my feet."

The Marx Brothers

L eonard, Adolph, Milton and Herbert Marx were all 're-christened' in 1914 by the vaudeville comic, Art Fisher and known as Chico, Harpo, Groucho, Gummo and Zeppo, went on to become five of the most anarchic and successful loons ever to hit the stage and screen.

The names are said to derive from their true natures – Chico, for example, always had an eye for the ladies, or chicks; Harpo played the harp, badly; Groucho was the insulting wise-cracker, and Gummo favoured soft rubber shoes. Each character existed in his own right,

but also as part of a well-balanced team producing shows and films that became classics of wild and illogical humour. Gummo left the act at an early stage and Zeppo, who played the romantic lead in five of their films, eventually left, seemingly at odds with the increasingly zany style of the others.

Their Life and Work

The Marx Brothers emerged into the world in New York in the last

decade and a half of the 19th century, the children of emigres from Europe, Minnie and Sam. The various brothers worked on a range of skills – music, singing and dancing – and their first real collaborative effort was a 1918 show called *Mrs Green's Reception*. The first real success came with *I'll Say She Is* in 1924. In truth it was a flimsy story but, dramatically enlivened by the brothers mad-cap humour, it was a big success on Broadway. While playing in *Animal Crackers*, a long-running show, they were contracted to make their first film, *The*

Cocoanuts, in 1929. Groucho played a hotel owner facing bankruptcy whose only hope of salvation is to woo the wealthy Mrs Potter, a hotel guest. *Animal Crackers* followed a year later. It was one of their best, introducing the song *Hooray For Captain Spalding*, at which point Groucho famously replied: "Hello, I must be going..."

Moving to Hollywood, they next appeared in their first film written expressly for the cinema – *Monkey Business* – which includes the famous scene where the brothers all try to get through customs using Maurice Chevalier's passport. *Duck Soup*, in 1933, was better structured than most of their offerings which tended to the anarchic, and features a celebrated sequence where two people are looking at one another, although each believes they're looking at a mirror.

Their very finest films are widely conceded to be *A Night At The Opera* and *A Day At The Races*. Later films seemed pale imitations by comparison, and after *The Big Store* in 1941, the brothers split up and went their separate ways. Groucho and Chico appeared on the radio, and Chico toured as a pianist in a band that also included Mel Torme on drums. Harpo also toured and had various roles in films and plays. After the war, they had two more stabs at film-making, neither being a success. Groucho's later career was spent as a TV host for a game show called *You Bet Your Life*, in reality a vehicle for his wisecracks. One such gem came when greeting a contestant who said she had something like 22 children. How comes? asked Groucho. I love my husband, the woman replied. Yes, and I love my cigar, retorted Groucho, but I take it out once in a while.

Chico (Leonard Marx) died in 1961, Harpo (Adolph [called Arthur] Marx) in 1964, Groucho (Julias Marx) and Gummo (Milton Marx) in 1977, and Zeppo (Herbert Marx) in 1979.

> ## Key Films
>
> The Coconuts (1929);
> Animal Crackers (1930);
> Duck Soup (1933);
> A Night At The Opera (1935);
> A Day At The Races (1937).

Performance Extracts →

From *The Cocoanuts*, 1929:

MR HAMMER (GROUCHO), PROPRIETOR OF COCOANUT MANOR, A FLORDIA RESORT, ATTEMPTS TO GIVE DIRECTIONS TO CHICO.

Hammer: Now, here is a little peninsula, and here is a viaduct leading over to the mainland.
Chico: Why a duck?
Hammer: I'm all right. How are you? I say here is a little peninsula, and here's a viaduct leading over to the mainland.
Chico: All right. Why a duck?
Hammer: I'm not playing Ask-Me-Another. I say, that's a viaduct.
Chico: All right. Why a duck? Why a... why a duck? Why-a-no-chicken?

Hammer: I don't know why-a-no-chicken. I'm a stranger here myself. All I know is that it's a viaduct. You try to cross over there a chicken, and you'll find out why a duck. It's deep water, that's viaduct.
Chico: That's-why-a-duck?
Hammer: Look... suppose you were out horse-back riding and you came to that stream and wanted to ford over these, you couldn't make it. Too deep.
Chico: But what do you want with a Ford when you gotta horse?
Hammer: Well, I'm sorry the matter ever came up. All I know is that it's a viaduct.
Chico: Now look... all righta... I catcha on to why-a-horse, why-a-chicken, why-a-this, why-a-that. I no catch on to why-a-duck.

Hammer: I was only fooling. I was only fooling. They're going to build a tunnel in the morning. Now is that clear to you?
Chico: Yes. Everything – excepta why-a-duck.

Jackie Mason

"Nobody makes me laugh harder." – Mel Brooks.

"A person who's funny always is an idiot, because it means he can't identify with reality. What kind of idiot is always funny?" – Jackie Mason.

Jackie Mason is a veteran stand-up comic with trenchant opinions on a wide range of subjects, in particular politics and the differences between Jew and Gentile. His scatter-gun monologues attack the hypocrisies of society, its pretensions, restrictions and contradictions. Indeed, so forthright has he been that he's allegedly received death threats, had bullets fired into his home, been involved in a mystery car crash and beaten up by a stranger.

He'll readily challenge the assumptions of US foreign policy and, less controversially, poke fun at Jewish characteristics, such as buying a status-symbol boat but never learning how to sail it.

His Life and Work

He was born Jacob Moshe Maza in Wisconsin on June 9th, probably in 1930, although he is reluctant to specify the year. His father was an orthodox rabbi who had emigrated from Russia, and in the very religious family his three elder brothers all became rabbis and his two sisters married rabbis. Growing up on the Lower East Side of New York, Mason says he spent most of his childhood in the

(c.1930-)

temple, becoming a cantor at the age of 18 before going on to take a BA in psychology at the City College in New York. He then completed a seminary course at Yeshiva University and became a rabbi at the age of 24.

Unhappy with his calling, Mason began to tend towards more secular employment, for example as social director at Jewish resorts in the Catskill mountains, and even began to stand-in for comics at the hotels – although keeping this a dark secret until after his father's death in 1957, at which point he became a full-time comedian. As brash as they come, Mason got mixed receptions in the early days, but a pivotal booking was one night in 1960 at the Slate Brothers comedy club in Los Angeles. He stayed three months. Steve Allen, who had his own TV show at that time, saw Mason and booked him for two appearances. This led on to him playing much better live venues like Copacabana and the Blue Angel nightclub, as well as other TV spots with Gerry Moore, Perry Como and Jack Parr.

In the mid-'60s he visited Britain, appearing on BBC TV's *Sunday Night At The London Palladium*, and also releasing a book and two records. By now his act was a thoroughly polished, though very sharp routine which included a spot-on Ed Sullivan impression. Sullivan himself saw it and invited him onto his show. There would be 30 in all, but one stands out... President Johnson had booked prime-time TV for a live address to the nation. When the picture cut back to the show, Mason was left with only two minutes instead of his normal six. Sullivan raised two fingers to indicate this, and Mason responded by joking directly with the audience and raising various combinations of fingers himself. The audience loved it; Sullivan didn't, cancelling all future appearances by Mason and stopping his payments. Americans sue as readily as breathe, so Mason instantly slapped a law suit on Sullivan, although it was later withdrawn and peace broke out again.

Among many other people, Mason's humour took the rise out of Frank Sinatra, and Mason claims he had calls threatening dire consequences if he used Sinatra's name again. In November 1966 three shots were fired into Mason's home. No one was hurt, but later Mason was hospitalised after a head-on car crash in which the woman driver of the other car fled. In 1967 he received serious facial injuries after a beating from a mystery assailant. He also landed himself a law suit from

Key Films

The Stoolie (1972);
The Jerk
(1979, with Steve Martin);
Love For Sale (1988).

CBS in 1969 over some pithy remarks about US Administration policy in Vietnam. Mason believed this further contributed to public perception of him as a 'censored comedian'.

Despite setting up his own company, JaMa Productions Inc. with Leon H Charney, Mason's attempts in film and TV in the early 1970s were poor, and he was forced virtually to begin again as a stand-up in the clubs and hotels. It was not until 1986 that he found the right recipe for another big success. Jyll Rosenfeld, his manager and girlfriend, proposed a one-man theatrical show, scripted by Mason. *The World According To Me* ran for six triumphal months in LA before transferring to Broadway where it ran for almost three years, collecting a Tony Award en route in 1987. The show also did well in London in 1989.

Performance Extracts

"You never saw a Jew before...? This is it. You must be a gentile – your clothes don't match."

"A Jew can't fix anything. If a car breaks down a gentile is under it in two minutes. If a Jewish car breaks down it takes him three hours to open the hood, and then when he does he looks down and says, "Ay, is it busy here..."

"Any gentile home is a workshop. A Jewish home is a museum. A gentile has a house to live in. A Jew has a house to show it to you."

Walter Matthau

"A palette with every colour you want. He has enough talent to make four big stars. He's as deft at comedy as he is at drama."
– Billy Wilder.

It took Walter Matthau a long time to gain serious public recognition and affection, the big breakthrough coming with Neil Simon's play, *The Odd Couple*, which later went on to be made into a film and a successful TV series. Now, however, Matthau's lugubrious rubbery face, the hang-dog expression and perfect comic timing, have become firm favourites in a string of light comedies.

(1920-)

He certainly never set out to become type-cast as the crafty, wise-cracking city survivor, but reluctantly accepts that that is precisely what has occurred. "I've developed a definite character and I have to pay the price. I can't play any dramatic roles, let alone the great ones any more: yet I would like to." That said, he hasn't helped himself expand his range, turning down many TV drama offers on the dubious grounds that actors of his stature just don't do TV. He argues that TV is the least satisfactory medium for an actor because the highly compressed time-scale hinders or even negates proper characterisation. In truth, he doesn't much care for films either, saying only in the theatre is he "comfortable, relaxed, fulfilled and delighted."

His Life and Work

Walter Matthau was born in New York, on October 1st 1920, the son of an emigre Russian priest, who'd moved to Finland and Lithuania where he met his wife. When Matthau was three years of age, his father left the family home. Like Jackie Mason, Matthau grew up on the Lower East Side. Aged seven, he discovered Shakespeare and began to recite poetry in school assemblies, later entertaining friends with impressions of famous film stars and appearing in

amateur dramatic productions. When 11, he found work as an ice-cream seller in the Yiddish theatres along Second Avenue, and witnessing actors at work fuelled his latent showbiz ambitions which led him into some small roles in Yiddish musicals. Graduating from high school in 1939, he had a succession of odd jobs while trying unsuccessfully to join theatre groups, and ended up as a boxing and basketball coach.

During his war service, Matthau won six battle stars, but the stars he still most hankered after were those on the stage. Back in New York, he studied at the dramatic workshop of the school for social research and actually first trod the Broadway boards in 1948 as a candle bearer in *Anne Of The Thousand Days*. In his own estimation, his first good role was that of detective Sam Dundee in the 1951 production of *Twilight Walk*. After several years in straight dramas, he played in *Guys And Dolls* earning praise from critic Walter Kerr, who said he had made a "surprisingly easy transition... from dramatic roles. He slouches, sneers and beats his weary breast with the confidence and energy of a trained vaudevillian." Matthau went on to win the 1959 New York Drama Critics Award for his part in *Once More With Reeling* and in 1962 collected a Tony Award for Best Supporting Actor in *A Shot In The Dark*.

Key Films

The Kentuckian (1955);
The Fortune Cookie (1966);
Guide for the Married Man (1967);
Kotch (1971);
Charley Varrick (1973);
The Front Page (1974);
The Sunshine Boys (1975);
The Bad News Bears (1976);
House Calls (1978);
California Suite (1978).

Neil Simon had seen Matthau in *Guys And Dolls*, and teamed him with Art Carney in his Broadway play, *The Odd Couple*, about the domestic tribulations of two divorced men who set up home together. Matthau played Oscar, the slovenly sportswriter, Carney the fussy newswriter, Felix. In the film world, director Billy Wilder became a great fan, guiding him through *The Fortune Cookie*, for which Matthau won an Oscar for his portrayal of a conniving, shyster lawyer, and also *The Front Page* and *Buddy Buddy*. A string of hits though the 1970s cemented Matthau's star status, with Oscar nominations for *Kotch* and *The Sunshine Boys*.

Somewhat stuck in the same screen persona, his work through the 1980s was mediocre, and seldom crossed the Atlantic to reach British audiences, except on video release.

Performance Extract

From *The Odd Couple*:

Oscar (MATTHAU): "I can't take it any more, Felix, I'm cracking up. Everything you do irritates me.

And when you're not here, the things I know you're gonna do when you come in irritate me. You leave me little notes on my pillow. I told you 158 times I

cannot stand little notes on my pillow. "We are all out of corn-flakes F.U." It took me three hours to figure out that F.U. was Felix Ungar.

Rik Mayall

"My comedy is a lot less pointed than other people's – the meaninglessness of my comedy is really the message. There's hardly a constructive message in there..." – Rik Mayall.

Rik Mayall's range is impressive: he can convincingly portray characters spanning the spectrum from utter yob to Conservative Member of Parliament – though he might argue that is a tautology.

A mainspring of the 'alternative' set, Mayall's early comic characters included a contemporary 'angry young man'; Kevin Turvey, the Birmingham bore; and

one half of the Dangerous Brothers – lunatic stuntmen Richard and Adrian – in partnership with long-time collaborator, Ade Edmondson. This team, together since university, is equally flexible – performing anything from Beckett's impenetrable stageplay, *Waiting For Godot*, to the positively lavatorial sitcom, *Bottom*, on BBC TV.

His Life and Work

Rik Mayall was born on 7th March 1958. His father ran the drama department at a teacher

training college and stimulated an initial interest in the performing arts in the highly intelligent child, who began at King's School, Worcester, two years early, and went up to Manchester University at 17. Mayall collected a 2:2 degree in drama studies, but of far greater long-term significance is that it was there he met and began to work with Ade Edmondson. Together with others, they formed an improvisational group called Twentieth Century Coyote, performing lunchtime theatre and shows entitled *Dead Funny*, *Who Is Dick Treacle?* and *King Ron And His Nubile Daughter*.

(1958-)

Mayall toured the United States with the Oxford and Cambridge Shakespeare Company and on returning, picked up again with Edmondson, producing occasional shows, while working most of a year in a foundry to try to clear his debts. They took one show, *Death On The Toilet*, to the Edinburgh Fringe Festival in 1979 and scored a hit. Mayall played both God and Death in the show, with Edmondson as a man called Edwin. They succeeded Hale and Pace at the Woolwich Tramshed, but since most of their work was, at this stage, deriving from Irish playwright Samuel Beckett's complex writings, it was largely unintelligible to most audiences. Trying a totally different tack, they created the manic Dangerous Brothers and, in addition, Rik developed a character who would recite truly awful poetry. In the early 1980s, London's Comedy Store was the place for all the up-and-coming comics, but soon another venue opened above a strip club – the Comic Strip. Quickly becoming regulars there, Mayall and Edmondson began the productive cross-fertilisation of ideas with other 'founder members' of what would become the 'alternative set' – Alexei Sayle, Dawn French, Jennifer Saunders and many more.

The Kevin Turvey character was created especially for TV when Mayall was invited to take part in *A Kick Up The Eighties*, also starring Tracy Ullman, but the genuinely innovative idea was a sitcom which Mayall and his then girlfriend Lise Mayer planned to write. *The Young Ones* featured four particularly obnoxious denizens of a student house. With the aid of Ben Elton, on the writing side, the pilot went out in 1982 with Mayall as a sociology student, Edmondson as Vivian the dangerous punk, Nigel Planer as Neil the hippy and Chris Ryan as Mike, the bossy organiser. Critic Philip Purser wrote: "What they are inviting you to laugh at or be shocked by, is a lurch through life without any saving graces or niceties. Watching them is like watching the monkeys at the zoo." For all that, the BBC commissioned two series. Meanwhile, the Comic Strip team won a deal for six short films for Channel 4. A series of tours and appearances on *Saturday Live* filled in any gaps in filming.

Mayall and Elton co-wrote a follow-up to *The Young Ones* called *Filthy, Rich and Catflap* but it didn't crackle. *The New Statesman*, a Laurence Marks and Maurice Gran script, was a different type of challenge for Mayall in

1987. Still profoundly unpleasant, but this time in a £500 suit, here he played the Tory MP Alan B'Stard, who lived up to his name with a series of utterly unscrupulous scams and scandals. The Comic Strip maintained its lure for Mayall however, and he appeared in their films *Eat The Rich* and *More Bad News*, a parody of a heavy metal band tour.

In the 1990s, came the Hollywood expedition, for *Drop Dead Fred*, in which Mayall, in the title role, is the imaginary friend of a young girl. When she grows up, he returns to haunt her.

Key TV/Films

TV: A Kick Up The Eighties; The Young Ones; Filthy, Rich and Catflap; The New Statesman; Bottom.

Films: Eat The Rich; More Bad News; Drop Dead Fred (1991).

Performance Extract

From *A Kick Up the Eighties*:

My name's Kevin Turvey... and here's a good one – "Why does Mrs Thatcher always wear barbed-wire underwear?" She doesn't – it's a joke. I thought, this week's subject is sex, which is slightly embarrassing, so I thought I'd start with a bit of a joke, right. Well, not a bit of a joke, the whole of a joke... a bit of a joke would be no good really... not unless it was the funny bit... so this week, I thought, how am I going to find out all about sex? And I thought, I know, I'll become a prostitute. That's what I did right, – I went out and bought myself a handbag, put it on my shoulder and hung around outside Tesco's, right, for about a day..."

Max Miller

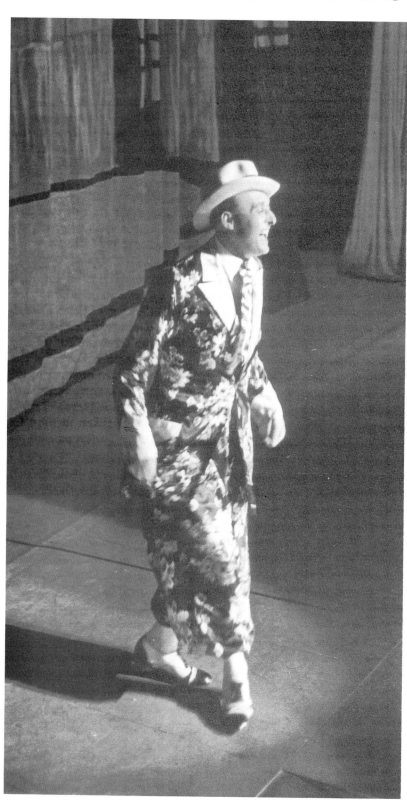

"I know exactly what you're saying. You're saying to yourselves – why is he dressed like that? I'll tell you why I'm dressed like this... I'm a commercial traveller and I'm ready for bed." – Max Miller.

"When he was on stage he generated a sense of danger. You thought this was somebody who is dicing, gambling, and is going to get away with it." – John Osborne.

Max Miller, the original 'Cheekie Chappie', brought a new form of humour to the music halls in the '30s and '40s – risque jokes. With his white trilby hat, white shoes, loud shirts and louder ties and plus fours, he was an outrageous sight and possessed the garrulous patter of a salesman. Like all the best performers, he had a natural gift for comic timing, enabling him to build one laugh right on top of another, keeping up a dizzying momentum.

The saucy stuff did land him in occasional trouble with reactionary magistrates and once, notably, with 'the powers that be''when he was felt to have overstepped the mark in a Royal Variety Performance. A measure of how tame it would be considered now though, is that Max Miller died in the year the prosecutor in the *Lady Chatterley's Lover* obscenity trial still felt able to open his concluding remarks with "Is this a book you would wish your wife or servants to read..." The key to Miller's risque material

Catchphrase

"There'll never be another, will there lady?"

His life and work

Thomas Henry Sargent was born in November 1895, near Brighton. His father had been a comedian before going on to work on the railways and the young Max learned to read music at an early age from an old cornet instruction book in one of his father's chests of old songs, sketches and jokes. Father determined the boy should have a trade, and got him apprenticed to a blacksmith, and later as as caddy at the local golf course, but Miller's goals lay elsewhere. He ran away from home, joining the original Billy Smart's Circus. In the Army, Miller was regularly punished for bad behaviour, but at least enjoyed performing his Dad's old material for his fellow squaddies in the unit's concert party, The Lightenings.

Back in Brighton in 1919, his father persuaded a local concert party promoter to give his son a job for the season. Here Miller met Kitty Marsh, a contralto, who became his stage partner for a while, and later his life partner, as wife and manager. After touring with various shows, he extended his experience with troupes run by Fred Karno and Tom Arnold, before landing a role as Tipperary Tim in a Francis Lidler revue. Miller wore a loud, not to say deafening, flowery chintz plus fours suit, and the Cheekie Chappie was established. He kept the outfit, later adding the trademark white trilby worn off-centre and later the white shoes, dazzling silks and kipper ties.

An almost permanent fixture at the Holborn Empire for years until it was bombed out in 1940, Miller had his act well polished. He'd parade around in his flamboyant suit for a full minute, then open with – "Well, what if I am...?" Then straight into the fast-talking patter, the cheeky smile and the ribald gags. He'd often let the audience complete the last few words of his saucy ditties, then accuse them of having the dirty minds.... To break up the stream of stories, there'd be a song or two and a little dancing too.

A favourite ploy was the two joke books – one white, with the clean ones in, and one blue.... Which one do you want? he would ask his audience, who invariably bellowed "the blue one, Max." This idea was developed after the run-in with the Royals, when he explained his cheekiness

Key Films

The Good Companions (1932);
Channel Crossing (1932);
Friday The Thirteenth (1933);
Princess Charming (1934);
Things Are Looking Up (1935);
Educated Evans (1936);
Get Off My Foot (1936);
Take It From Me (1937);
Don't Get Me Wrong (1937);
Thank Evans (1938);
Everything Happens To Me (1939);
The Good Old Days (1939);
Hoots Mon (1940);
Asking For Trouble (1943).

by saying he'd brought the wrong joke book with him that night. He made many recordings of his stage shows between 1939 and '57, and was also often on radio – once getting himself banned for going just that bit too far. It only served to increase his popularity in the theatres where he had become one of the highest paid variety stars. Max Miller's material had to be severely toned-down for his film work to get by the censor's scissors and because of this, although he made many, they never captured the magic of his theatre work.

He died on 7th May 1963.

Performance Extracts

I fell in love with Mary from the dairy
But Mary wouldn't fall in love with me;
Down by an old mill stream
We both sat down to dream:
Now on our farm, said Mary from the Dairy,

We've got the finest cows you've ever seen.
I don't do things by halves,
I'll let you see my calves
And they're not the same shape calves as Nellie Dean's.

Last night I had fun. I went out and I saw a light, up in a lady's room. I shouted up, I said - Put that light out. She said - What. I said – Put that light out. She said - You come an' put it out, you left it on... You've got to be careful, haven't you?

Spike Milligan

"Watching *Q5*, we almost felt as if our guns had been spiked... We had been writing quickies or sketches for some three years and they always had a beginning, a middle and a tag-line. Suddenly, watching Spike Milligan, we realised that they didn't have to be like that." – Terry Jones, of Monty Python.

Milligan's entirely valid claim to fame is the weird and wonderful humour of *The Goon Show*, broadcast on BBC radio throughout the whole of the 1950s. As part of a comic team also comprising Peter Sellers, Michael Bentine, Harry (now Sir Harry) Secombe and talented scriptwriter Jimmy Grafton, who was in many senses the paterfamilias, Milligan found his metier and became a hero to a set of mould-breaking writers, the Python team. Milligan both wrote and performed many of the leading parts, such as Major Bloodnock, the military idiot; Minnie Bannister, spinster of the parish; and most notably of all, Eccles, the very epitome of the Goons.

Despite his career having been blighted by severe bouts of depression, he has been amazingly prolific, also writing stage plays, and many books including several volumes of war and post-war memoirs, starting with *Adolf Hitler – My Part In His Downfall*, his first novel, *Puckoon* in 1965 and children's books such as *Startling Verse For All The Family* and *Unspun Socks From A Chicken's Laundry*. His humour is surreal, bizarre and, especially in the children's works, enchanting: "There are holes in the sky, where the rain gets in. But the holes are small, that's why rain is thin."

His Life and Work

Terence Milligan was born in India in 1918, the son of a British Army officer. He has described his time in the subcontinent as "idyllic" and the move to Catford, south east London, must have been as dislocating as moving in the opposite direction. As a youth, Milligan yearned for a trumpet, and through selling stolen fags from the cigarette factory where he worked as a packer, he finally acquired one. Thus, he spent his evenings playing jazz and his days in a variety of jobs.

Joining the Army in 1940, Milligan began to play in a band called The Boys Of Battery D during his time in Africa and Italy. He also became a member of the Central Pool Of Artists and played in numerous Forces variety shows, along with Harry Secombe. While serving, however, Milligan suffered shell-shock, the debilitating effects of which were to bring him later troubles.

He was invited by an ex-Army colleague, Bill Hall, to join his jazz trio in 1947 and worked

sporadically for a couple of years. Milligan, unsettled, moved into a little showbiz 'commune' in Notting Hill Gate, reuniting with Secombe and meeting Norman Vaughan. Both he and Vaughan then auditioned for the vacant resident comedian's spot at the Windmill Theatre – but both failed to get the job.

Arguably the critical introduction in Milligan's whole career came when Secombe took him along to Jimmy Grafton's pub. Michael Bentine was already known there, and soon after Peter Sellers bowled up. Grafton, ex-Army too, began writing with Milligan, praising his "great comic vision and originality." Working as a pair, they contributed to Derek Royal's *Hip Hip Hoo Roy* series. Now calling themselves The Goons, the quintet approached the BBC with plans for a show. A pilot was made and the hierarchy felt it too advanced, but offered them a second shot. The BBC wanted to call the show *The Junior Crazy Gang*, but compromised as far as *Crazy People*. To the Goons, it was the *Goon Show*, whatever they wanted to call it. Initially a group effort, Milligan came to play more of a leading role as the phenomenon grew over the years.

The original Goon show format was five sketches interspersed with musical items; the humour was irreverent, subversive, anti-Establishment and included ad-libbing and loud sound effects. The first series claimed audiences of a million and a half; the second, three million; after that it was a national institution. The format evolved from individual sketches to broad thematic stories – Fred Of The Islands, The Mystery Of The Cow On The Hill and Where Do Socks Come From? By the fourth series, the show was being taped so the scope for ad-libbing grew yet further. This served to encourage a yet more loose style: characters would get rounds of

Key Films

Penny Points To Paradise (1951); The Bed Sitting Room (1969, with Peter Cook and Dudley Moore); Digby, The Biggest Dog In The World (1974); The Great McGonagall (1975, with Peter Sellers); Monty Python's Life Of Brian (1979); Yellow Beard (1983).

ecstatic applause as they read their first line of the script, but not their last. The BBC found itself often troubled by the material used, and Peter Sellers' impersonation of Winston Churchill was ruled out of order. The final show was The Last Smoking Seagoon, broadcast on January 28th 1960. Milligan had grown weary with the endless arguments with 'Auntie' over what could, and what could not be broadcast. Nevertheless, they all reunited for *The Last Goon Show Of All* as part of the BBC jubilee celebrations, recorded in front of a royal audience, Prince Charles having become a loyal fan.

Milligan went on to write a well-received play, *The Bed Sitting Room*, with John Antrobus in 1963, which was subsequently filmed by Peter Cook and Dudley Moore. His later work mainly comprised five series under the generic title "Q". There was Q5, and also Q6, Q7, Q8 and Q9 completed the series in 1980.

The psychological consequences of his wartime trauma have sadly caused a number of interruptions to his career. He claims the epitaph on his tombstone will read: "I told you I was ill!"

Performance Extract

From *The Goons*:

Eccles: Hello Neddie bach.
Seagoon: Oh, it's Eccles, the loony.
Eccles: Hello Neddieee – Hello Neddieee.
Seagoon: What the hell are you talking about?
Eccles: I've been taking talking lessons – I'm going to be an actor. To be or not to be Neddie.
Seagoon: Shakespeare eh?
Eccles: No dat was Hamlet.
Seagoon: Have you seen Richard the Third?
Eccles: No – he died before I was born.
Seagoon: Dead? He can't be –

why, only last week I saw him in a film.
Eccles: Must have been an old one. Friends, Romans and countrymen – lend me your ears. I come to...
Seagoon: Shut up Eccles.
Eccles: Shut up Eccles.

Monty Python's Flying Circus

"Python started as a result of all of us deciding that we were fed up with the shows we were writing for. Just sending in scripts and letting someone else do it for you." – Michael Palin.

"Our biggest thing really was getting rid of the punchline." – Graham Chapman.

It is wholly apt that Monty Python should follow Spike Milligan in this text, because Python occupies the position in TV history that the *Goon Show* does in the annals of radio. It changed the very meaning of comedy for a whole generation. James Joyce might well have en-

joyed Python's random shapelessness – but it went further; this was stream-of-unconsciousness writing.

The 45 shows recorded made superstars of the six writers – John Cleese, Graham Chapman, Michael Palin, Eric Idle, Terry Jones and Terry Gilliam. Sketches from their TV and film work remain etched on the memories of millions, not only in Britain, but around the world. Many have tried since, but nothing has surpassed it.

Its History

The Python team assembled in 1969, all having previously written for various BBC programmes, including *The Frost Report, At Last The 1948 Show* and *Do Not Adjust Your Set*. Barry Took, then a freelance producer, was asked to be the liaison man between the group and the BBC. They began by pooling existing material but were

unsure what form the embryonic show should take. *The Goons*, and Milligan's later Q5 show, were significant influences (see Terry Jones' quote in the Milligan entry). Choosing a title was a problem; they wanted something elusive and imprecise. Various options considered were Owl Stretching Time; A Horse, A Spoon And A Bucket; and even Bunn, Wackett, Buzzard, Stubble And Boot. The BBC management was equally confused, one suggesting the whole idea was a 'flying circus'. Palin had spotted a name, Gwen Dibley, in a WI magazine that made him chuckle. For a time then, Gwen Dibley's Flying Circus was a working title, but the names Monty and Python cropped up separately in conversation and finally the title was fixed.

The seamless notion derived from Gilliam's cartoon, *Elephants*, for *Do Not Adjust Your Set*, and the non-formulaic linking idea that came to be a hallmark, was born. The first series ran from October 1969 to January 1970 gaining a generally positive critical reaction, although – almost inevitably – the BBC was less sure. There were sketches with tag-lines, but they refused to become slaves to the punchline, sometimes abandoning an idea in mid-scene.

The second series was from September to December 1970 and its first show is specially famed for one of Python's most celebrated sketches – The Ministry of Silly Walks, with Cleese using every inch of his gangling frame so memorably that even today he is still "haunted" (his word) by requests to perform it. In 1970, a special compilation edition won Python a Silver Rose at the

Key Films

And Now For Something Completely Different (1971);
Monty Python And The Holy Grail (1975);
The Life of Brian (1979);
The Meaning of Life (1983).

Montreux Festival and they also released a film version of highlights – *And Now For Something Completely Different*.

By the third series, Cleese was wearying of the project and the comedy became increasingly weird and obscure. His last TV appearance with Python was in 1973, but he did tour with a stage version. A fourth series, made without Cleese who had left to write *Fawlty Towers*, was broadcast under the shortened title *Monty Python* from October 1974 but it was to be the last on TV. The team split up to develop individual projects, but reformed to make a second film, *Monty Python And The Holy Grail*, in 1975. There was to be a four-year gap before their next collaboration. As Chapman put it, with typical Pythonesque logic: "We must develop separately as individuals for the group to survive."

Each went into new ventures; Gilliam and Chapman with the films *Jabberwocky*, and *The Odd Job*, respectively; Cleese into TV's *Fawlty Towers*; Idle producing *Rutland Weekend TV*. Later, came Jones and Palin's *Ripping Yarns*. In 1979, their penultimate picture was released – *The Life Of Brian*, about the 13th disciple Saint Brian who was always just a little bit too late. The film caused a storm and was accused of being blasphemous, though that didn't prevent it doing very well at the box office. Their last was *The Meaning Of Life*, notable for one of the most outrageous scenes that can ever have been filmed. Terry Jones plays Monsieur Creosote, a gargantuan glutton. Arriving at a restaurant, he is greeted by the unctuous waiter, Cleese. Egged on by Cleese, Creosote gorges himself... and then explodes. It is a scene that will stick forever in the mind, and the throat, of anyone who has seen it.

Performance Extract →

CLEESE HAS BROUGHT A DEAD PARROT BACK TO THE PET SHOP TO COMPLAIN...

Cleese: Look, my lad – that parrot is definitely deceased. And when I bought it not half an hour ago, you assured me its lack of movement was due to it being tired and shagged out after a long squawk.

Palin: It's probably pining for the fiords.

Cleese: Pining for the fiords – what kind of talk is that? Look, why did it fall flat on its back the moment I got it home?

Palin: The Norwegian Blue prefers kipping on its back. It's a beautiful bird, lovely plumage.

Cleese: Look, I took the liberty of examining that parrot, and I discovered the only reason it had been sitting on its perch in the first place was that it had been nailed there.

Palin: 'Course it was nailed there, otherwise it would have muscled up to those bars and voom...

Cleese: Look matey, this parrot wouldn't voom if I put four thousand volts through it. It's bleedin' demised.

Palin: It's not. It's pining.

Cleese: It's not pining – it's passed on. This parrot is no more. It has ceased to be. It's expired and gone to meet its maker. This is a late parrot. It's a stiff.

Bereft of life, it rests in peace – if you hadn't nailed it to the perch it would be pushing up the daisies. It's rung down the curtain and joined the choir invisible. This is an ex-parrot!!

Palin: Well I'd better replace it then.

Cleese: (TO CAMERA) If you want to get anything done in this country you've got to complain until you're blue in the mouth.

Palin: Sorry guv, we're right out of parrots.

Cleese: I see, I see – I get the picture.

Palin: I've got a slug.

Cleese: Does it talk?

Palin: Not really, no.

Cleese: Well, it's scarcely a replacement, then, is it?

Morecambe and Wise

"We've done sketches where we share a double-bed and no one has ever suggested there was anything immoral in it. I think we're the only double-act, apart from Laurel and Hardy, to share a bed. The audience accepted it from Laurel and Hardy, and now they accept it from us. And it's a great gift." – Eric Morecambe.

Eric Morecambe and Ernie Wise were two of the most-loved comics on British television. While their double-act had undeniable echoes of both Abbott and Costello, and Laurel and Hardy, theirs was a peculiarly British style, which may explain why, though they did well in Australia, they never cracked America.

Although they didn't socialise much together off-stage, they worked together for over 40 years, and their obvious mutual respect was one of the keys to their enduring popularity. When fully developed, theirs was no straight man/funny man act – each had a fair share of the action, although Morecambe did largely monopolise the physical comedy. Among the amiable buffoon's repertoire of boyish pranks were skewing his glasses, catching an imaginary stone in a paper bag, the two-handed slap on Ernie's cheeks, slapping the back of his own neck,

and throttling himself. A richly comic element of their later shows was Ernie's proud presentation of "plays what I wrote", invariably murdering a classic. Some very celebrated guests appeared happy to make utter fools of themselves.

Their Life and Work

Eric Bartholomew entered the world in Morecambe, Lancashire, in 1926, and borrowed his stage name from his birthplace. He joined his father on stage at the age of seven in an act called Carson and Kid.

Ernest Wiseman was born the previous year in Leeds, the son of a railwayman and part-time entertainer in the Yorkshire clubs.

Eric and Ern first met at an audition for *Youth Takes A Bow*, a child talent show, when Eric was 13 and Ernie already a member of the troupe. During the war, Wise served in the Navy, and Morecambe was a Bevin Boy. In 1947, Eric auditioned for the role of 'feed' to a comic in Lord Sangster's variety circus in Godalming, Surrey. The comic turned out to be Wise, and the partnership began. After playing in various revues, they got a radio show, *You're Only Young Once*, and though it was only broadcast

Catchphrases

"short, fat, hairy legs"
"Arsenal!"
"What do you think of it so far? – Rubbish!"
"You can't see the join..."
(of Ernie's supposed toupee)

Morecambe (1926-1984), Wise (1925-)

in the north it led to their first appearance on TV. *Running Wild* went out on the BBC in April 1954 and was an unmitigated disaster. Ernie said: "We learned that you have to involve yourself in every stage of a show, particularly the preparation of material."

For the next seven years, they played the theatres but also toured Australia and made a surprisingly successful appearance on American TV, on the Ed Sullivan Show. Initially, their act would hinge around Wise exploiting the gormless Morecambe, but as their comic personas began to mature, they came to be more of a blend, both earning laughs. 1960 saw them on British TV again, this time with great success, in *Sunday Night At The London Palladium*, which led directly to a seven year contract with ATV. Favourite and regular elements were Wise promising Morecambe a role in a play for which he'd done a costume,

Key TV/Films

TV: The Morecambe and Wise Show.

Films: The Intelligence Men (1965); That Riviera Touch (1966); The Magnificent Two (1968).

only for Wise to shoot back with "We've run out of time."

With a new scriptwriter (Eddie Braben took over after Dick Hills and Sid Green went to Hollywood), the 'plays' idea was further developed. A prestigious actor would be invited to star in an Ernie production. Eric would fail to recognise them, or call them by the wrong name, fluff his lines, produce extraordinary props and generally wreak havoc, all the while insisting he was only trying to help. Among the many famous

names who risked their careers with this ultimate sacrifice were Peter Cushing, John Mills, Glenda Jackson and Vanessa Redgrave. Musical guests were not spared either – conductor Andre Previn almost escaped when he said: "I'll just get my baton... It's in Chicago," and the sight of Shirley Bassey putting her shoe through stage steps, breaking her heel and completing the song in workman's boots, was supremely comic.

In the 1970s, Morecambe and Wise were at the peak of their popularity and their Christmas Specials were required viewing. They transferred to ITV in 1978, where the shows had a glossier, more overtly showbiz feel to them, but Eric Morecambe's second heart attack (the first had been in 1968) forced them to slow the pace thereafter. On 24th May 1984, he suffered his third heart attack, and died.

Performance Extracts

Ern: What's in the box?
Eric: He just gave it to me.
Ern: Who?
Eric: Arthur Negligee. The antique expert in the next studio.
Ern: You mean, Arthur Negus.
Eric: Yes, I was watching his antique programme. Thought I might pick up a few jokes.
Ern: You're not short of antique jokes.
Eric: Is that it?
Ern: The antique programme, Going For A Song.
Eric: He sings as well? I didn't know that.
Ern: You're interested in antiques?
Eric: You've seen the wife...

Eric: It's amazing how much you can learn from one of your plays.
Ern: Learn?
Eric: Tutankhamen.
Ern: What about it?
Eric: I always thought it was Tooting Common.
Ern: Had to do a lot of research to write that play about Egypt.
Eric: Must have done.
Ern: Spent days at the British Museum.
Eric: No problems getting out?
Ern: I thought that Robert Morley almost did quite well.
Eric: Fair comment.
Ern: Quite well, considering he had such a big role.

Eric: Kept catching me with it every time he turned a bit sharpish.
Ern: That's not a very gracious thing to say.
Eric: I must be honest – a superb actor and one of the nicest men it's ever been my pleasure to work with
Ern: Yes, I suppose I must be.
Eric: I meant Robert Morley.
Ern: Oh, him. Great Actor.
Eric: Like 12 Glenda Jacksons in a trouser suit.

Eddie Murphy

"I'm going to be bigger than Bob Hope." – Eddie Murphy, as a child.

"... he gets away with the most strident material because his eyes tell the audience he's laughing. Eddie's eyes are the erasers for any misunderstandings." – Dick Ebersol, Producer on *Saturday Night Live.*

Like so many contemporary American comics, the deeply modest Eddie Murphy is a scion of that talent hot-house, *Saturday Night Live.* On that show in the early 1980s, he created an act mixing racial stereotyping and savage satire using a stable of impersonations and characters, including Tyrone Green, the illit-

erate author: "I hate white people because they are W-i-t-e..." Critics complained his characterisations were lacking in dignity and social awareness, to which Murphy countered that they were only abstractions and shouldn't be considered necessarily realistic.

His quick, smart humour won wide acclaim, and he transferred comfortably into films, making several huge box-office hits in the middle '80s, but struggled to maintain his standard towards the end of the decade. His live stage work was highly controversial, peppered with profanity, sexism and homophobia – particularly the tour and video – *Raw* – in 1987. In the 1990s, he has tried to renounce his fiery past, but remains proud that two boasts, made when still at school, have been honoured: that he would be famous by the time he was 19, and a millionaire by 22.

His Life and Work

Born April 3rd 1961 in Brooklyn, New York, Eddie Murphy is the son of a policeman and amateur comedian, and a telephone operator. His parents divorced when he was three, and after his father's death five years later, his mother was hospitalised. Murphy and his brother stayed with a woman he describes as a kind of "black Nazi" until the family moved to Long Island, when his mother remarried. At school, his best subject was comedy, and in 1976 he made his stage debut as compere of a talent show at the Roosevelt Centre. Performing occasional spots in clubs, Murphy's early act was basically stolen from his hero

(1961-)

Key Films

48 Hours (1982);
Trading Places (1983);
Beverly Hills Cop (1984);
Beverly Hills Cop II (1987);
Coming To America (1988);
Another 48 Hours (1990).

Richard Pryor, and liberally laced with invective.

In his later teens, he began writing his own material and appeared at Manhattan's Comic Strip. The owners of the club later became his managers. He was still at school at this time, and his studies inevitably suffered, requiring him to re-take his tenth-grade.

After a short period of theatre studies at Nassau Community College, he auditioned for *Saturday Night Live* who specifically wanted a new, black member of cast. He spent the 1980-81 season making regular appearances, but was one of only two (with Joe Piscopo) to be re-hired for the next season. Murphy became the star of the show, specialising in irreverent impersonations of singers like James Brown, Stevie Wonder and Bob Marley along with monologues from his own creations which included: the fast-talking pimp Velvet Jones; Little Richard Simmons, a blend of TV exercise man Simmons and the pop star Little Richard; a surly, tenement dwelling TV host, Mr Robinson; and militant film critic Raheem Abdul Muhammad.

In 1982, Murphy starred as a wise-cracking, quick thinking convict in *48 hours*, with Nick Nolte. A huge success, director Walter Hill felt confident enough to let Murphy make some script amendments and introduce some black dialogue. *Trading Places* was another smash hit the following year. Directed by John Landis, the film saw Murphy exchanging life as a street-bum for the pampered luxury life of a high-powered commodity broker, allowing Murphy's skills of characterisation full rein. These successes won Murphy a five-film contract with Paramount worth $15 million.

A concert tour with the Bus Boys and two record releases (one winning two Grammy nominations) followed in 1982-83, and the next year came the massively lucrative box-office smash, *Beverly Hills Cop*. These films mark the zenith of his career to date. *Best Defence* and *Golden Child*, with Mel Gibson, were noticeably less impressive, and by releasing two videos of his stand-up material (*Delirious* and *Raw*) Murphy again highlighted the homophobic, sexist, macho stud image. Critics suggested that Murphy was beginning to believe his own publicity.

1990 brought the release of *Another 48 Hours*, and rumours that Murphy was so disappointed with the finished product that he contemplated quitting showbusiness altogether. Latterly, he has appeared as a Pharaoh in the video to Michael Jackson's song *Remember The Time*, and Jackson has returned the compliment, singing *Whatzupwitu* on Murphy's third rock music album. Another track, *Yeah*, features Jackson again, Paul McCartney, Hammer, Stevie Wonder, Luther Vandross, Julio Inglesias, Patti LaBelle, Janet Jackson and Jon Bon Jovi. Proceeds from that song are to be the financial basis of Murphy's "Yeah" foundation.

Performance Extract ➔

From *Saturday Night Live*:

Murphy: Here's a message to all you white viewers. I'm Eddie Murphy. I'm 20 years old and a high school graduate. I attended Nassau Community College for about two weeks. No theatrical training whatsoever, yet, I am one of the stars of the new SNL. I make more money in a month than most white people in a year. In 1981, a good education is just about as important as a bucket of warm hamster vomit. So all you white kinds in college are wasting your time – you're either lucky or a bum. Stop kidding yourselves, drop out, drink some beer, get each other pregnant and play space invaders. You know you white kids take life so seriously – quit school and be successful like me.

WHITE MAN IN A CHAUFFEUR'S UNIFORM ENTERS

Chauffeur: Excuse me Mr Murphy, your limousine is ready.
Murphy: Thanks Sammy. Sammy went to Harvard.

Bill Murray

"Murray is a master of comic insincerity. He speaks in italics and tries to raise the put-down into an art form." – Frank Rich, *Time* magazine

"... there's a wild strain loose inside the doughy handsomeness which saves him from predictability." – Pauline Kael, *New Yorker*.

Producer Lorne Michaels has a lot to answer for – mainly, producing an entire generation of American comics on his inspirational show, *Saturday Night Live*. And we in turn, the viewing public, have a lot to be thankful for. Bill Murray is yet another

from the Michaels factory. His scruffiness, deadpan delivery and casual manner disguised a vibrant wit brimming with impudent and scornful wisecracks. Like Chevy Chase before him, when Murray settled into his stride he **was** *Saturday Night Live*.

Subsequently, Murray understood well the sensibilities of the youthful audiences his early film work was targeted at, but only hit the financial jackpot with his own movie, the outstandingly successful *Ghostbusters*, in 1984. One critic dubbed Murray "the irrepressible common man" and, indeed, he wasn't the type to take no for an answer, being far more

interested in the lady of the house, Sigourney Weaver, than in her meddlesome ghosts.

His Life and Work

Bill Murray was born the fifth child, in a family that would grow to nine, in a suburb of Chicago, Illinois, on 21st September 1950. His primary school was run by Franciscan nuns in Wilmette, and continuing his religious upbringing, he went to a Jesuit secondary school. In the Middle Ages, the Jesuits said "Give us the child, and we will answer for the man", so either their methods have changed, or Murray was a tough nut to crack. Not the most able of students, Murray was in fact described as lazy and only really enjoyed basketball and baseball, though he also acted in his high-school theatre group as a way of getting out of class for a few hours a week. He went on to enrol at Regis College, Denver, as a pre-med student, but two arrests for possession of cannabis brought that phase to a swift end. Aged 21, he joined his brother, Brian Doyle-Murray, in Chicago's well-known improvisational troupe, Second City. Others there at the same time included John Belushi, Harold Ramis and Joe Flaherty. Belushi moved to New York, and in 1974 invited Brian and Bill to join with him, Gilda Radner and Chevy Chase in making *National Lampoon's Radio Hour*, and it's subsequent revue. Murray performed as a city-dweller whose main excitement in life was the new products in his local deli, and also a voyeuristic priest satisfying his desires in the confessional.

The Murray brothers were recruited by Howard Cosell, a sportscaster, for a show he was developing. Lorne Michaels hired Belushi, Chase, Aykroyd and Radner for his rival show – which had the same title, *Saturday Night Live*. Cosell's show was only differentiated by having his name attached, but it folded after half a season, while Michael's project prospered. Bill Murray's chance came in 1977 when a disillusioned Chevy Chase left, and Michaels hired him as replacement. Among Murray's best characters on SNL were Todd Loopner, a 'nerdy' teenager; a gossip columnist who regularly became distraught at the misbehaviour of his celebrities; a self-consciously trendy film critic and a smarmy club singer.

Between seasons of SNL, Murray began to get involved in film work. Ivan Reitman (co-producer of *Animal House*) wanted Murray to star as the head coun-

sellor in a picture set in a boys camp. Murray initially refused, but after a re-write, took the role. *Meatballs* was the hit of the summer of '79. In quick succession, he played a journalist in *Where The Buffalo Roam*, had a cameo in Steve Martin's *The Jerk*, appeared with Chevy Chase in the limp golf-course comedy *Caddyshack*, was Dustin Hoffman's room-mate in *Tootsie*.

The *Ghostbusters* phenomenon took off in 1984. Written by Aykroyd and Ramis, it was an inspired treatment of the typical spooks movie. Ramis said: "We are taking a very mundane attitude towards the supernatural." Critics felt Murray stole the show, with his laconic asides. His deal with Columbia also guaranteed him a straight acting role in *The Razor's Edge*, a re-make of the 1946 Tyrone Power classic, but the film was a flop. Feeling in need of a break, Murray took time off to be

with his family, took golf lessons, lived in Paris for a spell and, in the way film stars do, bought minor league baseball teams. He did some stage work again: three W.B. Yeats plays and Brecht's *A Man's A Man, in New York*. He returned to films with *Scrooged*, and then *Ghostbusters II*. Asked if he was satisfied with it, Murray replied: "Not really, no. We really resisted it for a long time because we didn't want to be knee-jerk sequel guys." It only grossed half of the original. *Quick Change*, in 1990, marked Murray's production and directorial debut.

Key Films

Meatballs (1979);
Stripes (1981);
Ghostbusters (1984);
Quick Change (1990).

Performance Extract

From *Saturday Night Live*:

RADNER AND MURRAY NAKED IN A SHOWER, BUCK HENRY FULLY CLOTHED. MURRAY HOLDS A BAR OF SOAP AS IF A MICROPHONE...

Murray: (PART ANNOUNCING, PART CROONING) Ladies and gentlemen... "don't wanna leave her now" a very special guest... "you know I buh-lieve and how" my wife, Mrs Richard Herkiman, Jane Nash. Come on in, Jane... (LEADS HER IN)
Radner: Honey will you quit fooling around.
Murray: Say Jane, how d'you feel about singing a song

today, huh?
Radner: Richard, will you quit fooling around, I'm taking a shower.
Murray: Aw, come on honey, would you mind singing that wonderful morning song. (TO CAMERA) Come on, let's hear it for her (STUDIO AUDIENCE APPLAUD).
Radner: (RELUCTANTLY SINGING, HER FACE DRIPPING) "On a clear day, I will walk around you, and you'll see..." Oh Richard, stop it. You're being silly...

(MURRAY QUESTIONS HER ABOUT LOVING HIM, SHE SAYS SHE DOES...)

Murray: (TO CAMERA) Well, you know, folks out there, what my wife doesn't know is that I know she's been cheating on me for the last couple of years and... we've got behind the curtain a surprise guest... the man she's been seeing behind my back for the past two years.

(BUCK HENRY ENTERS IN COAT AND TIE, SHAKES HANDS AND STANDS BETWEEN THEM IN THE SHOWER)

Murray: Thanks for stopping by... Mrs Richard Herkiman and the guy she's been messing around with. Wooo. (AUDIENCE APPLAUD) Thank you everyone.

Bob Newhart

specific record. *The Button-Down Mind of Bob Newhart*, which came out on the Warner Label in 1960, comprised six of his monologue routines from his nightclub act. It was an instant success, as was its follow up, two years later, *The Button-Down Mind Strikes Back*. The record catapulted him into guest spots on the top TV shows of the day, and into the first of his own series. The monologues featured imaginary dialogue down the telephone with famous names.

Newhart has a thin, nasal voice and a very low-key brand of satire. In his TV shows, he tended to be reactive rather than proactive, playing approachable characters that others would bring their troubles to, such as a psychologist or the owner of an inn. The image was of Newhart, the normal guy, trying to keep afloat in an insane world. *The Newhart Show* ran on Channel 4 in the UK, in 1984.

His Life and Work

George Robert Newhart was born in 1929 in Chicago, the son of a engineer. At St Ignatius High School he played banjo and gained a reputation for first-rate impersonations of Humphrey Bogart, James Cagney and Jimmy Durante. He completed a degree in commerce (majoring in accountancy) from the University of Chicago in 1952, and joined the army for two years. He began further studies at Loyola University, but dropped out in 1956, taking a series of jobs including copywriter, cigar salesman and an accountant of sorts – if he could not balance the petty cash, he'd make it up from his own pocket.

"Newhart is so diffident he can bite the hand that feeds him and make it feel like a manicure." – Gibert Millstein, *New York Times* magazine.

"I've been doing the same thing for 25 years and I'm still getting away with it." – Bob Newhart

Bob Newhart is one of very few comedians who can put his success down to the release of a

(1929-)

In his spare time, he acted in amateur groups and together with his friend Ed Gallagher, tape-recorded long and funny phone calls, sending them to radio stations in a bid to break into showbiz proper. It worked in part, and DJ Dan Sorkin got Newhart a job on a local radio morning show. Far more important was Sorkin introducing him to the President of Warner Brothers Records. Newhart performed some monologues for him, and the rest, as they say, is history.

Typical of the Newhart subject matter is a monologue about the training of bus drivers, who are drilled in the art of pulling away from the stop just as frail old ladies approach. Newhart played many nightclub gigs, but grew to loathe performing in front of a drunken audience, so he was thrilled to sign for a weekly half-hour TV show on NBC, in 1961: "It was a case of me either standing still or taking a big gamble. If I hadn't taken a gamble a few years ago, I'd still be an accountant." *The Bob Newhart Show* launched in October with a flexible but highly topical approach. Each show opened with Newhart in one of his specialities – the phone dialogue. Despite winning an Emmy and a National Academy of TV Arts and Sciences Award in April 1962, the show's sponsors, Sealtest Foods, pulled the financial plug in June that year.

It would be ten years before Newhart had his own TV show again, but in the interim he appeared many times on other people's shows and toured extensively. In 1972 he was commissioned by CBS for his first sitcom, again simply called *The Bob Newhart Show*. In this, he played a Chicago psychologist sharing his surgery rooms with a single dentist and their joint receptionist. A tough, no-nonsense type, she was the principal comic pivot. A big hit, the show ran every Saturday night for six years.

Newhart's career evidently moves in ten-year cycles, for he repeated the pattern of making films, guesting and touring before returning once again to the TV, in 1982. With the even more pared-down title of *Newhart*, this CBS offering saw him starring as Dick Louden, successful writer of DIY books but deeply bored with his Manhattan existence. Louden and his wife buy a dilapidated inn in rural Vermont. Just as they're settling in, Louden is offered the job of fronting a local TV show. There was a marked similarity of style between Newhart's two TV sitcoms but his relaxed humour remained eminently watchable. Indeed, he won awards in 1984, '85 and '86, for *Newhart*.

Performance Extract

SPEAKING TO ABRAHAM LINCOLN ON THE TELEPHONE...

"Hi ya sweetheart, how's everything going? How was Gettysburg? Abe, listen, I got your note, what seems to be the problem? You're thinking of shaving it off? Abe, you're kidding aren't you? Don't you see that it's part of the image? It's right, with a shawl and a stovepipe hat. You didn't have a shawl? Where did you leave the shawl this time, Abe? You left it in Washington... What are you wearing, Abe? A Cardigan. Abe, don't you see that doesn't fit with a stovepipe hat? Abe, trust in us on this – that's what you're paying us for... Abe? Abe, you got the speech? You haven't changed the speech have you, Abe? Abe, why do you change the speeches? You **typed** it? Abe, how many times have we told you – on the backs of envelopes, it will look ad lib, as if you wrote it on the way over..."

Leslie Nielsen

"Leslie Nielsen will never again be offered a serous role." – David Zucker.

"To have had the remarkable stroke of luck of going into *Airplane* and beginning my career in comedy wasn't an ambition. It was a dream." – Leslie Nielsen.

Leslie Nielsen's inclusion in this anthology of comedy is entirely due to David Zucker, co-producer of the brilliant disaster movie spoof, *Airplane*. Nielsen had previously spent 30 broadly successful years as a straight character actor, invariably playing someone in a position of authority. The Zucker brothers wanted Nielsen to ridicule the wooden style of Hollywood third grade movies – stand still, stand up, deliver the line, move... repeat.

His commanding, even imposing figure worked so well in spoof-

mode because he has the ability to deliver the corniest line with perfect seriousness, as if it were a matter of life and death.

His Life and Work

One of three sons of a Royal Canadian Mounted Policeman, Leslie Nielsen was born February 11th 1926 in Regina, Saskatchewan, Canada. It was a talented family: one brother, Gordon, went on to be a prominent businessman, and the other, Erik, became Deputy Prime Minister of Canada. A younger half-sister is an artist.

He trained as an actor at the Neighbourhood Playhouse, in New York, and worked as an announcer on both American and Canadian radio stations. Working as a serious actor, he appeared in over 60 movies and many plays. His was a moderate success without ever becoming a star. Due to his physique and manner, he was inevitably typecast: "If they wanted someone to play a banker, scientist, professor, military commander or aristocrat, I'd get the call."

Offscreen, he was a natural comic, but steadfastly refused to try comedy in front of the cameras, considering himself to be first and foremost a dramatic actor. Some of his extensive TV work includes the role of Lt Price Adams, the head of a team of police utilising high-tech electronic gadgetry to hunt down criminals in *The New Breed*; also *Bracken's World* about the lives of people in the movie business, and a true-life documentary series, *The Explorers*.

Airplane was the turning point. Along with Robert Stack, Lloyd Bridges and Peter Graves, Nielsen wickedly sent up the ramrod-stiff types he'd played for years. Nielsen was the doctor on board a plane where the crew and most passengers were stricken with food poisoning. Sample dialogue: "How long before we get to Chicago? I can't say. You can tell me – I'm a doctor." Nielsen commented that he simply brought out the latent humour in the scripts, something he'd never before been allowed to do. From *Airplane*, Nielsen has gone on to numerous spoof roles, such as *Police Squad*, a send-up of 1960s police show, for ABC. The series was short-lived, but led directly to *The Naked Gun*, in 1988. This was a tacky spoof police thriller, also

starring Priscilla Presley. The same deliberate style animated a set a terrific adverts for Red Rock cider – "it ain't red, and there's no rocks in it".

Next came *Repossessed*, another spoof, this time of *The Exorcist*, in which Nielsen played an eccentric who is called out of retirement to help a housewife who's having a 'devil of a time'. Linda Blair, who played the possessed girl in *The Exorcist* also starred. The sequel to *The Naked Gun, Naked Gun 2½ – The Smell of Fear*, saw Nielsen again playing Lt Frank Drebin. The picture includes a scene in which he repeatedly knocks a lookalike Barbara Bush flat on her face. The President and the First Lady invited Nielsen to meet them, saying it was one of their most favourite movies.

Performance Extract

From *The Naked Gun*:

NIELSEN, AS LIEUTENANT FRANK DREBEN, VISITS THE HOSPITAL BED OF A BADLY WOUNDED COLLEAGUE ALONG WITH HIS SUPERIOR OFFICER, ED. THEY MEET THE WOUNDED OFFICER'S GRIEF-STRICKEN WIFE, WILMA. FRANK ATTEMPTS TO CONSOLE HER BUT MANAGES TO SAY ALL THE WRONG THINGS.

Wilma: He's such a good man, Frank. He never wanted to hurt anyone. Who could have done such a thing?
Ed: Well, it's hard to tell.
Frank: Could be a roving gang of thugs, a blackmailer, an angry husband, a gay lover...
Ed: Frank! Get a hold of yourself!
Frank: A good cop, needlessly cut down and ambushed by some cowardly hoodlum...
Ed: That's no way for a man to die.
Frank: You're right, Ed. A parachute not opening, that's the way to die. Getting caught in the gears of a combine. Having your nuts bit off by a Laplander... that's the way I want to go...

Richard Pryor

"The quick action and non-stop dialogue are like a blackface parody of a white, fast-talking '30s comedy, mixed with uniquely black bad taste jokes about blacks which take one back to the old days at the Apollo Theatre." – Penelope Gilliat, *New Yorker*.

"Pryor is a star – a black man who stands on stage and ticks off the foibles of 'white folks' and 'niggers'. It is as if absolution were being granted." – David Ehrenstein, *L.A. Reader*.

Richard Pryor's wild, raunchy stage-act as the self-styled 'Crazy Nigger' centres on the issues of drugs, police harassment, and politics. It has brought fame and controversy in about equal measure. The wide eyes, arching eyebrows and mobile features have led some critics to say he has the most expressive face since Chaplin. Though in his early days he was delighted to be compared with Bill Cosby, the uninhibited and incorrigible Pryor is black first and foremost, a comedian second. As a stand-up comic he delivered surreal monologues, developing characters from people he actually knew, to make his political points.

He became a successful movie star, writer, producer and director, despite a notorious cocaine habit and a volcanic temper. A cocaine-related accident in 1980 left him with third-degree burns over half his body and a one-in-three chance of survival, but he kicked the habit and remains one of the most inventive and offbeat live performers.

(1940-)

His Life and Work

Richard Pryor is an only child, born December 1st 1940 in Peoria, Illinois. A popular boy, if often late to school, one of his teachers bribed him with the chance to perform for his peers for ten minutes each Friday if only he got to school on time. With that incentive, Pryor got to show off his Red Skelton Jnr character and his Jerry Lewis impression. Leaving school at 14, Pryor developed his comedy and was MC for talent shows at the Carver Community Centre, encouraged by Juliette Whittaker, who became his mentor. He became a father aged 16 but persevered with his comedy, aided by veteran vaudevillian Ray Le Roy, a near neighbour. Pryor's own father threw him out and he joined the army, serving in Germany and performing in the unit's amateur shows. As a full-time comic, he moved to New York in 1963, inspired by Cosby's example, and started performing around the clubs, especially in Greenwich Village. His first TV booking came in 1962, and in 1965 he achieved what was then the summit of his dreams – appearing on the *Ed Sullivan Show*. The Cosby-Pryor comparison was often made around this time, with Pryor gaining due credit for being unmistakably black, while Cosby's act could be just as funny from a white man.

In Las Vegas, Pryor's visible irritation at the restrictions placed on him got him fired, but the unexpurgated live shows sold well when released as records in 1969 and '71. He grew to resent having to bottle up what he really wanted to say on stage. He claimed he had many characters in his head, but that they were all black ghetto characters, using bad language, living on the edge. The frustrations boiled over in 1970, in a Las Vegas hotel. In mid-performance he erupted, shouting "What the fuck am I doing here?" and stormed off stage. As a live performer, Pryor was effectively blacklisted, but did continue to make an impact in film work, particularly as the pianist beaten to death by dope dealers in *Lady Sings The Blues*. As compere of a show in the Watts area of L.A. Pryor's sharp observation of the problems faced by young blacks won him this critical approval, from Jay Cocks of *Time* magazine: "What makes the jokes sting is not punchlines, but lethal accuracy."

Pryor won an Emmy for his writing for Lily Tomlin in 1973, and released two further albums in 1974, one of which, *That Nigger's Crazy*, went gold, and the other won him a Grammy. A bitter disappointment was not getting the lead role in *Blazing Saddles*. Dispute continues as to whether it was because of his cocaine habit, or Mel Brooks' seeking to get total credit. Either way, Pryor has reputedly never forgiven Brooks. Universal signed Pryor in 1975 to write, perform and produce his own material and a string of films ensued. He rowed with NBC over the boundaries of taste and comment in his ten-show series in 1977, later cut to five. 1980 brought the burns incident, but he recovered and continued to work busily through the decade and on into the '90s.

Key Films

The Busy Body (1967);
Lady Sings The Blues (1972);
Blazing Saddles (1975);
Car Wash (1976);
Silver Streak (1977);
Greased Lightning (1977);
Stir Crazy (1980);
Harlem Nights (1990).

Performance Extracts

"I always wanted to be something. I never wanted to be white, but niggers sounds so rough... I tried black cat with neat hair. I thought that was a problem – hair – and if the hair was straight then they'd dig me. I got it processed. Wrong."

"I went to jail to find justice, and that's what I found – just us..."

Vic Reeves & Bob Mortimer

"Savoury snacks aren't funny in the slightest, really, are they? Hula Hoops, they're not funny.... Yes – actually – savoury snacks are funny, a subject for much mirth and merriment." – Vic Reeves.

"I suppose if you have to analyse our comedy, you'd have to say that it's useless." – Vic Reeves.

Vic Reeves, Britain's self-styled 'Top Light Entertainer' and partner Bob Mortimer brought a new kind of cult humour to theatre and TV in the late 1980s. It is not so much surreal, as plain daft. A brisk mix of old-time vaudeville, Edward Lear-type 'nonsense', classic music hall, send-ups, and off-the-wall zaniness. In large part, it is the theatre of the absurd, the humour deriving from the most mundane and ordinary of things: savoury snacks, meat products, even chives.... In addition to its two hosts, the show is peopled by some moderately-unhinged regular characters such as The Man With The Stick, and The Living Carpets.

Their Life and Work

Vic Reeves was born Jim Moir in Leeds, Yorkshire on 24th January 1959 and was brought up in Darlington. He left school at 16 without any qualifications and reputedly began his working life with two jobs that would have challenged anyone to find the funny side – clearing greenhouses of rotting cabbages and castrating pigs. Not unreasonably turning his

Reeves (1959-), Mortimer (1959-)

back on such delightful employment, Reeves came to London as part of a dismal punk rock band, *Hot Murder*, in 1978. When it swiftly folded, Reeves was asked by a friend to help run an alternative comedy venue in south London, The Goldsmith's Tavern. Auditioning dozens of acts for the club, he rapidly decided he could do every bit as well and probably better. Soon he had his own show at the Tavern, which is where he met Bob Mortimer.

Mortimer is also a northerner, born 23rd May 1959 and brought up in Middlesborough. Another failed punk rocker – Mortimer's band was called *Dog Dirt* – but obviously keen to work in comedy, he had become a solicitor. A regular at Reeves' gigs, he

was an enthusiastic heckler, so working on the principle of if you can't beat them, get them to join you, Reeves invited him to be part of the act.

Their joint effort became a cult phenomenon with a large and loyal following. It transferred to the Albany Empire theatre under its now famous title – *Vic Reeves Big Night Out*. The approach was new and distinctive – Reeves would sit behind a desk as a bewildering array of strange characters appeared around him. Les is one such. He wears a white coat, is bald and has large glasses. The Living Carpets like the audience to stick strips of underlay to their heads when they come on stage. Why, no one knows. A favourite is a suited man, who ambles on with a paper bag on his head carrying a large stick. Reeves will ask his audience: "What do we cry when we see this Man With A Stick?" and they dutifully reply: "What's on the end of the stick, Vic?" Others features include Judge Nutmeg, Novelty Island, The Ponderers and Donald and David Stott. Audience participa-

tion is positively encouraged, and Reeves' show began to gain the same sort of cult following that *The Rocky Horror Show* still possesses.

Word went round the TV companies after Adam Ross (brother of Jonathan) saw the show, and Channel 4's Michael Grade paid a royal visit. He loved it, commissioning the pair for an ecstatically-received TV series, broadcast in 1990. A sell-out tour followed, a New Year's Eve special for C4, and then a second series of eight, in 1991. A second tour, this of 40-dates, will produce a video release.

Reeves must have felt like Midas in 1991. Everything he touched turned to gold – his pop single *Dizzy*, with *The Wonderstuff*, shot to number one in the charts, and a book built on the show's characters was also published. In 1992 Reeves and Mortimer were given a special BAFTA award for originality.

Performance Extracts

Vic: So, Man With The Stick, come in and put your stick down. I believe you're now going to tell us a bit about yourself and your good friend Terry.

Man With Stick: Yes, I am indeed, Vic. Some say that he treats me bad, but if you've got someone that you like, that can make you laugh all the time, then they're worth having. Terry's hilarious and he's popular with the lasses and all that.

He's very good with voices. Once he pretended to be the boss at work and said "You're sacked." So I left, and didn't get my proper job back. Then he often pretends to be a lass. He goes – "Man With A Stick, show us your willy." and I think it's a lass, so I get it out, and it's usually the boss..."

Vic: And are you going to reveal what's on the end of your stick? No? What a surprise... Well,

lay your stick low and come on over here.. Nice to see you, poppet, you're looking good.

Man With Stick: Always a pleasure, Vic, always a pleasure. Actually I'm a bit out of breath. I've just got here on my invisible horse. Ask the people if they like it, Vic.

Vic: People won't be able to see it.

Man With Stick: Why's that like?

Vic: Because you parked it behind the invisible steam-roller.

Both: Oooooh.

Joan Rivers

"That awful, vulgar, loud woman on stage – that's not me – I wouldn't want to be her friend." – Joan Rivers.

"Jane Fonda didn't get that terrific body from exercise. She got it from lifting all that money." – Joan Rivers.

"If I thought I would hurt anybody, I'd go crazy. That's why I pick on the biggies – they can take it. Comedy should also be on that fine line of going too far... otherwise it's pap." – Joan Rivers.

If Joan Rivers ran for President she might or might not make it to The White House, but she would certainly never be off the news bulletins. Everything she says is a soundbite, and 'bite' is the operative word. Dubbed, with good reason, 'the bitchiest woman in comedy', Rivers' rasping voice and outrageous insults have made her a real star in a country which, more than most, loves to mock the failings and foibles of its celebrities. To balance her attacks on others, she is also pretty blunt about herself: "My body's falling so fast, my gynaecologist wears a hard hat."

Catchphrase

"Can we talk...?"

But beneath the armour-plating, lies a warm and caring human being. Surely...?

Her Life and Work

Joan Molinsky was born in 1933, to an upper-middle class family in Brooklyn, the daughter of a GP. A small role in Mr Universe fuelled her existent desire to act, but to please her family, she enrolled at the Connecticut College for Women and later at Barnard College in New York, graduating in English and Anthropology in 1954. Pressurised by her parents to take a safer career option, she

(1933-)

became a publicity assistant and later a fashion coordinator, and married the heir to a successful clothing store business. The marriage crumbled within a year and was dissolved in 1958. Six months after the divorce, she cut herself off from her family and plunged into an acting career.

The seven years of hard work to establish herself are described in her best-selling autobiography, *Enter Talking*, published in 1986. To survive, she worked as an office temp by day and a lowly actress by night. Turning to comedy in 1960, initially merely as a money-earning prop for her serious acting ambitions, she played in strip-clubs, Mafia-owned venues and Catskill resorts, often being booed off stage.

Focusing more on the comedy side, she was cast in *Talent 60*, a Broadway revue, and this led to a critical break – two appearances on *The Tonight Show*, hosted by Jack Parr. Her first was interrupted by news flashes about a plane crash, and Parr didn't much like her anyway. Nevertheless, she had had her first whiff of national exposure, and wanted more. Discovering Lenny Bruce in the club scene around Greenwich Village, she found his comedy inspiring and began to use the same intensely personal and painful type of material and to address the audience directly. She toured with Jim Connell and Jake Holmes as Jim, Jake and Joan for two years (1963-4) but left to go

solo with a booking at the Duplex club. The owner said of her: "Untried and a little raw. Brilliant though. And she had the fastest comedy mind I'd ever seen." Carson's agent, Roy Silver, took her on and helped smarten up her material, leading eventually to an appearance on *Tonight* with Johnny Carson, in 1965. She was billed as a comedy writer who would discuss her life and career. It was tour de force, as she recounted her mother's attempts at marrying her off and the story of the motorist who ran over her wig and apologised for killing her dog. Suddenly, she was hot property on the club circuit and NBC put her under contract, and in 1968 created her own programme, called simply – *That Show*. It was a morning slot, opening with a Rivers monologue followed by ad-lib conversation with audience and guests, and ran until 1971.

Throughout the 1970s, Rivers was a regular guest host on *Tonight*, ultimately becoming its permanent guest host from 1983-86. Also in the '70s, Rivers wrote and starred in *The Girl Most Likely To*, a TV-movie about an ugly young student having plastic surgery and being transformed into an absolutely stunning beauty. It claims to be the most-screened film on American TV.

Rivers' stage material is very direct. She often works out much residual hostility about her unhappy childhood, when she was fat. Also strongly featured are the

Key TV/Films

TV: That Show (1968-71); The Girl Most Likely To (1973); An Audience With Joan Rivers; Can We Talk?; The Late Show Starring Joan Rivers.

Films: Mr Universe (1951); The Swimmer (1968).

brutal one-liners: about an over-weight Elizabeth Taylor – "mosquitoes see her and shout... buffet." In 1984, she published a book *The Life And Hard Times Of Heidi Abromowitz*, the story of her fictitious 'former best friend', which held the top slot on the New York book sales list for 18 weeks. She also visited Britain for the LWT series, *An Audience With...* gaining the highest viewing figure of the intermittent series. On the strength of that, the BBC signed her for six, shows entitled *Can We Talk?*

In the United States, *The Late Show Starring Joan Rivers* began in 1986, but ratings tailed off in '87. Eventually, the show was axed. Around the same time, Edgar Rosenberg, Joan Rivers' second husband, to whom she had been married for over 20 years, committed suicide. Rivers began the long haul back from personal and professional crisis with a successful run on Broadway, and collecting an Emmy for Best Talk Show, in 1990.

Performance Extracts ➤

"I was my own buddy at camp... in my class picture I was the whole front row."

"When I was little I had to beg a boy to play doctors with me. He finally agreed, but sent me a bill."

Will Rogers

"Will Rogers was probably the most-beloved man of our time... He was the most charitable, most tolerant man I have ever known. There wasn't an atom of envy in his system." – Eddie Cantor.

"I depend on the newspapers for most of my inspiration. Some days there is material for several good lines." – Will Rogers.

Think of Will Rogers and you think of the comic cowboy. Initially a star of silent pictures, he later transferred so successfully to the talkies with his brand of topical, acerbic gags that deflated the pretensions and dishonesties of politicians that he was seen as a statesman for the common man and was even urged to run for President. Rogers, however, was having none of it: "There's always too many comedians in Washington – competition would be too great for me."

At his peak he was compared to Mark Twain, being well-known not only as a comedian and film star, but as a journalist and writer.

His Life and Work

Born in Oklahoma in 1879 when the West still was pretty wild, Will Rogers hated schooling as a child, preferring to practice the very real cowboy skills of lassoing, riding, roping and branding. His showbiz association began in 1905 in a vaudeville show at Hammer-

(1879-1935)

Key Films

Laughing Bill Hyde (1918);
Water Water Everywhere (1919);
Scratch My Back (1920);
Connecticut Yankee in King Arthur's Court (1921);
Judge Priest (1934);
Steamboat Round The Bend (1935).

stein's Roof Gardens as a rope-spinning cowboy. Rogers is thought to be the first, and who knows, even the last, person to lasso a horse on stage. Together with Buck McKee, who rode the horse in the act, he performed at what were then called 'supper shows', new acts that went on during intervals between the established performers. To begin with, Rogers' act was limited to demonstrating his skills in silence. One trick was to rope the horse and the rider simultaneously, but separately, with two different ropes. A contemporary supper show performer suggested he should announce the trick beforehand, to build it up a little. The first time he tried this, the audience laughed... but far from being pleased, Rogers was irritated that they were chuckling at what he considered a straight introduction. He dropped the idea for a spell, but was later persuaded to re-introduce some patter. Showing obvious signs of being a competent ad-libber when he chose, the first gag he cracked on stage was when a trick went wrong and the rope ended up wound round himself. "A rope ain't so bad to get tangled up in, as long as it ain't round your own neck."

Rogers' act became more popular as he developed the asides, and in 1917 and 1918 he began appearing in the *Ziegfeld Follies*, and in 1921 in the *Ziegfeld Midnight Frolic*. With his dry patter focusing on political matters, and his mastery with the ropes being fully honed, Rogers seldom bothered to rehearse, preferring to spend the days studying the papers for new material, especially anything he could find to denigrate the Republicans.

In 1918 he made his film debut, encouraged by Sam Goldwyn, starring in *Laughing Bill Hyde*. In all he made around 24 silent films and rather fewer talkies. In the mid-20s, he remained as the big star of the *Follies*, but went back into movies in 1929, becoming one of the biggest money-spinners for Fox. His cinematic skill was to use the wisecracks very sparingly, instead conveying the image of a simple character full of emotions. Establishing his range, he didn't only appear in cowboy-mode. Rogers also variously played a tramp, a pig farmer, shop owner, country doctor and even a banker.

Rogers was perceived as something of a national hero in the '30s, being invited no fewer than five times to The White House to meet President Roosevelt. No other comic was so frequent a visitor. An illustration of his popularity is that there is only one statue of a comedian in Statuary Hall – that of Rogers, unpressed trousers and all.

Will Rogers also wrote successfully, publishing a series of books under the generic title, Rogerisms, including *The Illiterate Digest* and *Letters Of A Self-Made Diplomat*. When he was killed in a plane crash in 1935, he was mourned by the whole nation. In his short career he had achieved much, including touring as a lecturer and being Mayor of Hollywood. His son, Will Rogers Jnr, tried to continue the act, but was never so successful, although he did appear as his father in the 1950 bio-pic *The Story Of Will Rogers*.

Performance Extracts

TO A CONVENTION OF BANKERS:
"You're as fine a bunch of men as ever foreclosed on a widow. I am sure glad to be with you Shylocks..."

"We are a nation that runs in spite of and not on account of our government."

AFTER PLAYING POLO WITH THE PRINCE OF WALES:
"The Prince was well-mounted. He knows good horse flesh when he sees it. I was ridin' a coupla' dogs. One I could have got off and outrun myself."

Leonard Rossiter

"Leonard was one of the great farce actors of all time. He was nervous, vulnerable, a slave-driver, but no more punishing to others than he was to himself in the search for perfection." – Frances de la Tour.

"There is something birdlike about that side-long glance, rolling eye and beak of a nose. His Rigsby reminds me of a parrot sliding along its perch while mulling over some scandalous phrases." – Shaun Usher, *Daily Mail*.

"As the central character (Perrin), the bored ice-cream executive, Leonard Rossiter has the splendidly mobile features of a man suffering a terminal case of social indigestion." – Peter Dunn, *Sunday Times*.

It takes considerable skill to play an appalling snob, who is bigoted, sex-obsessed and cowardly, and yet win the audience's love by showing that character's desperate vulnerability. Leonard Rossiter pulled it off with consummate professionalism in the 1970s' sitcom *Rising Damp*. He topped even this with one of the very finest portrayals of the full mania of the male menopause in *The Fall And Rise Of Reginald Perrin*. As the bureaucracy-bound middle manager of Sunshine Desserts who fakes his own death but returns to found his own business empire, Rossiter was magnificent. In truth, Perrin –

as the series was known for short – was over-reliant on schoolboy humour (Reggie's visualisation of his mother-in-law as a hippo, and the whoopy cushions) but a virtuoso display from Rossiter saw it become another big success.

Though best remembered for his comedy work, Rossiter was previously a fine straight actor, having learned his craft in regional repertory companies, where, he said, he "developed a frightening capacity for learning lines.

The play became like elastoplast, which you just stuck on and then tore off."

His Life and Work

Born in Liverpool on October 21st 1926, Leonard Rossiter's father served as a volunteer ambulanceman during World War Two and was killed in 1942. Leonard wanted to study modern languages at Liverpool University and was

(1926-1984)

offered a place, but his recently widowed mother was unable to support him, so after National Service, he went to work for Commercial Union Insurance. Six years in the Claims Department unwittingly provided real-life experience that he would draw on in mocking the mundane in Perrin: "Twenty-two minutes late again – buffalo on the tracks at New Malden." Rossiter became interested in drama through a girl-friend of the time, a keen amateur actress. Between 1949 and '54 he appeared in around 35 amateur productions and found his day job was interfering with what he loved most: the acting. Turning professional in 1954, he moved to join the Wolverhampton Rep Company and played in some 75 productions there. Collecting further experience at Salisbury Rep, he was at the Bristol Old Vic Company from 1959 to '61. While there, Peter Hall, then director of the Shakespeare Memorial Theatre invited him to join, but Rossiter declined, saying: "Never leave a pond until you're the biggest fish in it."

Rossiter got his first TV role in 1963, as a straight actor in *The Buried Man*, about a dissatisfied Yorkshire Miner. He played Detective Inspector Bamber in *Z Cars* and got roles in shows such as *Steptoe And Son. Drums Along The Avon* was an important BBC play of the period, dealing with race relations, and he collected three awards for his starring role in *The Resistible Rise of Arturo Ui* in 1969.

It was *Rising Damp* that made him a household name. Rossiter played Rigsby, the conceited, mean, sneering, sleazy landlord, always bursting uninvited into his lodgers' rooms in the hope of 'catching them at it'. Usually unshaven, clad in grubby cardigan, he nevertheless persuaded himself he was God's gift to women, eternally lusting after Miss Jones (Frances de la Tour). The late Richard Beckinsale, playing an idol student, and Don Warrington, as a much-insulted black man, also co-starred. *Rising Damp* ran for four years from 1974 and a film version was made in 1980.

The Fall and Rise of Reginald Perrin overlapped with *Rising Damp*, beginning in 1976. Along with Pauline Yates as his long-suffering wife and John Barron as C.J. his authoritarian boss ("I didn't get where I am today, Reggie, by not recognising a good dessert when I see one.")

Key TV/Films

TV: Rising Damp; The Fall and Rise of Reginald Perrin.

Films: A Kind Of Loving (1962); Billy Liar (1963); Barry Lyndon (1975); Rising Damp (1980); Water (1985).

Rossiter played Reginald Iolanthe Perrin with touches of almost Cleeseian lunacy.

Rossiter's later work never matched these two triumphant peaks, although a series of commercials for Cinzano in which he invariably tipped the drink over Joan Collins kept him firmly in the public mind until his death in 1984.

Performance Extract

From *Rising Damp*:

RIGSBY (LEONARD ROSSITER) IS THE UNSCRUPULOUS AND SLIMY LANDLORD OF ALAN (RICHARD BECKINSALE) AND OTHERS.

Rigsby: When did you last study? The only thing you study is your navel. You even shave lying down. When did you last go to college? They must have forgotten what you look like.
Alan: Of course they haven't. I go regularly.
Rigsby: How can you – your hair's never dry.
Alan: Oh, it's my hair is it? Well, let me tell you you, Jesus Christ had long hair.
Rigsby: Don't you go comparing yourself to him – have a bit of respect.
Alan: Well, it's true. He did have long hair.
Rigsby: He didn't have a hair dryer... didn't give himself blow waves.

Rowan & Martin's Laugh In

"We didn't sing, didn't dance, didn't do impressions. We just developed this wonderful ability to read each other's minds. We never had anything written down." – Dick Martin.

Dan Rowan and Dick Martin's hit show was innovative and chaotic. Similar in some respects to the British *That Was The Week That Was*, the *Laugh In* was even more frenetic – they aimed for a laugh every 12 seconds. There was a constant barrage of jokes, flung out from a huge cast scattered all over a complex three-dimensional set. Cameo appearances from politicians or famous faces was an integral element of the mayhem. The show was particularly characterised by the use of a large number of catchphrases which became integrated into everyday usage by millions.

Their Life and Work

Dan Rowan was born in Beggs, Oklahoma, in 1922. Both parents appeared in a carnival-type revue, and the young Dan joined them on stage as soon as he had learned to sing and dance. Orphaned when he was 11, he was later adopted and at 19 took himself off to Los Angeles, hitch-hiking all the way. In California, he worked as an apprentice scriptwriter for Paramount Pictures, but the war intervened. Post-war, he settled down, married and became a full-time car salesman.

Dick Martin was also born in 1922, in Michigan. Always wanting to become a comedian, Martin

Catchphrases

Sock it to me;
Veeerry Interestink, but stupid;
Look it up in Funk and Wagnall's;
Here come de judge;
I'll drink to that;
You bet your sweet bippy;
Here in beautiful downtown Burbank;
I don't want to hear that...

(and many more).

Rowan (1922-), Martin (1922-)

got himself a job as a staff writer for the *Duffy's Tavern* radio show at the age of 22. He worked with several comedy partners, including Archie Lewis (billing themselves as The Real Martin and Lewis) but with little success. A writer by day, he was also a barman by night.

Rowan, bored with selling cars, set about becoming an actor in the early '50s. A friend, the actor Tommy Noonan, saw a comic potential in Rowan and introduced him, at a party, to Dick Martin. They struck up a good relationship and started writing and performing together. To begin with, Rowan was the comic and Martin played the straight man. Unfortunately, Martin could never remember a line unless it was funny, so they switched roles. Performing in a variety of modest venues, they found improvisation worked best, with Rowan making a straight-forward observation which Martin would then humorously invert, twist and play with verbally. Despite being contracted by Universal to make the Western spoof, *Once Upon A Horse*, they remained competent but not outstanding comics, never short of

work but in need of that one big break.

It came in 1966 when Dean Martin saw their show, and invited them onto his. During Dean Martin's summer break, they were chosen to host the replacement series. In 1967, they starred in a one-off special, produced by George Schlatter for NBC. The loose-format and ferocious pace struck the right notes, and a weekly series was commissioned. The first regular *Rowan and Martin's Laugh In* was broadcast on 22nd January 1968. An instant success, it shot to the top of the ratings almost immediately. Strongly topical, it featured a vast cast of over 40, but only four stayed with it through the entire six-year run – Rowan and Martin themselves, Gary Owens and Ruth Buzzi. Among the many top names who appeared at various times were Goldie Hawn and Lily Tomlin.

A regular device was the "sock it to me" line followed by a bucket of water or a pie in the face; others included the cocktail party, the Flying Fickle Finger Of Fate Award, Laugh In Looks at the News (Past, Present and Future),

Key Films

Once Upon A Horse (1957); The Maltese Bippy (1969).

Hollywood news and the joke wall at the end of each show. Goldie Hawn was the inevitable dumb blonde, Lily Tomlin the sarcastic telephone operator, Arte Johnson the heavily-accented German peering out through a pot plant and saying: "Veeerrry interestink – but stupid." The pace never slackened, but after two years at the top of the ratings, its popularity tailed off as the best of the early talent left to pursue solo careers and other ventures.

In 1974, Dan Rowan retired and Dick Martin went into directing TV comedies.

Performance Extracts ➤

DICK MARTIN BRINGS YOU NEWS OF THE PRESENT:
TV and movie-star Dean Martin narrowly escaped injury early this morning when he was found asleep on the Hollywood Freeway. When asked about it, Martin answered: "I can't understand it. I always sleep on the Santa Monica Freeway."
London: When queried about the recent rash of bank robberies in

England, Prime Minister Harold Wilson replied: "Well it does seem to indicate renewed confidence in the British pound..."

DAN ROWAN BRINGS YOU NEWS OF THE FUTURE:
Dublin 1988; With marriage in the Church recently sanctioned, the Archbishop and his lovely bride, the former Sister Mary Catherine, said, "this time it's for keeps."

GAGS:
"A friend of mine is afraid to fly, so he took a train and a terrible thing happened... a plane fell on it."
"In Florida, they use alligators to make handbags. Isn't it amazing what they can teach animals to do...?"

Saturday Night Live

"SNL's contribution to television has a lot to do with its spontaneity and the danger of doing it live." – Mitch Glazer, scriptwriter.

Saturday Night Live is a landmark show in American TV history. Beginning in the mid-70s, it was a live 90-minute show built around comedy, satire, zany humour and originality. SNL has proved to be the launchpad for a whole generation of American comics, in much the same way that *The Frost Report* and *That Was The Week That Was* did in Britain.

Among the long list of those who have gone on to carve major careers after appearing on SNL are Chevy Chase, Bill Murray, John Belushi, Eddie Murphy, Billy Crystal and latterly, the Wayne's World duo.

Its Origins and History

The key figure in the SNL story is producer Lorne Michaels. Toronto-born, he was comedy writer for Woody Allen, Phyllis Diller and Rowan and Martin before, at the age of 30, persuading NBC of the merits of a new style of show: fresh, outrageous, designed to bring the trendy urban viewer back to the network through the unpredictability of being live. Michaels got a provisional go-ahead and began assembling a team of writers and performers: Gilda Radner, Jane Curtin, Garrett Morris, John Belushi, Dan Aykroyd, Chevy Chase who were known collectively as the Not Ready For Prime

The Wayne's World duo of Mike Myers (left) and Dana Carvey (right) first hit the screens on Saturday Night Live.

Time Players. The very first show went out on 11th October, 1975.

Most of the performers also wrote, but in addition there were Michael O'Donoghue (as head writer), Rosie Shuster, Suzanne Miller, Tom Schiller, Alan Zweible and Don Novello.

Each week a guest host presented the show, beginning with George Carlin, and the list went on to include Buck Henry, Elliott Gould, Lily Tomlin, Dick Cavett, Steve Martin, Eric Idle, Richard Dreyfuss and Paul Simon. Non-showbiz hosts were also used – New York Mayor Ed Koch, for instance – but the most unusual must be Mrs Miskel Spillman, an 80-year old viewer who won the show's own 'Anybody Can Host' competition. Jim Henson and his Muppets were regulars in 1975-76, and major rock stars like *The Rolling Stones* and *Blondie* appeared, often alongside bizarre or totally unknown acts.

Many famous 'characters' were developed on the show – Chevy Chase as the earnest newsreader, and also as President Ford; Dan Aykroyd as the candidate; Gilda

Radner as Barbara Walters; and above all, Belushi and Aykroyd as Jake and Elwood – the Blues Brothers. In their identical outfits – Ray-Bans, black suits, ties and hats – they became the show's most popular pair, going on to make the brilliant cult movie of the same name which features the ultimate car chase.

At its peak in 1977 SNL's ratings were beating those for the *Tonight* show, but as cast members left to pursue individual projects the glorious anarchy of the first few years started to dissolve. When Lorne Michaels moved on in 1980, the ratings plummeted. Neither Jean Doumanian's nor Dick Ebersol's' teams could match the earlier successes, despite bringing in much fine new talent, including Eddie Murphy. The President of NBC threatened to axe the show in 1985, but Lorne Michaels returned to steer his ailing baby back towards the top of the ratings. Recently, a major success to rival that of the *Blues Brothers*, has been that of *Wayne's World*. It is a study of modern teenage American life as seen

through the eyes of two nerds in love with Alice Cooper, with Wayne played by Mike Myers and Dan Carvey as Garth. Talking in heavy metal speak, Wayne and Garth have become SNL favourites, and moved most successfully into film.

Performance Extract

A MESSAGE FROM PRESIDENT BUSH, TO PROVE HE'S FULLY FIT.

"Good evening. I have recently experienced what my doctors called aortic fibrillation – my heart going too fast... too fast... fast... scared some people but no, that heart beat is normal, normal, right down there. A whole normal area there (POINTS TO HEART) being monitored at all times. You see, doctors have implanted a tiny cardio device down in this whole thing over here (POINTS TO HEART) and as you can see the beat is steady. (VIEW OF HEART MONITORING EQUIPMENT) Let me turn up the volume, there. Here we go, you can hear it. (SOUND OF NORMAL HEART BEAT) Kind of odd isn't it, kind of gives you the creeps.. a little icky. Now let me show you how this thing works here. Mitzy Gaynor (HEART BEAT QUICKENS)... (HEAVY BREATHING)... That's a normal elevation for a healthy heterosexual man... bring it down, down... down. In a black satin teddy (HEARTS BEATS VERY FAST)... down... down... down. Turns out it was caused by something called Graves Disease... scary name... but not that bad. (PROCEEDS TO LIST PAST PRESIDENTS WITH MORE SERIOUS ILLNESSES, INCLUDING JFK HAVING THE CLAP THEN CLIMBS ONTO TREADMILL AND STARTS TO RUN) Does that look like a man about to die?'"

Alexei Sayle

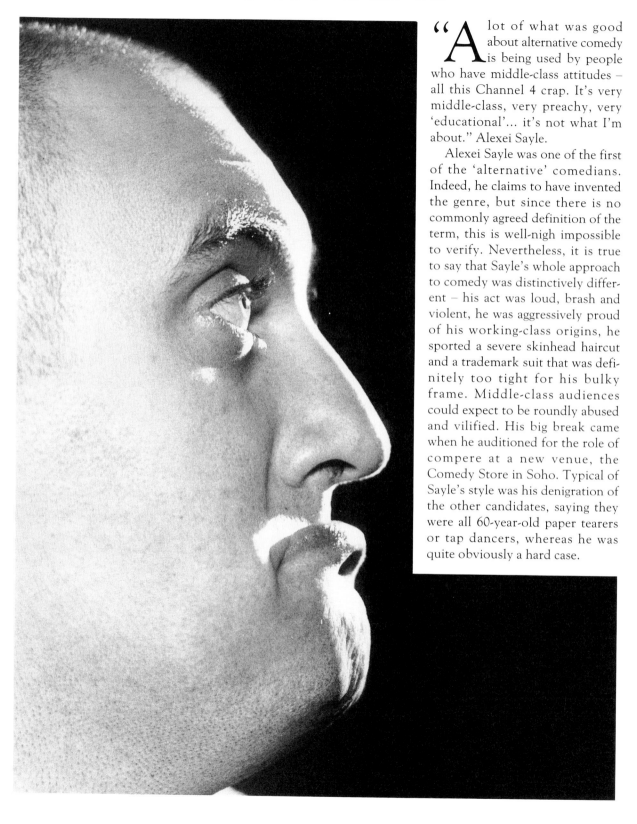

"A lot of what was good about alternative comedy is being used by people who have middle-class attitudes — all this Channel 4 crap. It's very middle-class, very preachy, very 'educational'... it's not what I'm about." Alexei Sayle.

Alexei Sayle was one of the first of the 'alternative' comedians. Indeed, he claims to have invented the genre, but since there is no commonly agreed definition of the term, this is well-nigh impossible to verify. Nevertheless, it is true to say that Sayle's whole approach to comedy was distinctively different — his act was loud, brash and violent, he was aggressively proud of his working-class origins, he sported a severe skinhead haircut and a trademark suit that was definitely too tight for his bulky frame. Middle-class audiences could expect to be roundly abused and vilified. His big break came when he auditioned for the role of compere at a new venue, the Comedy Store in Soho. Typical of Sayle's style was his denigration of the other candidates, saying they were all 60-year-old paper tearers or tap dancers, whereas he was quite obviously a hard case.

(1952-)

His Life and Work

Born in Liverpool in 1952, Sayle was christened Alexei after his maternal grandparents who had fled Russia before the First World War. His father was a Communist railwayman, his mother a Lithuanian Jewess, working for a football pools company. As a child, Sayle spent a number of holidays visiting East European countries.

At 17, he went to the Chelsea School of Art, to study painting. On leaving three years later, he had a succession of jobs (caretaker, school 'dinner lady', and a labourer on the Jubilee Line) but was sacked from every one. An old friend, Chris Cocker, invited him to be part of his Brechtian cabaret troupe, touring for a year. When the troupe split, Cocker and Sayle began trying their hand at comedy. Sayle was teaching General Studies at Chelsea by day, and performing comedy by night. Then came the Comedy Store audition....

What made Sayle stand out was his sheer physical presence, his high-speed rantings and his willingness to broach subjects hith-erto largely ignored. Sayle has said that two distinct groups developed at the Comedy Store: the vibrantly left-wing comics and the more bizarre and experimental type such as Mayall and Edmondson. Sayle found these less 'bitchy' than the political comedians (though his own work was largely based in the politics of poverty) and when a rival club, the Comic Strip, was established, he moved there. His star firmly in the ascendant, Sayle began extending his act and touring, often as support act to bands. TV exposure was also developing with appearances on *OTT* with Lenny Henry and in *Boom Boom Out Go The Lights* with Tony Allen, Keith Allen and Rik Mayall. He also popped up in *The Young Ones* and in the *Comic Strip* films.

Having given up live performance in 1985, he concentrated on writing: he published a novel, *Train To Hell*; had columns in both the *Sunday Mirror* and *Time Out*; and brought out two more projects – *Alexei Sayle's Great Bus Journeys Of The World*, and an illustrated book, *Geoffrey The Tube Train And The Fat Comedian*. Sayle also got roles in movies, and had his own TV series *Alexei Sayle's Stuff* in 1988, with a second series in 1991. His role as the devious forger in the TV drama *Selling Hitler* won him wide critical acclaim and in 1991 he toured Australia, his first live work for six years.

Catchphrase

"Who is that fat bastard?"

Performance Extracts

From his early years as a stand-up:

"This gig is actually in aid of a charity called Help A London Child – Kill A Social Worker... a very good cause, I think you'll agree. Although I am very alternative and do have my own roller skates and everything, there's one thing about the whole scene I can't get behind - and that is all the people taking drugs... and not giving me any, the bastards. I think, if you want to get out of your head, what's wrong with going out and having 93 pints of real ale, you know, Scruttock's Old Dirigible, with the twigs and bits of beak still in it..."

"They fucking love me down the Arts Council, you know... down Piccadilly with the ponchos and the lapsang souchong, you know... and the trousers tucked into the boots. They say, here's a working-class half-wit – let's patronise him. I live in Fulham, right? I fucking love going down the Riverside Studios, you know what I mean... seeing an avant-garde Polish mime troupe doing all the old bollocks..."

Peter Sellers

"I'm a classic example of all humourists – only funny when I'm working." – Peter Sellers.

For someone who created one of the funniest screen characters of all time, the hapless, bumbling Inspector Clouseau in the *Pink Panther* films, Peter Sellers also produced an awful lot of dross. The extremes of his work reflect the extremes of his personality as a man – brilliant, charming and inspiring one minute, volatile, philandering and tempestuous the next. At root, he was a deeply insecure individual, constantly in need of reassurance, but regularly losing his temper, his friends and his wives in the search for perfection.

His Life and Work

Peter Richard Henry Sellers was born in Southsea, Hampshire on the 8th September 1925, into a theatrical family. Gaining an early taste for the stage, by the age of 18 he could play drums, piano and ukelele, and was drumming with several bands. Joining the forces entertainments troupe, ENSA, he performed for the troops during the war and on quitting the Army was entertainments manager at a holiday camp for a year. A successful audition for the Windmill Theatre gave him the confidence to ring the BBC producer Ron Speer, mimicking the voices of the well-known broadcasters Richard Murdock and Kenneth Horne, praising the young Sellers, and recommending him for a job – which he got.

Jimmy Grafton's pub had a small coterie of comics who

drank and wrote there – Milligan, Bentine, and Secombe for three. When Sellers joined the group, they made a pilot's recording of a programme they wanted to call the *Goon Show*. The BBC liked it, but insisted on calling it *Crazy People*. The innovative show was packed with offbeat humour, lots of silly voices quick-fire repartee. The *Goon Show*, as it subsequently became known, was a huge hit,

running from 1951 to 1958. The film *Points To Paradise* (1951) utilised the Goonish characters to the full – Secombe was a simple-minded pools winner and Sellers a wool-gathering major related to Bloodneck. When John Redway, who had been a casting director, went independent he put Sellers into the movie *Orders Are Orders* as a private soldier in the story of an American film unit infiltrating

(1925-1980)

a British barracks. *The Ladykillers* in 1955 was an important film for Sellers. It was his only Ealing Comedy, but in it he appeared alongside Alec Guiness who epitomised everything Sellers was striving for as an actor – chiefly the ability to become somebody else.

With *The Goons* thriving, a hit record (*I'm Walking Backwards For Christmas*) and his radio show Finkel's Cave, Sellers was becoming a star. *The Naked Truth*, a black comedy in which he played several roles, established him as a serious actor, and Peter Hall, the theatre director, cast him on stage in *Brouhaha*. Sellers however began to tinker with characterisations, making his performance ever more Goon-like. Nineteen-fifty-nine brought the important picture, *I'm All Right Jack*, which won Sellers a British Academy Award for his portrayal of Fred Kite, the communist shop steward who sighed when he thought of Mother Russia.

Sellers personal life was in turmoil. His first wife, Anne Hayes, was growing weary of his behaviour and divorce was looming, but before the final split, he went to Hollywood to make the first, and best, of the *Pink Panther* films, for Blake Edwards. Sellers said of his most famous role: "I'll play Clouseau with great dignity, because he thinks of himself as one of the world's best detectives."

He appeared in many films throughout the '60s, '70s and '80s – among the most notable being *Dr Strangelove*, from the Peter George novel *Red Alert*, *There's A Girl In My Soup*, further *Pink Panther* films, and in 1979, *Being There*. In this he played an illiterate gardener who becomes a national celebrity on account of his homespun philosophising. This role won Sellars an Academy Award as best Actor. His final picture was *The Fiendish Plot of Dr. Fu Manchu*, released two years after his death in 1980.

Peter Sellers was a troubled man, suffering from repeated bouts of depression and was almost child-like in his insecurity. He had a total of eight heart

Key Films

Orders Are Orders (1954);
The Ladykillers (1956);
I'm All Right Jack (1959);
Two Way Stretch (1960);
Lolita (1962);
The Pink Panther (1964);
Dr Strangelove or How I Learned To Stop Worrying And Love The Bomb (1964);
What's New Pussycat (1965);
Being There (1979).

attacks, and had four wives, including Britt Ekland. Barry Took has likened him to a chameleon, and indeed Sellers' anguish and uncertainty can be seen in his own bittersweet comment "There is no me. I do not exist. There used to be a me, but I had it surgically removed."

Performance Extracts

From *What's New Pussycat*:

SELLERS, AS PSYCHIATRIST DR FRITZ FASSBENDER, ACCIDENTALLY MEETS ONE OF HIS PATIENTS – PETER O'TOOLE – IN A STRIP CLUB. AS THEY TALK, THEIR EYES NEVER LEAVE THE SHOW.

Sellers: Aaaaaaaaah...
O'Toole: Ooooooooooh...
Sellers: I vas really interested, you know, in your case. It intrigued me, those things you said about vat happens and all of zat, and

I... er... decided to follow you here.
O'Toole: Er... if you followed me here, how did you contrive to be here before me?
Sellers: Er... I followed you very fast...

From *The Case of the Muckinese Battlehorn*:

SELLERS, AS SUPERINTENDENT QUILT, AND SPIKE MILLIGAN, AS SERGEANT BROWN, ENTER A ROOM TO LOOK FOR CLUES.

Milligan: (POINTS DRAMATICALLY TO FLOOR) Look, Sir! An impression of a heel!
Sellers: (STUDYING ORNAMNET WITH MAGNIFYING GLASS) Very clever, Brown, but we haven't time for your impressions now.

Phil Silvers

"Silvers was an old vaude-villian. He knew how to get a laugh even if he was only in front of the camera crew." Bob Foster, TV Critic.

Phil Silvers began his career in vaudeville, where he developed a unique comic persona, that of a lovable conman and trickster always plotting, always scheming and always on the make. It was here that he adopted the horn rimmed spectacles "to add something to my sort of blank face," he explained.

This persona was later developed to become Sergeant Bilko, the cynical wiseguy in *The Phil Silvers Show*. The TV role brought him international admiration.

"Engaging bespectacled Phil Silvers who works like a truck horse at the speed of a race horse and with the timing of a steeple-chaser." *Time.*

His Life and Work

Born in Brooklyn on May 11th, 1912, to Russian immigrant parents, Philip Silversmith was the youngest of eight.

From an early age his singing ability was remarked upon and by the age of 11, he was regularly singing at the local movie house whenever anything went wrong with the projector. At 13, Silvers made his debut at the Palace Theatre, Manhattan, with the vaudeville act Gus Edwards' School Days Revue. He toured with them until his voice broke three years later.

As the popularity of vaudeville declined, Silvers began playing night clubs and making two-reel movies. In 1934, he joined the Minsky burlesque troupe, eventually becoming the star. It was at this point that he added the spectacles. In 1939, he left to star in *Yokel Boy*, an unsuccessful musical, but his performance attracted the attention of MGM and he was given a contract.

His movie debut was in *The Hit Parade* (1940). Between 1942-45 he appeared in over 20 movies, usually in a supporting role. He joined Sinatra for a USO show in the Mediterranean in 1945. But the musical *Top Banana* in 1951 was the turning-point of his career. On Broadway, the show was an instant hit and Silvers later

(1912-1985)

toured the country with it, before making a film version in 1954. The TV offers flooded in.

He signed with CBS in 1954. Writer/producer Nat Hiken began looking for a suitable sitcom vehicle for CBS's newly-acquired star. Between them, they hit upon Ernest T Bilko, the eternal loser who always dreamed he was a winner. It took months for the series to be shaped. CBS were nonetheless confident of the project and asked for 21 half-hour episodes. Originally entitled 'You'll Never Get Rich', the first show was broadcast in September of 1955.

As the cynical wiseguy Sergeant Bilko, Silvers played the little man against the system. The army was riddled with bureaucracy and thus the perfect place for a conman to hustle in. The supporting cast included Private Duane Doberman, played by Maurice Gosfield and Colonel John T Hall, the unit's ineffectual commanding officer, played by Paul Ford. The story dealt with a section of the army in peace time, after the Korean War. While they are waiting for their 'freedom call', the men in the ranks play endless poker, run pointless drills and suck to the officers. Bilko ran the motor pool and was constantly looking for ways to part the soldiers from their paychecks,

normally through poker, pool or raffles.

The Phil Silvers Show was one of the first to use black actors as a matter of course. Among the staff writers on the award-winning show was the now famous playwright Neil Simon and Dick Van Dyke, and Alan Alda also made appearances. After 138 episodes, the last Bilko was broadcast on September 11th, 1959.

In 1963, *The New Phil Silvers Show* was made for CBS. The characters were similar, but Harry Grafton (Silvers) was now a civilian in charge of Osborne Industries. It was nowhere near as successful as the original and ran for only a year. Silvers continued to guest star on other television programmes and from 1969 to '71 played Shift Shafer in *The Beverly Hillbillies*.

Although he continued to tour and appear on stage and in various films, including *How The Other Half Loves* and *A Funny Thing Happened On The Way To The Forum* both in 1971, Silvers never achieved the same success after *Sergeant Bilko* and there were constant rumours about how lonely and underworked he was. When *The National Enquirer* described him as "a lonely has-been", Silvers successfully sued them for ten million dollars. His autobiography, cynically titled *The*

> ## Key Films
>
> Tom, Dick And Harry (1941);
> You're In The Army Now (1942);
> Cover Girl (1944);
> It's A Mad Mad Mad Mad World (1963);
> A Funny Thing Happened On The Way To The Forum (1966);
> Won Ton Ton (1976).

Laugh Is On Me, was published in 1974.

Phil Silvers died on November 1st, 1985.

Performance Extract →

From *The Phil Silvers Show*:

Colonel: Bilko, you know I've tried to arrange the military schedule of this post so as not interfere with your poker games.

Bilko: Sir, I'm merely trying to create an atmosphere for my men.

Colonel: I know very well the atmosphere you're creating round here. They're starting to call this post Little Vegas....

Smith and Jones

"We make a good team. I'm laid back, Griff is edgy and tense but drives straight to the heart of any problem." Mel Smith.

"Mel's the man about town who couldn't care less. I'm the boring, domesticated Mr Average. I tend to be the hysterical, neurotic one." Griff Rhys Jones.

Mel Smith and Griff Rhys Jones first made a major public impact on *Not The Nine O'Clock News*, but seemed somewhat overshadowed by the other members of the team, Rowan Atkinson and Pamela Stephenson. Smith is wry, relaxed and sarcastic, Jones frantic and frenzied. Though they have made many programmes together, each has a separate and successful career in his own right.

Their Life and Work

Griff Rhys Jones, the son of a doctor and a nurse, was born 16th November 1953, went to Brentwood School in Essex and then on to Cambridge University, where he read History. While there he joined the Footlights Club and performed alongside Clive Anderson and Rory McGrath. After graduating, Jones got a job at BBC radio, where he produced Rowan Atkinson's Radio 3 series. He also continued to perform with Anderson and McGrath in their show called *An Evening Without*.

Mel Smith was born 3rd December 1952, and grew up above his father's betting shop in Chiswick, west London. He went up to New College, Oxford to read experimental psychology and went on to direct at theatres in Bristol, Sheffield and London. He directed for six years before ever stepping out in front of an audience.

In 1979, producer John Lloyd was assembling a team for a new satirical sketch show built on topi-

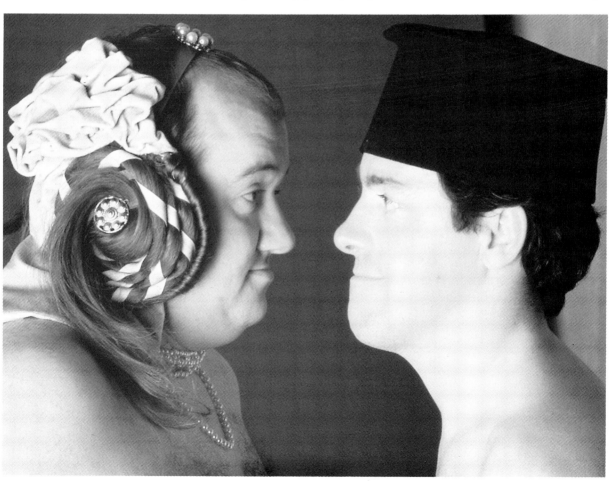

Smith (1952-), Jones (1953-)

cality. *Not The Nine O'Clock News* made instant stars of the extraordinary Atkinson and the outrageous Stephenson. Four series were made, all highly successful, and yet Smith and Jones remained less noticed. Opposites attract, it is said, and certainly the pairing of the intense and agitated Jones with the laconic Smith has become a major force in modern comedy. 1983 saw their first series together, rather than as part of a larger team, in *Alas Smith and Jones*. A favourite set-up involved a very tight head-to-head shot, the two characters talking intently about matters of great import (sex, often). The lack of movement and sharp focus centred attention on the sharp scripts. This recurring set-up is their principal trademark. They made four series for BBC2 under the "Alas" title, before crossing to LWT for two series of *The World According To Smith And Jones*, in 1986-87. Jones has subsequently described this work as "embarrassing tat." Returning to BBC1 in 1989, they made two more series, called simply, *Smith And Jones*, produced by their own company, Talkback. Both had featured separately and together, in numerous TV commercials, so in 1980 they had formed their own business, Not Any Old Radio Commercials, later to be renamed Talkback.

Their forays into the film world as a team have had mixed results. The first effort, *Morons From Outer Space* in 1985, with Jimmy Nail, Joanne Pearce and Dinsdale Landen, was an utter flop, but when they teamed up in the film of Tom Sharpe's novel, *Wilt*, in 1989 they recorded much greater success, while not quite capturing the frantic logic-chopping lunacy of the book. In all Sharpe's novels, names are clues: thus Jones, as Henry Wilt, is the henpecked college lecturer deeply disillusioned with the thankless task of trying to introduce day-release plumbers and meat-packers to the joys of classic literature. Fantasising about murdering his over-bearing wife Eva, he buries an inflatable sex-doll in a foundation shaft, and is arrested for murder... his interrogator, Smith, is Inspector Flint, as determined as he is stupid.

Smith and Jones have written books together and recorded albums too – *Bitter And Twisted*; *Scratch And Sniff*; and others. They won an Emmy for *Alas Smith And Jones*, a British Comedy Award for *Smith And Jones*, and individual awards.

Working apart, each has a considerable range: Jones has appeared in plays as varied as *Charley's Aunt*, *Wind In The Willows* and *Twelfth Night*, and

Key Films

Morons From Outer Space (1985); Wilt (1989).

also in the opera *Die Fledermaus* and in a TV version of another Tom Sharpe novel, *Porterhouse Blue*. He has also directed.

Mel Smith's career has included film direction (*The Tall Guy*, written by Richard Curtis), acting roles in *Muck And Brass* and in *Colin's Sandwich*. He has continued to direct in the theatre, and is Assistant Director at the Royal Court, and Associate Director at the Crucible and Young Vic theatres in London.

Performance Extract

Talking in a head-to-head about sperm donation.

Jones: Do you have the lights out there? When you're...?
Smith: No, no. There's nobody there but you.

Jones: Well where was this woman then, while you're...?
Smith: Don't know. Might be anywhere. Probably shopping.

Spitting Image

"The whole thing sounds common, vulgar and an insult to the Royal Family." Barbara Cartland.

"There are only two programmes that matter to a politician – *Question Time* and Spitting Image." Gordon Brown, M.P.

"Please could I have a copy of last night's show. I didn't see it, but apparently I gunned down Robert Runcie." (the Archbishop of Canterbury). Mrs Mary Whitehouse on the telephone to the Spitting Image production offices.

If there were prizes for controversy, Spitting Image would walk off with the lot. It is hard to decide which is the more cruel – the caricature latex puppets or the words they utter. Some of the most vitriolic characterisations have been of Roy Hattersley's spittle problem, David Steel living in David Owen's pocket, Kenneth Baker as the slug, Norman Tebbit as the Chingford skinhead and Gerald Kaufman as Hannibal Lecter from *The Silence Of The Lambs*. Most controversial of all

however is their treatment of the Royal Family. This generates more protest mail than any other topic on television. It is a show which one either loves or hates; there is no middle ground.

Its History

The Spitting Image idea began with Martin Lambie-Nairn of LWT, responsible for the graphics on their current affairs shows. A regular listener to Radio 4's satirical news-based show, *Week Ending*, he felt that television should have its equivalent. In 1981 he dreamed up the idea of an adult version of the *Muppets*, and approached Peter Fluck and Roger Law, cartoonists and puppeteers specialising in Plasticine models of politicians. Fluck and Law had first met aged 16 at the Cambridge Art School and worked together and separately on various projects down the years. They enthusiastically agreed to Lambie-Nairn's proposal, and brought in Tony Hendra, an Englishman who'd worked for some time in the United States on the *National Lampoon* magazine. Hendra suggested expanding the original news-only idea to include other areas – showbiz, sport, the business world, movies etc. John Lloyd, of *Not The Nine O'Clock News* fame, was appointed producer and after long negotiations Central TV funded a half-hour pilot. Called UNTV, this was never screened, but featured the Secretary General of the United Nations watching a bank of TV

monitors showing broadcasts from around the world. Among the clips were puppets of President Reagan giving a fireside chat, Tebbit and Thatcher opening the mail in the UK, and a royal corgi seizing a royal baby and tossing it off a balcony. Central loved it and wanted 26 weekly shows. Lloyd pleaded for and won a reduction to 13.

The first to be broadcast went out on 6th February 1984, receiving very modest notices from the Press. Changes were made to the writing team, with Rob Grant, Doug Naylor and Ian Hislop coming in. Within a year, Spitting Image had won over both the public and a sceptical Broad-casting Press Guild who, in February 1985, gave the show the Best Light Entertainment Award. Later that year, it won a Bronze Rose at Montreux and first prize in the Banff TV festival in Canada. The voices of the characters were obviously important, and the highly skilled team of mimics included at various times Steve Nallon as Mrs Thatcher, Chris Barrie as Reagan,

Prince Charles and Neil Kinnock. Others were Enn Reitel, Jan Ravens, Jon Glover, Harry Enfield and John Sessions. One-off specials were produced for the 1987 General Election, the tenth anniversary of Mrs Thatcher's time as Prime Minister, and for Reagan's retirement.

After the fifth series many of the original writers moved on and a new crew including Mark Burton, John O'Farrell and Pete Sinclair came in, with significant contributions also from Stuart Silvere, Steve Punt and Geoff Atkinson. The show was the subject of a *South Bank Show Special* in which its 'victims' were confronted by their puppets and Mary Whitehouse was told to lighten up by Pope John Paul II.

Performance Extract

The Queen is Dead, by Burton/O'Farrell.

INTERIOR, BUCKINGHAM PALACE. A DOOR CREAKS OPEN AND PRINCE CHARLES PUTS HIS HEAD AROUND.

Charles: Mother?

IN THE FOREGROUND, THE QUEEN IS SLUMPED FORWARD IN A CHAIR. A BELL TOLLS IN THE DISTANCE.

Charles: (RUSHES UP TO HER) Mother? (HE SHAKES HER)

Mother? Oh, my God.... Andrew, Edward, everybody come quickly.

THE OTHERS RUSH IN, LOOKING CONCERNED.

Andrew: (FEELING HER PULSE) She's... dead.
Charles: But, but, she can't be... (MORTIFIED) It's a national tragedy... But I must be strong... for... I, I must now lead... I... I am King (GROWING IN STRENGTH) after all these

years... King at last... The Queen is dead... Long live the King.

PAUSE

THE QUEEN SITS UP AND BURSTS OUT LAUGHING, THEN THE REST OF THE FAMILY JOIN IN TOO.

Charles: Oh... I always fall for that one.

Jacques Tati

"Making people laugh is a wonderful profession."– Jacques Tati. "Observation is everything." – Jacques Tati.

"Tati's most original idea is that the world around him is funny. As a result, he invented a form of comic story in which the central character merely wanders about and sets people laughing." Pierre Etaix, long-time collaborator.

Jacques Tati was a tall, angular man and a superb visual comic in the tradition of silent films. He

(1908-1982)

only made five major films in his career, but each could justly be described as classic. The key character is that of Monsieur Hulot, a gentle French eccentric sadly observing the erosion of old values. A complete perfectionist, Tati would spend years making a film, devising the ideas, writing them up, preparing the ideal locations, directing and performing. To enhance the realism of his pictures he would often use non-professional actors.

His Life and Work

Born Jacques Tatischeff in Le Pecq in France on October 9th, 1908. His father had his own picture-framing business and was deeply disappointed when the young Jacques decided not to enter the family firm. Briefly a rugby player, Tati entered the French music hall circuit in the early 1930s with an act that mimicked and parodied the sports stars of the era. He would perform anywhere, including circuses in those tough times, but did appear on the same bill as Maurice Chevalier in 1935 and won some positive notices for his performance in the ABC revue. Seeking to record some of his best routines for posterity, Tati drifted into the world of short films, landing roles in two films directed by Claude Autant-Lara: *Sylvia et la Fantome* in 1944 and *Le Diable au Corps* in 1947. These experiences convinced him that film should be his chosen medium.

Tati appeared in the short film *L'Ecole des Facteurs* in 1947, and this was made up into a feature length picture two years later, *Jour de Fete*. Here, Tati plays a postman

who, struck by the modern efficiency of the American postal system, tries to streamline his own operation.

The first picture he took full control of was *Les Vacances de Monsieur Hulot*. Four years in the making, it introduced the character he would play for the rest of his life. The accident-prone Hulot is not a comedian as such, he rather stumbles through life, constantly aspiring to social graces and usually failing, illustrating the comedy that surrounds him. In *Les Vacances de Monsieur Hulot*, his attempts to learn tennis and to ride are hilariously chaotic and come to a climax when he sets off the fireworks stored in an outhouse. With his shabby clothing, silly hat, too-short trousers, pipe and umbrella, Hulot was an international success.

The perfectionist in Tati saw Hulot could go on to other situations, but spent two full years walking the streets of Paris with Jean L'Hote, author of the book *Mon Oncle*, in search of ideal locations. Though Tati directed, Hulot was not the main character. Instead, he weaves in and out of the storyline, eternally confronted by the new affluence of the middle-classes. Two versions of *Mon Oncle* were shot – one in French and the other in English.

His third venture brought disaster. Unable to find the right settings for *Playtime*, he paid for a stretch of wasteland at Vincennes on the outskirts of Paris to be developed into 'Tativille'. After six years work, the film was released in 1967. Its commercial failure put Tati deep into debt.

The bubble appeared to have burst, but a Dutch company

Key Films

Jour de Fete (1949);
Les Vacances de Monsieur Hulot (1953);
Mon Oncle (1958);
Playtime (1967);
Traffic (1971);
Parade (1973).

funded *Traffic*, the story of the transportation of a car/caravan from Paris to Holland for the Dutch motor show. Hulot is the hero.

His final picture to be completed was *Parade*, a 60-minute film with Swedish financing in which two children visit a circus and see Monsieur Lloyd (Tati) presenting and performing the various acts himself. This picture won the Grand Prix du Cinema and also a gold medal in Moscow.

He was working on another film – *Confusion*, with American writer Jonathan Rosenbaum – when he died, on November 5th 1982.

The Three Stooges

"The public upon which the screen depends for its existence appears to be divided into roughly two groups: one composed of those who laugh at The Three Stooges, and the other made of those who wonder why." – *Motion Picture Herald*, 1937.

The Three Stooges were among the finest physical comedians of their time. Masters of burlesque and vaudeville, they were superb clowns and slapstick comics. Many attribute their success to their unpretentious view of their own work – that it was knockabout comedy in its own right, not needing complex ideas.

Their career spanned nearly 50 years in all, and their influence is still seen today, as in *Lethal Weapon II* where Mel Gibson is addicted to watching their films.

Their Life and Work

The Three Stooges took a long time to become an established trio. When they did, in 1933, they were Moe Howard, his younger brother Jerry (who was known as Curly) and Larry Fine. Prior to this, a third Howard brother, Samuel (known as Shemp) had

been involved but left to go solo. Moe Howard was born in 1905, Curly Howard and Larry Fine, both in 1911. MGM put them under contract to appear with comedian Ted Healy in film shorts. One of their best collaborations was *Dancing Lady*, which also starred Clark Gable and Joan Crawford. Set back-stage at a musical, Healy was Gable's right-hand man, and the Stooges were

seen basically wreaking havoc among the scenery and equipment. After this the threesome began to go it alone. They all appeared in *Woman Haters*, but as individuals rather than as a group. Assuming more control of their projects, they moved on to make *Punch Drunks*, and famously, *Men In Black* – a spoof of the movie *Men In White*. This two-reeler was their first and only nomination for an Academy Award.

Dozens more were to follow as they were now contracted to Columbia for eight shorts year. This allowed them plenty of time to continue touring vaudeville halls with their live act.

In 1935, they had a new director, Del Lord, who in the first of two stints with them, added a subtler touch to their flamboyant slapstick style. In 1945, Edward Bernds directed what many consider to be their finest short, *Micro Phonies*, but disaster struck two years later when Curly suffered a stroke and was forced to retire. His older brother Shemp returned to the trio as his replacement, and Curly died in 1952. That same year The Stooges experimented with the first comedy 3D films, under the direction of Jules White, producing *Spooks* and *Pardon My Backfire*.

Shemp died in 1955, and Joe Palmer stood-in briefly before Joe Besser took over for a further two years. Besser had previously worked with Abbott and Costello, so he certainly knew his business, but when his wife fell ill, he too retired to care for her. Critics argued that The Stooges golden era had passed. By the mid-50s, their low-budget approach was looking tired and stilted, and the

Key Films

Over 200 shorts and nearly 40 feature films.

Shorts: Woman Haters (1934); Uncivil Warriors (1935); Ants In The Pantry (1936); Rockin' Through The Rockies (1940); Micro Phonies (1945).

Features: Soup To Nuts (1930); Dancing Lady (1933); Start Cheering (1938); My Sister Eileen (1942); Have Rocket Will Travel (1959); The Outlaws Is Coming (1965).

market for shorts was fast disappearing. Their contract with Columbia ended in 1957 and The Stooges were effectively unemployed, and were said to be on the point of disbanding. Columbia, in an inspired move, repackaged 28 of their early shorts for television, and found 75 buyers around the world. The Stooges were a huge success all over again.

Naturally delighted, Columbia signed them up for a series of feature films, beginning with *Have Rocket Will Travel*. They started to appear on television, and were even turned into a successful TV cartoon series of 160 episodes. Larry Fine suffered a stroke in 1970, and although Moe valiantly tried to keep going, bringing in Emil Sitka, one of their long-time supporting cast, the magic had gone. Fine and Moe Howard both died in 1975.

Tom and Jerry

"I knew that no matter where you ran it, the minute you saw a cat and a mouse, you knew it was a chase." – Joe Barbera

"We have discovered the harder they hit, the louder they laugh. So we didn't change our formula." – Bill Hanna

Few comic characters are instantly recognisable all over the world. Fewer have a universal comic touch. Fewer still remain as funny over 50 years on. Of human comedy stars perhaps only Chaplin passes all three tests. Then there is Tom and Jerry.

They first fought their eternal conflict on February 10th, 1940, when the cat (then named Jasper) chased the innocent mouse up and down the house, sending pot plants left, right and centre. Jasper is put 'on probation' by the house-keeper, so the little mouse does his utmost to land him in it, throwing glasses off the sideboard, shoving dishes from the sink... *Puss Gets The Boot* was the title of the very first Hanna-Barbera collaboration for MGM. For 18 years, this duo produced the finest of animations. Later efforts by others were pale imitations, but

the indestructible Tom and Jerry remain classic entertainment for children of all ages.

Their History

The year was 1939, and although the world was on the brink of war, Hollywood was booming. Magnificent films like *Gone With The Wind* and *The Wizard Of Oz* were pouring out of the big studios. Disney had achieved a smash with *Mickey Mouse*, and Warner had *Bugs Bunny*. MGM wanted a slice of the action. Gambling, they teamed Bill Hanna and Joe Barbera though neither had a successful track record in cartoon work.

Hanna was born in New Mexico in 1910, working initially at the Harman-Ising studio washing used celluloid for re-use. Promoted to the ink and paint area, he soon became a cartoon director.

Barbera was born in New York, in 1911, and from an early age was a talented artist. He was employed in a bank, but loathed it, preferring to sell cartoons to newspapers and magazines. Fascinated with animation, he took an evening class in the subject and secured a job as a painter at the Famous Studios where *Popeye* was made, and went on to the Van Beuren studio where he became an animator within six months.

They first met at Terrytoons in 1937, but didn't work together until two years later. Their brief was to come up with a cartoon so vivid, that it leapt off the screen. They settled on animals with an inborn sense of conflict – either a fox and a dog, or a cat and a mouse. The storylines were to have a sense of justice.

Puss Gets The Boot was a success. The cat character clearly sought to ingratiate himself with authority figures, while the innocent mouse only retaliated when provoked. MGM thought its initial success was a flash in the pan, and despite holding a staff competition to rename the characters, put the project on hold, until the head of an important chain of theatres in the south wrote asking when the new cat and mouse cartoons would be available. Tom and Jerry was up and running, so to speak.

Initially, Hanna and Barbera were required to obtain storyline approval from animations chief Fred Quimby, but rapidly established their own autonomy. For twenty years they were their own bosses. Subtle amendments were made to the base drawings over the years – the outlines were sharpened, Jerry gained a little weight to be more cuddly and Tom's face grew grey with just a white muzzle. Clearly, the musical arrangements and sound effects were vital components of the action. Scott Bradley was the musical supremo, and his scores helped *The Cat Concerto* and *Johann Mouse* to win Oscars.

Classics include *Mouse Trouble* (1944) in which Tom gets a book on how to catch mice, but Jerry has shrewdly already studied it, and leads Tom a merry dance.... *The Cat Concerto* (1946) sees Tom as a piano virtuoso in concert. Jerry is sleeping in the piano, naturally awakens and begins to wreak havoc with Tom's recital. Tom and Jerry, on film, won seven Academy Awards in all. In 1954, Cinemascope was introduced allowing even greater definition, but despite this MGM decided

in 1957 to shut the cartoon division. Hanna and Barbera set up their own business, making limited animation Tom and Jerry cartoons, but in 1960 MGM revived their interest, asking Gene Deitch to produce 13 shorts – but these all fell short of the original standard. Chuck Jones took over in 1963, and though better, his 34 cartoons still weren't right and in 1967 MGM again dropped the series.

Hanna-Barbera tried to resurrect the ideas by casting Tom and Jerry into a new children's show in 1975, and MGM leased the characters to CBS for their own show in 1980. None of these gambits paid off. Nothing could equal the sheer exuberance and fun of Hanna-Barbera's 1940-1958 originals.

In an attempt to revive the careers of the world's most famous cat and mouse act, Turner Entertainment, under the guidance of special consultant Joseph Barbera, launch *Tom and Jerry – The Movie* in 1993. A major departure from their traditional roles in many respects, this full-length, animated musical adventure has the former adversaries teaming up as friends and, for the first time, talking and singing. Richard Kind supplies Tom's voice while Jerry benefits from the talents of actress Dana Hill.

Lily Tomlin

"A goddam national treasure." – Richard Pryor.

"One of the funniest women in the world." – *New Yorker*.

Lily Tomlin's place in the history of American comedy is assured. Equally effective on stage, television and film, this versatile comedienne came to prominence in *Rowan and Martin's Laugh-In* with an extensive stable of characters, including her hugely popular Ernestine, the spinster telephone operator and Edith Ann, the uninhibited child.

Constantly reappraising her material throughout her career, Tomlin has set an example for other female comics. She will not perform in anything she considers demeaning to her sex.

Her Life and Work

Mary Jean Tomlin was born in Detroit, in 1939. Her childhood heroines were Lucille Ball and Imogen Coca. At high school, she was a cheerleader but was eventually dropped for being too vulgar. On graduation, she entered Detroit Wayne State University and began pre-med studies, where a yearning to perform led to an appearance in a very mediocre university revue. She was its only saving grace, performing a character that she later revived on TV, that of Mrs Earbor, the tasteful lady and a member of the country club set. After the revue, Tomlin was invited to perform in local coffee bars and on local radio and TV talk shows.

At the end of her second year at University, she decided to give up her studies and go to New York to try to carve a career for herself as a comic.

Her progress was slow to begin with and to support herself, Tomlin worked by day as an office temp, while gaining the occasional tryout at the Improv Club. To make ends meet, she also began making TV commercials, but she

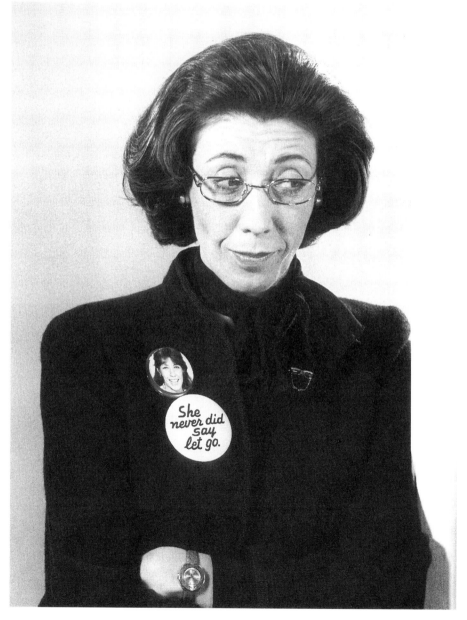

She never did say let go.

(1939-)

did not enjoy the experience, however lucrative.

In 1966, Lily Tomlin got her first big break. Following a series of appearances on Gary Moore's TV show, she was signed by a talent agency. Inspired by Elaine May and the monologues of Ruth Draper, Tomlin's repertoire of characters was now developing apace.

After watching the budding comedienne on *The Mary Tyler Moore Show*, producer George Schlatter booked Tomlin for *Rowan And Martin's Laugh-In*. Within months, she had established herself as a regular. Her wide array of characters fitted perfectly into the show's zany format. Ernestine, the power-mad and subconsciously erotic telephone operator, soon became the audience's favourite, with lines such as "one, ringy dingy... two, ringy dingy: a gracious good afternoon to you" and "have I reached the party to whom I am speaking?" Others included the tasteful lady; the inarticulate fast talker, Suzie Sorority; and Edith Ann. In 1971, she released her first comedy LP, *This Is A Recording*, which heavily featured Ernestine. It won the best comedy album of the year award from The National Academy of Recording Arts and Sciences. Her second LP, *And That's The Truth*, featuring Edith Ann, was released in 1972.

Tomlin continued to appear on *Laugh-In* until 1973, and at nightclubs in Greenwich Village, California and Washington. She also appeared at New York's Carnegie Hall.

In 1972, Tomlin came to England to appear in the Royal Variety Performance. When *Laugh-In* came off the air in 1973, she was given her own one-hour comedy-variety show on CBS-TV, *The Lily Tomlin Show*. Guests included Richard Pryor, who also helped her write the script. She did *Lily*, a second special, in November of the same year.

"She makes, unmakes and remakes her various selves with a kind of ecstasy, a metamorphic bliss, that only the great actors have," wrote Jack Kroll in *Newsweek*.

Tomlin's first film was Robert Altman's *Nashville* (1975), in which she played a white gospel singer. She earned several awards plus an Academy Award nomination for the supporting role. *The Late Show* (1977) directed by Robert Benton and co-starring Art Carney followed.

Also in 1977, Lily Tomlin conquered Broadway with her solo show, *Appearing Nightly*. She performed all her characters and was on stage for almost two hours with very few props. The show was a big hit. "She is at once so likeable and so tireless in her attack that the evening never wears thin," wrote Brendan Gill, *New Yorker*.

She co-starred with John Travolta in *Moment By Moment*, in 1979, but this was not one of her

Key Films

Nashville (1975);
Nine To Five (1980);
All Of Me (1984);
Lily Tomlin (1987).

best. However in 1980, Tomlin made *Nine To Five* with Dolly Parton and Jane Fonda. After *The Incredible Shrinking Woman*, she returned to TV as the host of *Saturday Night Live*.

Tomlin teamed up with Steve Martin for *All Of Me*, in 1984, and won an Emmy nomination the same year for her portrayal of Ernestine in *Live... And In Person*, for NBC. She went to the awards in character.

She also teamed up with writer Jane Wagner in 1985 to produce another solo stage show, *The Search For Signs of Intelligent Life In The Universe*, which examined modern life. This time, she presented a whole new set of characters, including Trudy, a dim bag lady; Kate, a bored socialite; two prostitutes and a punk rocker. Parts of the show were edited together with interviews and backstage shots to produce the 1987 film *Lily Tomlin*.

In 1988, she appeared with Bette Midler in *Big Business*.

Performance Extracts

"Every time I see a yield sign on the highway, I feel sexually threatened."

"I'm worried that the person who invented leisure suits, will tell us what to do with our leisure time."

"If love is the answer, could you rephrase the question?"

Tracey Ullman

"Miss Ullman is the sound you don't know you're missing until you've heard it." – James L Brooks.

"I try hard not to conform, I can't bear to be smug, complacent....You'll never see me on the cover of *Family Circle* judging a toy competition." – Tracey Ullman

Tracey Ullman, please note, is a comic actress. She is not a comedian, she says because "I couldn't get up and tell a joke to save my life." Nevertheless, her characterisations, including Elizabeth Taylor and Margaret Thatcher, are damn funny. Other characters are modelled on more ordinary folk she has personally encountered – a frumpy British clerk, a snobby radio psychologist, a Yuppie mother and a sweaty New York postal worker.

Ullman is a good singer, with four top ten hits to her name, and can claim a unique achievement – the video for her 1985 hit featured the ex-Labour Party leader Neil Kinnock.

Her Life and Work

Tracey Ullman was born in Slough, Berkshire in 1959, the daughter of a lawyer, originally from Poland. He died when Tracey was six, and her mother raised her and a sister in Hackbridge, south London. Aged 12, Tracey won a scholarship to the Italia Conti Stage School. She has described herself as the 'ugly kid' who never got sent to auditions, so she concentrated on character acting. A loud, often difficult pupil, after four years she was expelled.

(1959-)

At 16, she went to Berlin and was in the chorus line for Gigi, returning after six months to join the dance troupe *Second Generation*. Ullman then appeared in a number of West End shows including *Elvis*, *Grease* and *The Rocky Horror Picture Show*. An important breakthrough came in 1981, winning the London Theatre Critics Award for her performance as Beverley, a born-again Christian and nightclub singer, in the improvisational stage play *Four In A Million*.

After a listless six months, she won a part in the BBC TV series *Three Of A Kind*, with Lenny Henry and David Copperfield. Her best sketch in the series was an inversion of the Benny Hill style in which she pinched mens' bottoms, leered at them and gazed down their trousers. She was also noted for her portrayals of air-head debutantes ("Okay, soopah, yah, right, okay yah Roz") dumpy housewives and inarticulate teenagers. Other shows included *A Kick Up The Eighties*, with Rik Mayall, and *Girls On Top*, with French and Saunders.

Switching into the music business, she recorded successful hits, including *They Don't Know About Us* and *Move Over Darling*. The former included a cameo from Paul McCartney and went on to be one of the most popular songs on MTV and introduced her to the American public. McCartney cast her as the tatty slut in *Give My Regards To Broad Street*, and, having set up home in Los Angeles in 1984, she broke into Hollywood by appearing with Meryl Streep in *Plenty*. Failure to capitalise on this, save a small role in Whoopi Goldberg's *Jumpin' Jack Flash*, brought disillusionment until her agent suggested sending tapes to James L Brookes, creator of the *Mary Tyler Moore Show* and also *Taxi*. He was impressed: "I was just startled at the size of the talent. I got chills." Brooks became her mentor, and, taking his time to find the right vehicle, launched Ullman in her own show in 1987.

An instant success, it received five Emmy nominations after just a few short months. but when shown in the UK it sank without trace, being judged too American in style. Her American show was also the first showcase for the cartoon, *The Simpsons*. The show ran successfully until 1990, with *The Best of Tracey Ullman* also going out that year.

Back in England, her producer husband Allan McKeown is a director of Meridian Broadcasting which won the former TVS franchise for southern England in 1992. He is aiming to relaunch her UK career with *A Class Act*, satirising the British class system, due for transmission in late 1993.

Performance Extract ⟶

From *I Love You To Death*, 1990:

ULLMAN PLAYS ROSALIE, A WOMAN WHOSE HUSBAND, JOEY, IS CHEATING ON HER. SHE AND HER MOTHER, NADJA, DECIDE TO STOP HIS WOMANISING – FOR GOOD.

JOEY (TO A POLICEMAN): Some maniac in an Abraham Lincoln mask, tries to brain me with a baseball bat. That's the whole story.

Nadja (TO JOEY): Ya... er... could you see vot he look like?

Joey: Yeah, he looked like Abraham Lincoln – coming up to bat.

(LATER)

Rosalie: Mama, what kind of way is that to kill somebody – a baseball bat? Now I know why you think murder's the national pastime.

Nadja: Baseball bat's is vot's cheaper than gun.

Rosalie: Oh, and I suppose Abraham Lincoln is cheaper than George Washington?

Mae West

"It isn't what I say, but how I do it. It isn't what I say, but how I say it, and how I look when I do it and say it." Mae West.

"It's hard to be funny when you have to be clean." Mae West.

Mae West was the original, man-mocking sex symbol. She scandalised America with her provocative routines and suggestive persona. In many regards a model for all female performers, she wrote most of her own material, and produced her own films. The shock-value was that she talked about sex in a way women had never before dared to. Her

Catchphrases

"Come up and see me sometime..."

"Goodness had nothing to do with it."

scripts implied much, but actually gave the censors – a constant threat – nothing with which to prosecute her. Her performances oozed sexuality, but never degraded or debased women.

Her Life and Work

Born in Brooklyn in 1893, Mae West was the son of a boxer turned detective. While still a small child, West would go to the

matinees of vaudeville shows with her mother, and was treading the boards in Brooklyn before she was seven years old. She married actor/dancer Frank Wallace in 1911 but even aged 18, she had come to realise that conventional songs and routines didn't suit her, so she began writing her own material, which she used for the first time in *A Winsome Widow*, appearing with her sister, and dressing as a man.

During the 1920s West wrote her own plays, consistently receiving dreadful reviews. The titles suffice to suggest the topics – *Sex*, a play about prostitutes, *The Drag*, which features homosexuality, *The Wicked Age*, *The Constant Sinner*, and *Pleasure Man*. *Sex* was actually raided by the New York police, earning West a $500 fine and ten days on Welfare Island. Her most successful play was the 1928 *Diamond Lil*, and included her most famous line, when she invited a Salvation Army captain to "Come up and see me sometime..." The Diamond Lil type, the bad girl with a heart of gold, the workshy, blonde, femme fatale became West's best known persona, and one she would play over and over again.

The first of her numerous films was *Night After Night*, with her then boyfriend George Raft, in 1932, complete with another immortal line: "Goodness had

nothing to do with it." West wrote and produced a series of films for Paramount whose success can only have been enhanced by that 'forbidden fruit' mentality boosted by the strenuous campaigns of religious objectors. To be fair, she gave them plenty of ammunition – playing Eve in a radio broadcast to Don Ameche's Adam in the *Garden of Eden*, her steamy dialogue caused uproar and she was banned from the radio. An apology to listeners was broadcast the next week.

My Little Chickadee, with W.C. Fields was another important film, but as they each wrote their own dialogue it seemed at times as if it was more competition than cooperation. She played a lion tamer in *I'm No Angel* opposite Cary Grant and then appeared in the adaptation of her own play *Diamond Lil*, filmed as *She Done Him No Wrong*. Singing often in her movies, she regularly hired the very best of musical accompanists, including Duke Ellington and his orchestra.

The Heat's On, in 1953, ended a successful run in the movies, and West returned to touring with her shows, such as *Catharine Was Great* which ran on Broadway for six months, and a stage revival of *Diamond Lil* in 1949. During the '50s, she introduced an array of muscular young men to her shows, one of which, Paul Novak, remained her companion until her

death. She published her autobiography *Goodness Had Nothing To Do With It* in 1959, and, possibly unwisely, returned to the screen in 1970 with the movie *Myra Breckinridge*, in which she played a casting agent.

Mae West, sexual icon to a generation, died in 1980.

Key Films

Night After Night (1932);
My Little Chickadee (1940);
I'm No Angel (1933)

Performance Extracts

"Sex and I have a lot in common. I don't want to take any credit for inventing it, but I may say, in a manner of speaking, that I have rediscovered it."

West: My, you're a tall boy.
Boy: Yes ma'am. I'm six feet, seven inches.
West: Let's forget about the six feet and concentrate on the seven inches.

"It's not the men in your life that counts. It's the life in your men."

"Say, is that a gun in your pants pocket, or are you just pleased to see me?"

Robin Williams

"...**a** pastiche of mime, light-speed improvisation and complex clowning." *Time* magazine.

"You're only given a little spark of madness. You mustn't lose it." Robin Williams.

Robin Williams shot to stardom with his portrayal of Mork, the alien visitor to Earth, in *Mork and Mindy*. Prior to that he was a stand-up comedian notable for his Chaplinesque trousers, loud shirts and wide red braces. He has been described as "insanely funny" and is certainly a brilliant improvisational comic, a fluent ad-libber, and able to contort his features quite extraordinarily.

Though now a major Hollywood hot property, many consider his most inventive work was much earlier in his career – the unstructured, free-form, live stage-acts.

His Life and Work

Robin Williams was born in Chicago in 1952. He had a highly affluent, but lonely childhood. His father, a Ford Motor Company Vice President, was 50 when Robin was born and was always a remote figure to the boy. There were two half-brothers from a previous marriage, but they had both grown up and left home, so Williams was often alone. To while away the hours he created imaginary playlets and acted out all the parts himself. A further dislocation was that the family

Catchphrase

"na-noo-na-noo"

(1952-)

moved often during his child-hood, but while Williams was at senior school, his father retired, settling in Marin County, California. Williams attended Redwood Public School, known for its relaxed attitudes and emerged as the fat kid, but voted by his classmates the most funny and most likely to succeed.

He briefly studied political science and also theatre, then enrolled at the famed Julliard Academy where he was tutored by John Houseman. He quit before completing his course, in pursuit of a girl he'd fallen for in San Francisco. When the love affair failed and he couldn't get straight acting roles, he joined a comedy workshop and began playing in the clubs. He met Valerie Velardi, a dancer later to become his wife, and she helped him with his routines. Encouraged by Valerie, he went to Los Angeles. and went on stage at the Comedy Store on an 'open mike' night and soon became a regular at the club, where his extempore style was highly regarded.

TV producer George Schlatter spotted him and, having per-suaded him to shave off the beard and cut his long hair, hired him for a short-lived and surreal new talk show, America 2Night. Another TV producer, Garry

Marshall, at the time producing Happy Days, wanted to make an extraterrestrial show and audi-tioned Williams. On being asked how an alien would sit, Williams up-ended himself and sat on his head... Mork and Mindy was premiered in 1978. Williams played Mork, the alien visitor who spoke in a language filled with odd phrases – like "na-noo-na-noo" – gets drunk on cream-soda and wears his watch on his ankle. Within a year it claimed an audi-ence of 60 million a week.

Williams continued in the clubs too, creating characters such as Grandpa Funk, a battered old geezer; Andrew the six-year old psychologist; a spastic French waiter; the blues singer Benign Neglect; the Reverend Earnest Sincerely, plus a host of bizarre takeoffs like Shakespeare and sound effects to Japanese movies.

His film debut came in the 1980 flop Popeye, but when Mork and Mindy finished in 1982, he went straight into The World According To Garp. By now Williams had a bit of a reputation as a lover of parties and he was with John Belushi on the night he died. Garp, he said, helped him to slow down and re-evaluate his lifestyle.

Good Morning Vietnam made Williams a Hollywood star and won him an Oscar nomination. He

Key Films

Include: Popeye (1980); Good Morning Vietnam (1988); Dead Poets Society (1989); Awakenings (1990); The Fisher King (1990); Hook (1992).

played Adrian Cronauer, a DJ broadcasting to the troops. It was a role tailor-made for Williams, allowing him to utilise all his skills to improvise whole scenes. Dead Poets Society was his next big hit, in 1989, when he played John Keating, a renegade English teacher in a highly traditional boarding school. Since then he has also appeared in Awakenings, The Fisher King, and Steven Spielberg's updated version of Peter Pan, called Hook.

Performance Extracts

On the Falklands War:
"Having Alexander Haig negotiate the peace is like having Charles Manson as a male nurse... Do you ever have this feeling that when Alexander Haig was in office, he would wander into the Oval Office at night, and go – shh, Ron, just let me push one damn button..."

On San Francisco:
"People in San Francisco are so damn nice they don't flash, they just describe themselves to you."

On the wealthy:
"...the sort of people who don't get the crabs, they get the lobsters."

Norman Wisdom

"...a kind of bashfulness verging on mental deficiency." Penelope Gilliatt.

"All my comedy is about being just an ordinary person and if I do things that are a bit over the top, the key is that they could happen." Norman Wisdom.

"A lot of what I do appeals to children – the slapstick, the slipping on banana skins... anyone who doesn't have a child's sense of humour is not a very happy person." Norman Wisdom.

Norman Wisdom, like President Ford of America, made a career out out of falling down.

Clad in his trademark too-tight grey suit and cap, Wisdom is famed as the little man who usually wins through in the end. He'd strut and swagger briefly, bump into a quirk of fate and soon be slipping and sliding all over the place. Relying on pathos to win the hearts of his audiences, Wisdom was a master of slapstick and, much like The Three Stooges, didn't feel any need for elaboration.

Catchphrase

"Mr Grimsdale – don't laugh at me 'cos I'm a fool."

His Life and Work

Norman Wisdom was born in Paddington, London, in 1920. His parents divorced when he was nine and young Norman was packed off to live with guardians at Deal, on the Kent coast. His father stopped paying for his upkeep however, and he was thrown out. Leaving school at 14, he had a variety of jobs – errand boy, trainee waiter, hotel page boy – before a friend suggested they

become miners and Wisdom walked from London to Cardiff in search of work. In the event, he found employment as a cabin boy on a ship to Argentina, where he learned to box. He later joined the Army as a band boy, learning to play clarinet, saxophone, piano and drums. Despite being diminutive in the extreme – he stood 4ft 10 1/2 inches and weighed 5st 9lbs – he found people laughed with him rather than at him.

Leaving the Army in 1946 after ten years service, he set out in search of a showbiz career. At this stage he was performing in a small bowler, striped football shirt and trousers half way up his legs. He briefly switched to a Chaplinesque baggy suit, but in 1949 found the persona that would make him a star. Appearing in Scarborough on the same bill as the magician David Nixon, Wisdom volunteered to be his stooge and went out to buy a suitable costume – the 'Gump' was born.

Wisdom's act was developing – he had a laugh that rose from a gentle chuckle into rabid hysteria, a constant ear-to-ear grin and acrobatic hops and skips of his little legs that forever sent him sprawl-

ing. He toured extensively around the country and made his first television appearance in 1948, and his first Royal Variety performance in 1942, which led to his first television series. The Rank Organisation signed him up on a contract for seven years at a film a year in 1953.

The first was *Trouble In Store* in which he fell about to great effect and sung the song that would become his catchphrase and also a chart hit for over a year, *Don't Laugh At Me 'Cos I'm A Fool*. Wisdom played the same 'Gump' character in most of his films thereafter, as a milkman, reporter, soldier, sailor and window cleaner.

In 1963 Wisdom appeared alone on stage, save for compere Bruce Forsyth, at the London Palladium for a full hour during which he re-papered the entire set. Wisdom played the employee and Forsyth the foreman in a celebrated sketch which culminated in a chase through the audience and orchestra.

Lest anyone think Norman Wisdom's art was mere clowning, a reminder of his talent is that he won an Oscar for his performance in *The Night They Raided Minsky's*,

Key Films

Trouble In Store (1953);
Follow A Star (1959);
On The Beat (1962);
A Stitch In Time (1963);
The Night They Raided Minsky's (1968);
Double X (1992).

in which he co-starred with Britt Ekland and Jason Robards.

Growing weary of the 'Gump' character, despite, or perhaps because of, a tedious TV series called *A Little Bit Of Wisdom*, he hung up the suit and cap for good, and sought out serious roles. In 1981 he struck gold. Stephen Frears moving and award-winning television play *Going Gently* saw Wisdom as a terminal cancer patient. Fulton Mackay and Judi Dench also starred.

Wisdom is also a singer and songwriter of some note. In 1991 he was working on an album produced and arranged by Rick Wakeman, and he has sung with The Human League on *The Things That Dreams Are Made Of*.

Performance Extract

From his stage show:

NORMAN STARTS TO ARGUE WITH HIS ORCHESTRA'S CONDUCTOR AFTER THE MUSIC HAS STOPPED.

Norman: Did you stop the band?
Conductor: I did.
Norman: Well, what for?
Conductor: The band needs a break... now, can you play the drums?

Norman: What do you mean?
Conductor: Vibraphones, timpany, orchestra stuff...
Norman: Oooooooh... classical percussion! It's funny you should mention that.
Conductor: Why?
Norman: Can't play 'em.
Conductor: Would you like to earn £5?
Norman: Your joking. I'm not broke, I'm mangled.

Conductor: Good. Let's make a start, shall we?
Norman: Wait a minute! I want my money first! Anyone who takes me for a fool is making no mistake!

Victoria Wood

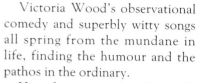

"Most of my inspiration comes from way back, during my childhood in Bury and schooldays. From stuff that's all tucked at the back of the head." Victoria Wood.

"I could never write normal songs about love or anything. I had to write songs about something that had happened, like the death of Guy the gorilla." Victoria Wood.

Victoria Wood's observational comedy and superbly witty songs all spring from the mundane in life, finding the humour and the pathos in the ordinary.

Her characters are often afflicted by varicose veins and dropped wombs. they have spare tyres instead of waists, spots and still shudder with embarrassment at their teenage gaffes... the very familiarity, and the fine detail, make her work directly relevant to all.

Her Life and Work

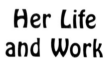

Born 19th May, 1953, in Bury, Lancashire, the daughter of an insurance underwriter, Victoria Wood went to grammar school and then Birmingham University to read drama and theatre arts. While there, and indeed before, she was writing plays and songs. Graduating in 1974, she failed in a bid to enter drama school but a BBC producer saw one of her shows and invited her to audition at Pebble Mill, the BBC's Midlands studio. She wrote the occasional songs for regional magazine programmes, and went on to compete in *New Faces*, victoriously.

Moving into TV work, much too soon in her own opinion, she did a show with Lenny Henry and Marti Caine that amounted to simply regurgitation what she'd done previously with-

(1953-)

out any structure or theme. An important meeting came about through her appearance in the revue *In At The Death*, at the Bush Theatre, in London. Also in the cast was Julie Walters.

Wood's first significant play, *Talent*, in 1978, was the tale of the glamorous girl and her dumpy friend both entering a talent show. Wood was the plump girl, Walters was the pretty one. The play won the Most Promising Playwright award and was later bought by Granada TV. Her second play, *Good Fun*, was part-musical, and included one of her best songs, *I've Had It Up To Here With Men*. Writing all her own material, Wood then embarked on a highly productive phase, returning to TV with *Wood and Walters* in 1982. She said "some bits of it were good, and some were deadly" but it nevertheless gained a BAFTA nomination. Interspersing TV work with live

tours, she honed the wry style and pithy lyrics that were to be her hallmark. Beneath the comedy there was always an edge, as in the warning in the song about marrying young: "A life full of nothing, it's stupid, it's painful... don't do it."

Her burgeoning TV career continued with *Victoria Wood As Seen On TV*, for BBC2 in 1985 with a second series the next year. This series included the wonderful Acorn Antiques spoof on soap operas. The scripts were later published in her book *Barmy*, in 1987. The two series collected several BAFTA awards, but having written every last word of it, Wood was fatigued and found the sketch format too constrictive, so she again turned to touring, and took part in Comic Relief.

A different sort of style emerged in 1990 in her Alan Bennett-type series of six short playlets, each telling the story of a

different character, called *Victoria Wood Now*. She followed this with a virtuoso performance in the LWT occasional series *An Audience With...*, a 90-minute special. Continuing to entertain across the spectrum, she had a successful season of live shows at the Strand Theatre in 1991, and a Radio 4 compilation in 1992.

Performance Extracts

Wood: Did you go to see Macbeth?
Walters: Mmm. Wasn't a patch on Brigadoon. There was some terrible woman kept washing her hands, saying she'd never get them clean. I felt like shouting out – try Swarfega. We walked out in the end.
Wood: Why?
Walters: Someone said womb.
Wood: (ASTOUNDED) No...

"You know they say – see Venice and die. See Morecambe and you feel as if you already have... no, it's a very jolly place. It's one of the few resorts where you can get

a kiss-me-quick hearing aid... and there's a pier – well it's like a council house on a stick... I tell you, things are very wild in Morecambe on a Saturday night. You get old men dipping their Garibaldis into another woman's Horlicks."

From *I've Had It Up To Here*:

"I've not had a punter yet
That didn't leave me cold and wet.
I'd be happier you know
If we could only go
From the foreplay
Straight to the cigarette.

"I studied the symptoms for pregnancy. Moody, irritable, big bosoms. I have obviously been pregnant for 20 years."

"I didn't use to bother about my body until I first wore ski pants and somebody asked if I'd had my thighs lagged for the winter."